A rare and evocative portrait of a young woman and her extraordinary experiences with an ancient African culture that has never before been revealed to the white man's world with such candor and honesty.

Lona B. Kenney was a teenage opera singer when she married a specialist in tropical diseases. Before joining her husband at a small post in the Belgian Congo, she learned Bangala, the *lingua franca* of the Western Congo. This and her ready and reverent acceptance of the ways and rituals of the inhabitants of a neighboring village (the *mboka*) created a close relationship between them and her. It enabled her to understand and share their tribal lives as few other whites have been able to do.

In the jungle, with little to remind her of Western civilization, she approached her new friends at the *mboka* with characteristic sincerity and total lack of preconception. She opened her mind and heart to their myths, customs, and wisdom. Above all she grew to know intimately a group of remarkable human beings: Molali, the palm-wine entrepreneur; Molali Moke, his small son; Baloki, his beautiful daughter; Lisengo, Baloki's lover; Mafuta, the lecherous chief; and the witch doctors, Djito and Mokolo.

Disregarding old-school colonial officials and traders, Lona Kenney overcame all barriers in getting to know the people of the *mboka*. Children always escorted her around the village and helped her sympathetically as she tried to draw closer to their lives; she even swam naked with them. She undertook rites demanded by

(continued on back flap)

MBOKA

Books by Lona B. Kenney:
A CASTE OF HEROES, A Novel
MBOKA, A Congo Memoir

MBOKA

A CONGO MEMOIR BY
LONA B. KENNEY

CROWN PUBLISHERS • NEW YORK

I took poetic license in writing this memoir.
Names, some of the locale, and the sequence
of events have been changed. Any resemblance
of the people described in this book to actual persons
is purely coincidental.

Library of Congress Catalog Card Number: 72-84300
ISBN: 0-517-50037X
Printed in the United States of America
Published simultaneously in Canada by General Publishing Company
Limited

To my dearest husband, Michael, without whom there would be nothing and to the memory of my beloved friends, Dr. Elias Bronberg and his gentle wife Natalie, my parents, without whom there wouldn't be me.

". . . Whereof what's past is prologue,
what to come in yours and
my discharge."

Shakespeare, *The Tempest*

CHAPTER I

It was still early evening, and Michael, my doctor-bridegroom, and I lingered in the large living room of our brand-new house at the small government post of Busu Melo, the *chef-lieu* (headquarters) of the Ngombe Territory deep in the bush of equatorial Congo. The shutters of the room's two windows, devoid of any mesh, were wide open, although we both realized how unreasonable it was in this malaria-infested region to expose ourselves to the incessant mosquito bites. But the blinding light of the Coleman pressure lamp was supposed to discourage the mosquitoes, and high boots worn over slacks were meant to keep them from biting our legs, although that was in theory only. What we should really have been doing was call it a day, for I had just joined Michael a week before, and he was scheduled to start on a swing through the interior at sunup and wouldn't take me along.

Naturally, we could continue our conversation in bed, under the protective canopy of its mosquito net. But perhaps we were putting off getting under the huge white dome, because it was such a sticky night, and we knew how uncomfortable we would feel inside the net in our overheated bedroom with its shuttered windows. The mosquito net was an absolute must. And the second rule was that one did not sleep with one's windows open in the African jungle, no matter what the temptation to let in a breath of air.

Or maybe we didn't move from our morris chairs because we were absorbed in a discussion of the jungle drums, sounding so clear in the uncommon stillness of the evening. Unmistakably, these distant tom-toms came from somewhere other than our own hamlet of Busu Melo, barely a few hundred feet outside our garden. The chief of the territory and his wife, Monsieur and Madame Van Derveer, were back at the post following an inspection tour, and from what I had heard, they would not stand for our own villagers' participation in this nocturnal broadcast, which would then be virtually next to their bedroom. The drums probably originated in another village, a steady rhythmical staccato of two sounds: one high-pitched, the other low.

"Darling, do you think they're simply amusing themselves, or are really signaling something?" I asked Michael.

"I'm quite sure they're transmitting messages," he said. "If you listen carefully, you'll hear fainter signals from somewhere else, much farther away. That's how the villagers communicate from place to place. In Yakata, the Mongo people are real drum specialists and they can reach the other end of the territory in no time. They beat huge drums made of hollow tree trunks plugged at both ends, with a lengthwise slit on top. Their drums sound just like these here, and the sound carries for many kilometers."

"Kilometers? How do they manage to beat these tremendous drums without hurting their hands?"

"They don't beat that type of drum with their hands, silly. They use something like huge wooden drumsticks, shaped like bottles, and they bang away on their drums real hard . . ."

I listened for a moment. Perhaps I did hear some other,

weaker, higher pitched sounds. Or maybe it was only the malaria-suppressive quinine we always took at dinner, which made my ears buzz.

"Do you understand what they're signaling?" I asked.

"N-no," Michael confessed. "The villagers won't reveal their code to any white man. They don't even teach it to their women. But of course I've only been here a few months myself," he added.

"It's like listening for hours to coded short-wave messages without being familiar with the code." I was disappointed, because I was convinced that Michael knew everything.

"Speaking about codes," Michael said, "when I was in Yakata, I tried to apply the Morse code principle to the tom-toms. You know—the high sound for a dot, the low for a dash. I would ask a villager to drum on the wooden tom-tom the name of a chief I know and would jot it down in Morse. Then I'd ask the man to drum other words I know. He would oblige, and the other villagers would laugh and laugh. But I still couldn't figure out how their code system works. Maybe they were confusing me on purpose."

We sat quietly, listening, and the drums seemed louder now, for the hissing of our lamp had grown softer with the falling pressure, and we were both too lazy to get up and pump up the lamp a little.

"But I have no doubt that before long, with that musical ear of yours, you'll get the hang of their telegraph system," Michael said. "You have to start somewhere to learn about tribal customs." He knew that that was why I was so eager to come to Africa.

To be sure, coming to the Congo was only the consequence of a logical sequence of events. At least the first part of it was—marrying Michael, a physician graduated in Switzerland, but specialized in tropical medicine at the Ecole de Médecine Tropicale in Belgium where he had been working after graduation with the world-renowned Dr. Rodhain, the director of the school and at one time chief of the medical services in the Belgian Congo.

My meeting Michael on the French Riviera was truly the work of destiny. I was studying singing and had made my operatic debut in Italy, and I had come to Nice to join my vacationing parents just as Michael had arrived there from Brussels on a spur-of-the-moment holiday. We fell in love and married, all within a few weeks.

Perhaps it was while listening to Michael talk about the medical research he intended to do in Central Africa, with its still many incurable tropical diseases, that I had first developed an interest in this land. But what interested me most was its indigenous population, unspoiled by the corrupt influences of the "civilized" man, the Africans' strange tribal ways of life, their natural impulses and beliefs. Thus both of us were attracted to the same source, although not quite for the same reasons, yet with an equal degree of anticipation.

When, on Nice's sunlit Promenade des Anglais, Michael and I discussed the possibility of going to the Congo, everything seemed perfectly sensible. The voyage to the exotic African continent appeared as an extension of the dolce far niente on the azure Mediterranean coast. It was agreed that I would pursue my career, spending the winter opera season in Europe and joining Michael for summer somewhere in the Congo where he would be stationed. There, in addition to satisfying my interest in the people, I would also have the opportunity of enriching my linguistic repertoire—acquired in the half-dozen countries where I had studied since early childhood—by learning a couple of Congolese dialects. Michael would spend his winter leave with me somewhere in Europe, maybe in Rome or Paris, or wherever my singing engagements might take me. It appeared that simple.

The first uncertainties set in on our arrival in Brussels. "As a first-term appointee, your husband will most likely be stationed in some swampy, God-forsaken region, even if he does work with Rodhain," a veteran colonial had said, chilling our enthusiasm.

"A colonial government physician doesn't get a winter vacation every year," had added another well-wisher. "You stay put for three years and like it."

But I was still in my teens. And Michael, although quite a few years older, was also an impractical dreamer. Everything would work out just fine. I was already studying Bangala. This dialect was chosen not because we had any idea where Michael would be sent, but because Bangala, a phonetic language, was much more primitive and easier to learn than Swahili, the general language of the eastern Congo. Another reason was that it had been in use for some time by various African tribes to enable them to communicate with one another in their travels and trading. Some of them, initially speaking different dialects, had finally begun using Bangala among themselves. It was derived not only from many African dialects, but also included a number of borrowed and corrupted English, French, and Portuguese words. Bangala was the official language of the colonial army, as well as of the missionaries over a vast area of the west. After the introduction of some basic grammar, the polished Bangala was called "Lingala" by the missionaries, but it was still the same language. Therefore, studying it seemed more practical, with a considerably lesser investment of time and effort. In a relatively short time, because of my special affinity for languages, I was enjoying how surprised the small group of retired old colonial physicians were at my fluency in Bangala. They met regularly, club-fashion, in a small café off the Place de Brouckère in Brussels, and Michael and I came there to soak up some second-hand Congolese atmosphere from the old-timers who told many pretty tall tales about their life in the Congo.

Although uneasiness sometimes won over the unrealistic

optimism of youth while we listened to these accounts, we went ahead with our somewhat fantastic plans. Finally, Michael left for the Congo alone, and according to our timetable I was to follow him in the spring, at the end of the opera season, to resume our interrupted honeymoon.

Michael's very first letter from Léopoldville dispelled all illusions regarding his appointment, which he had received in a sealed envelope aboard the Congo-bound steamer. It was not in "Léo," as the capital was called by Europeans living in the Congo, nor was it in any large city, and in fact, not in a city or town with well-equipped hospitals and laboratories, so important for medical research. But from what people in Léo said, the territory of Ngombe was something akin to paradise. A road that ran its length, with practically all its villages lining it, made a car a welcome necessity. And there was a new house waiting for the doctor. And the large palm-oil company compound of Mongana, at one end of the territory, with its up-to-date conveniences, where one might spend weekends, and finally the town of Lisala, the district capital, straight across the Congo River from Mongana, made Busu Melo appear like a pleasant suburb of a large center.

That Michael's territory was no paradise became clear from his second letter from Busu Melo. The new house existed on paper only. However, construction had started under Michael's personal supervision. It also became obvious almost immediately that his job was a semi-itinerant proposition and that he could spend little time in the new house at Busu Melo, traveling as he had to all over the Ngombe Territory, and even beyond. This free medical care provided by the Belgian government for all Africans was of course fine indeed, but it posed a personal problem for us and we had to reach a difficult decision. There were only three alternatives. Michael could break his contract and return to Europe—which we could hardly afford, and, more important, knowing Michael's passion for tropical medicine, I would not let him jeopardize his career at its very start. It would also mean the end of my ambition to learn about the Africans firsthand. The second alternative was to follow Michael on his trips after joining him in the Congo, but this meant exposing me to hardship. It meant spending days in dank, roach-and-spider-infested stopover huts, being subjected to the rigors of the equatorial jungle. Michael would never stand for this. Not while there was the magnificent palace built especially for me in the safe Eden of the *chef-lieu* at Busu Melo. The final choice was for me to stay put at the government post, while Michael traveled, doing his best to return home as often and as soon as he could, which appeared practicable.

The beautiful, relatively hard Busu Melo dirt road hemmed in by rows of stocky *élaïs* (oil palms) or winding picturesquely through a dense forest or hamlets with their predominantly cassava plantations was fine. It was certainly good enough for the thirty or so kilometers an hour Michael could make in his tenth-hand Chevy, which he had just bought at an exorbitant price. And so, this was what we had finally agreed upon. There were other redeeming features as well. "You'll find the Ngombe very interesting. I think you will like it here," Michael had written. . . .

He had evidently not changed his mind about it.

"You'll see, you'll enjoy knowing the villagers and learning about them," he said, as though reading my thoughts.

Since my arrival in Busu Melo, vague doubts that had been troubling me from the moment I set foot on Congolese soil seemed to spring into sharper focus. Now I had mixed feelings about our being here. Michael's duties in the territory hardly allowed him time to do the research he had been so looking forward to. And, after a few days in Busu Melo, I still hadn't figured out where to start looking into the tribal ways of life in the region.

The hamlet of Busu Melo, whose men wore either loincloths or white man's cast-off trousers and most of whose women were draped in *pagnes* (a sarong-like strip of cloth wrapped loosely above the bosom), consisted of a single row of square thatched mud huts on either side of the main road. It was too accessible to everyone at the post and too exposed to the eye to stimulate any uncommon curiosity. Most likely I would do a lot better if I could get to know villagers living somewhere off the road, in the real bush.

The distant drums were still sending their messages, and for some seconds we silently listened to them.

"Any idea where these tom-toms are coming from?" I asked.

Michael reflected a moment. "Perhaps from the village in the middle of the swamp down between our road, which sits on a high crest, and the Congo River."

"Have you ever been there?"

"No, never, though I probably should have. But I can only use my car to visit the hamlets lining our road, and the rest of the time I must tramp knee-deep in bog and mud. So, when I'm here, where I can take care of the villagers from all over the Busu Melo area at my own dispensary, I'd rather do just that."

"Then you know some of these villagers?" I persisted.

"I suppose I must have seen a few of them. They're different from the Ngombe of Busu Melo. Some of them look and sound like the riverside people I saw between the Congo and Ubangi rivers when I was on an inspection tour there."

One of our old colonial friends in Brussels, who had had some personal experience with the riverine people, had mentioned more than once the little-known inhabitants of the Congo Ubangi region isolated from the rest of the equatorial Congo by the flooded forests. In his opinion the whole population there would eventually die off from sleeping sickness and other tropical diseases.

Michael had apparently noticed my interest in what he told me about the village in the swamps.

"I wouldn't want you to try to hike there, hear?" he said. "It must be a kilometers-long, hairpin trail, and it's probably boggy and not quite safe . . . Why don't you start by getting to know the villagers right here in our own backyard. They have all kinds of very good drums too. The minute Van Derveer leaves the post the villagers will go to work on their tom-toms."

"Maybe I'll do that," I said without much conviction, remembering the jungle drum I had seen and heard in Léo at a dance in a public square of the African quarter. I had been sightseeing with an older couple who had taken me under their wing, to protect "the little one" during my stopover in the capital. The Africans in that open square, men in European clothes and women wearing either bright *pagnes* or a dress here and there, danced something reminiscent of a foxtrot to the sound of an ear-splitting band, made up of a mixture of wind and string instruments and, in addition to the conventional band-type drum, a large African tom-tom. Although I was told that it was indeed authentic, it somehow sounded like just another drum, and its beat, submerged by the cacophony of the rest of the band, had nothing in common with the nostalgic and mysterious sounds now filling the Busu Melo night.

"You don't want to catch malaria in that swampy village, *mon bébé*. The mosquitoes down there must be a thousand times worse than they are here—infected mosquitoes!" Michael went on cautioning me.

There might be more infected mosquitoes in that jungle village, I thought, but there couldn't possibly exist insects anywhere in the world more ferocious than those right here in our living room.

"Let's go to bed," I said, skirting the issue.

Much later, before we had fallen asleep, Michael was probably still fretting about my hiking to that distant village while he was away. Or perhaps he didn't like the idea of leaving me behind in Busu Melo and was trying to reassure me. "After all, besides the villagers, there are a few Europeans to see at the post," he said, before sleepily kissing me good night. "You'll get along with them just fine."

CHAPTER II

That my social life in Busu Melo was to be a failure became unequivocal the next day, after Michael's departure, when I dutifully called on the ample, aging wife of the chief of the territory.

She greeted me on her front *baraza* (veranda), then, rushing to its side, started to shout in the direction of the backyard. There, under a luxuriant clump of banana trees, stood the family outhouse with a sentimental heart-shaped vent cut out of the upper part of its rustic wooden door.

"Monsieur Van Derveer," she called to her closeted husband, "hurry it up in there, the doctor's wife is here!"

"You won't have to call your husband out in the toilet when you have company," she remarked after crossing back to where I was waiting. And gazing down at me with mock compassion, she added sweetly, "You won't have to, *ma chère*. Your toilet is practically in your living room."

She was referring, of course, to the uncomplicated plumbing device installed in a small cubicle in my bungalow, consisting of a toilet seat fitted over a pail, removable from the outside through a small, hinged door. There always was a can of sand handy for "flushing" the toilet, which reminded me of the sandbox for my childhood cat. Primitive as it was, this fixture was the last word in comparison with the *potopoto* (mud) outhouse which was a part of the jungle-post architecture. Above all, this arrangement eliminated the necessity of having to face the equatorial night in all kinds of weather, with its insects, snakes, and what not. Regardless of Madame Van Derveer's sneering at it, it was certain to be copied by others, including herself. Despite other limitations, like having to be sure to remember not to use the "toilet" at the hour when the "Sanitary Brigade" came around to empty it, my husband's practical idea was a convenient innovation in the interior.

The "Sanitary Brigade" consisted of two prisoners shackled to each other by a length of chain linked to loose metal rings around their necks. Wearing brief loincloths or shorts and black-and-yellow striped sleeveless T-shirts, they walked Indian file, a large, empty iron oil drum, with its top cut out, dangling from a bamboo pole they carried slung across their shoulders. The "Water Brigade," a similar team, brought water from the small clean stream behind the vegetable garden to every government bungalow in an identical drum, and I could only hope that there had not been an accidental mix-up of these containers.

"My, aren't you skinny!" said Madame Van Derveer, continuing to smile patronizingly at insignificant little me and bringing to bear the authority of her two hundred pounds, while I was busily thinking of what to reply to her attack on my bungalow's most luxurious feature.

"I'm not skinny all over," I protested, sticking out my chest.

"How can you be an opera singer when you're so scrawny?"

Madame Van Derveer had that old-fashioned notion about opera singers having to look something like herself to be able to sing. But my slenderness had not stood in the way of my so far brief but rather successful operatic career.

"You think it wise to be all skin and bones?" she insisted, ignoring one of the measurements in my favor, still without inviting me to sit down.

"No," I said angelically. "In fact, I understand local people have an old saying that 'While a sick fat person loses weight, a sick thin person dies.' I guess it would be wiser to be fat."

It was childish of me to antagonize the first lady of the Busu Melo Territory. But then, I was very young.

Luckily Madame Van Derveer was not listening to me. Perhaps she, too, was still thinking about my toilet that was "practically in my living room," for she abruptly changed the subject.

"Monsieur Van Derveer is considering switching houses with your husband," she informed me. "Wouldn't that be nice for you? Imagine—living in the house of the chief of the territory."

"Over my dead body," I said.

From the expression on Madame Van Derveer's face I could tell that she had no objection to that clause of the transaction. I cooled off instantly. It was certain that the chief of the territory would not attempt to pirate the new bungalow that my husband had so painstakingly planned and built for me. In the improbable event the exchange should take place, we would get the termite-infested old "residence" lost in the post's vegetable garden.

Termites in tropical regions are unlike those in temperate areas. They may ignore a structure for quite a while, but once they invade a house, it is literally doomed. They insidiously destroy it from within. Sometimes the slightest pressure would cause a door, whose whole inside had been devoured, to cave in like an eggshell. Perhaps the Van Derveers' house was not really at that final stage yet, but it was getting there.

The fat old Monsieur Van Derveer, whom the local Africans had aptly nicknamed *"Alembi te?"* (Is he not tired?), was really the least likely man to make trouble, and definitely not one to become involved in an obviously losing fight. The funds for the construction of new quarters had been allocated in Coquilhatville, the capital of the Equatorial Province, for the doctor's house in Busu Melo and not for the chief of the territory, who already had one. And although practically the whole investment in the new house amounted to the prisoners' labor and the local soldiers' supervision, the official memorandum spelled out the orders that could not be changed without a new mountain of red tape. Besides, Monsieur Van Derveer would have found it difficult to explain why the doctor should have spent all his free time at the post to personally supervise the construction and improvements of a house if it was not intended for him.

"House or no house, you won't like it here, *ma chère*." Madame Van Derveer's prediction put an end to my thoughts. She was evidently already scheming how to make her forecast become a reality, for she was rather absentminded for the remainder of my visit and did not detain me when I decided to leave.

I tried to think of what the wife of the chief of the territory could do to make life miserable for me. Whatever it was, I was prepared to face it in order to keep my bungalow.

The coveted house would more than likely have raised my eyebrows in other circumstances. There had been enough locally made bricks for the floors only; the walls were built of piles driven vertically into the ground, with the empty spaces filled with *potopoto*, Congolese style. Remembering my horror of the narrow windows of medieval fortresses we had seen on our recent tour of France, Michael had bay windows built. This had been easy, considering that no panes or screens were available in the territory anyway. One of the most desirable and unusual features of this luxury dwelling, in addition to the bay windows, were *potopoto* ceilings that prevented the dust from the thatched roof and the inevitable bats' droppings from continually showering the rooms.

"House or no house, you won't like it here, *ma chère*," Madame Van Derveer's warning kept popping up in my mind.

And from that day on I thought I felt her heavy hand

turning that unpleasant prophecy into reality. Certainly she may have increased the many nuisances that really were problems in the jungle. Like the delays with which the "Water Brigade" brought me the daily supply of water from the creek; the shortage of fresh vegetables from the huge governmental garden dominated by the administrator's bungalow; the Van Derveers' chickens—apparently obeying the same orders—pecking out every last seed I had planted in my flower garden. It was true that my own two new pets, a white hen and a black rooster whom I named Desdemona and Othello, joined the plundering enemies, making it impossible for me to complain about the ravages to Madame Van Derveer, should I have decided to face her again. Though it was quite unlikely that I would, for worse than anything was the wagging of Madame Van Derveer's venomous tongue, which one could avoid only by avoiding her.

There were of course a few other people stationed in Busu Melo, but they were not at the post all the time. Michael's Belgian assisting *agent sanitaire,* Monsieur Leport, was constantly traveling slowly somewhere along the road, only occasionally to reappear at Busu Melo. It was too bad, for one could invariably count on Leport for entertaining scoops. Sometimes I suspected him of being in league with some mysterious jungle newsmongering service, for he not only knew all the latest local gossip, but also always managed to learn what was happening in the distant capital of Léopoldville. He had greeted me on my arrival in Busu Melo with the story about some "clumsy oaf of a greenhorn" in Léo, who had rushed a traffic-accident casualty to a hospital in one of the cars designated for the official motorcade in honor of visiting dignitaries, ruining the upholstery with the man's blood. It so happened that the "clumsy oaf of a greenhorn" was none other than Michael himself. He had been driven about in a government car during his briefing in Léo, and had, that particular morning, come across a motorcycle smashup on the road and had taken the dying African to the hospital.

But Leport was away, and the Fallets, the young assistant administrator and his pretty and bosomy bride, were also absent on a few weeks' inspection of the interior. Madame Fallet and I had had a chance to chat briefly on the day of her departure, when she paid me an unexpected visit, probably to open her heart to somebody. It seemed that Madame Van Derveer felt that Madame Fallet ought not to pick the choicest vegetables from *her* garden, while Madame Fallet thought that just because Madame Van Derveer was the wife of the chief of the territory, she should not regard the government vegetable garden as her own personal property. Wasn't it being tended by the prisoners?

Paulette Fallet was bubbling over with indignation about it. "If it weren't for my Gaston, we wouldn't have a single prisoner," she said, curling up like a kitten in one of the morris chairs on my front *baraza*. "The natives don't call Gaston *Nkoi* (leopard) for nothing. The natives fear Gaston. You know, of course, what they've nicknamed Van Derveer? They call him '*Alembi te?*' Is he not tired? Chief of the territory, humph!"

"From what I hear, *le commissaire de district* thinks very highly of Monsieur Van Derveer as administrator." I couldn't help teasing little Madame Fallet, who was only a few years older than I.

"And why wouldn't the district commissioner think so?" she flared up. "Gaston does all the work, and *Alembi te?* takes all the credit. And he bothers my poor Gaston instead of being grateful. Do you know that now Gaston is afraid to step out of the office even for a second? Last week Gaston came home for a minute, and Van Derveer came charging right after him and lectured him in front of Kutu, our houseboy. Now what does he want Gaston to do—die from thirst? All Gaston did was to drop in for a glass of lemonade!"

Afraid of bursting into laughter, I looked away. I had already heard of that lemonade incident. To begin with, Fallet was not the lemonade type—no man in this territory was.

Besides, it was a thirst of a different nature that was driving the ardent Fallet to cross the road and pay his attractive young bride quick visits during working hours, because he claimed that "the night was made for sleeping." Michael said that, according to Leport, when Van Derveer had followed his assistant, he came upon a scene that had infuriated him. Leport thought that the devoutly Catholic Fallets, who desperately longed to have their first baby, seized every opportunity to try for it, while the Van Derveers, both two-hundred-pounders who had to enter their old Ford simultaneously from opposite sides to keep the car from tipping over, probably were enviously jealous of the younger couple's attempts. Didn't Monsieur Van Derveer, when Leport had inquired, upon the administrator's arrival in the territory, if he and Madame Van Derveer had any children, reply that he and his wife were not acrobats? Leport had laughed gleefully at recounting this titbit of the portly administrator's boudoir intelligence.

So, because of these circumstances, the Fallets might stay away from Busu Melo even longer than expected. Living out of the forever rusty iron colonial trunks was an insignificant drawback compared to all the stimulating advantages of unlimited time in a narrow folding cot screened from the rest of the world by a mosquito net . . . Those mosquito nets! In the equatorial Congo, infested with all kinds of insect life, one had the choice between the looser type of mesh, that armies of small gnats and even an occasional mosquito could easily penetrate, or the very tight sort that along with the insects kept out all air. I could imagine the Fallets bathing in their own perspiration during the hot, humid equatorial nights . . . and days.

But, anyway, my brief contact with Paulette Fallet had made it plain to me that we had nothing, except perhaps our isolation, in common. As for the three other people who now made up the rest of the permanent European population of Busu Melo, the three Portuguese traders, they lived almost like villagers with their Congolese *ménagères*, "housekeepers." This was partly by their own preference and partly because of a peculiar brand of colonial snobbery, but they kept to themselves most of the time.

Before long I knew that I would have a great deal of leisure on my hands. I also understood the actual meaning of the villagers' saying about the survival of the fattest—if not the fittest—in this territory. It clearly meant that unless one was prepared to die of boredom, one had better find a hobby without delay. And what easier and pleasanter hobby was there than indulging in hearty overeating. I was not ready, however, to give Madame Van Derveer the satisfaction of losing my waistline. Besides, my absorbing interest in Congolese customs would easily fill most of my time. My one and only self-imposed duty, which never varied during our stay in Busu Melo, consisted of packing Michael's overnight case for his short but frequent tours of the interior. The other "duties" somehow never materialized.

My well-meant plans for starting a garden fell through, for it soon became evident that the Van Derveers' chickens had powerful allies in the termites, which ate all the rose plants we had such a hard time getting. The sturdy bougainvillea was the only one to hold its own, but the help of two "gardeners" we had hired for a ridiculously low pay seemed more than adequate to look after the thriving crimson vines. And so, as far as gardening was concerned, all I could actually do was stroll among the symmetrical flower beds, with equally symmetrically planted agaves. A friendly agronomist, who had for a while been attached to the post, had landscaped the grounds for Michael with the precious red bricks left over from the floors and the square pillars that buttressed the thatched, projecting roof of our bungalow.

Naturally, I could walk not only in my own still young and bare garden, but also about the post—with its bungalows and stopover quarters. Busu Melo also boasted a small, temporary dispensary that we proudly called "Hospital" (supervised in Michael's and Leport's absence by an African *in-*

firmier, male attendant), and the Administration Office, with its crooked flagpole and sleepy and solemn barefoot sentry in front. There was the diversion of watching the tiny, sparrow-like birds, the "Republicans," building their nests that looked like strange fruits dangling from the stripped fronds of tall palms. One could also go to the local general store, midway between the government post and the village. There one could finger the multicolored calicos imported by the traders for the African women's *pagnes,* order a can of this or that, or buy the latest gadget from Léopoldville, like a bell worked by air pressure instead of the unavailable electricity.

There were other pastimes. Wearing a khaki shirt, breeches tucked into high boots, a pith helmet that was rather unnecessary in the thick forest, and carrying my twelve-gauge shotgun, I investigated the several trails leading away from the post. The gun had actually no purpose. I loved animals too much to be a hunter. And as for self-defense, loaded with buckshot, this weapon was no protection against wild animals. I knew there probably would be no need for a gun, anyway. Not that there weren't any animals around. The region was teeming with game. But unlike the well-publicized national parks or the plains in the northeast where one could see herds of game from a low-flying aircraft or even a car, here one did not run into wild animals on an afternoon hike. Yes, occasionally one would come across a passel of monkeys screeching in the trees; or a snake, undulating over a trail; or maybe even the hulking back of an elephant barring the way. Most likely, though, the only living creature one encountered on a walk would be the industrious ants forever hurrying somewhere, and beautiful, velvety black and brilliant blue butterflies hovering above the wall of tangled vegetation that obstructed the path on both sides and from behind which one suspected myriads of watchful eyes.

At first the silent, dark hairpin trails appeared too forbidding, and after a short walk I would gladly return to the security of the post. But with each passing day I would hazard

farther away from the familiar landmarks, combining the delight of discovering constantly new, eye-captivating spots with
savoring the satisfaction of escaping Madame Van Derveer.
She in her turn retaliated by being more and more intolerable
every time she managed to corner me.

CHAPTER III

I had been thinking a great deal of the old *mboka* (village) after discussing it with Michael the other day. He wasn't the only one who shunned the trail leading inland toward the swamps where that *mboka* lay near a *chenal* (watercourse) that apparently led nowhere. It seemed that none of the officials ever chanced the nearly two-hour walk to visit the hamlet. Instead, the villagers were summoned to appear at the government post whenever necessary. Naturally, with such an arrangement, the population census was less than accurate and the collected taxes far from the desired goal, but the governmental feet certainly remained drier. I was not afraid of the distance. I was a born hiker, and had often amazed my European friends by the many kilometers I could cover without tiring. Even Michael, who had done quite a bit of bicycling and skiing while living in Switzerland, and who was in top physical form, could hardly keep up with me on my long walks. However, the only visible path leading away from the main road was so boggy that in spite of my mounting curiosity it had initially discouraged my attempts to reach that intriguing community.

When I finally made up my mind to walk to the remote
mboka no matter what, I started out rather late, for it had
been raining since early afternoon and I had waited for the
rain to stop, forgetful of the abruptness of the falling tropical
night on the equator. Michael was away at Pimu, one of the
farther posts on his itinerary, and would not be back till the
following morning. Both our cook and houseboy had begged
off to trek to some African notable's wedding at the neighboring village of Busu Kwanga. It was depressing to picture myself all alone in my bungalow whose whitewashed walls were
still reeking of the *mpembe* (white clay). The only place in
the house with comfortable chairs and enough light from the
windows to read by was our living room. But stubbornly
growing from an undetectable crack in the middle of its cement floor there sprouted our very own termite hill that never
failed to hypnotize me away from my book.

Unlike the Van Derveers' old house, our new bungalow
was not really invaded by termites. Michael had told me that
the vertical piles, which made part of the framework, had
been coated with some kind of by-product of the palm-oil
refinery in Mongana, apparently distasteful to the termites. Our
own midget termite hill was probably accidental, since aside
from it there was no evidence of any invasion of other parts of
the bungalow. But whatever the cause of its springing out in
the middle of our living room, it seemed indestructible.
Neither scraping it off, nor trying to flood the possibly
kilometers-long subterranean tunnels through the barely visible
crack, did any good. The next morning it would be there once
again, a small hill with a rounded, sealed-off top, already hardened like the cement of the floor itself. All we could do was walk
around it.

It was with a lilting sense of escape that I ventured down
the hairpin trail, often so narrow that the tall plants watered
by the earlier rain brushed against me on both sides as I advanced. Soon my shirt was soaking wet. It was very quiet. The
village tom-toms, which were always audible even from our

baraza, had abruptly become silent after I had started on my walk, and without their guiding sound it was impossible to gauge my closeness to the *mboka.* It proved to be an almost two-hour hike and I began to regret straying so far at such a late hour, when unexpectedly the tom-toms resumed their wooden throbbing and a moment later I emerged near a village huddled in the center of a broad glade. It was a relief, for in seconds, although a full moon had appeared above the somber mass of the forest, it was dark.

The blaze of a huge fire somewhere in the hub of the tiny community illuminated the details of what lay before me, projecting dancing shadows of trees and dwellings. Smaller fires were in front of the rows of square windowless huts built of mud. They were erected a short distance from one another and their conical thatched roofs gave the hamlet the appearance of a tract of stacked hay. Some of the huts were shaded by clumps of banana trees, and there were cornfields to the right of the village. A rapid inspection did not yield anything more. At first sight the place looked deserted, but the now louder beat of tom-toms and the hubbub suggested that the villagers were celebrating nearby. There was a small, isolated fire built somewhat away from the rest of the hamlet. Drenched from head to toe now and shivering with cold, I approached it and, before going any farther, stripped off my clinging shirt and started to wring it out, listening to the loud uproar and watching the wind cast toward the brooding sky the long tongues of a huge, invisible fire. The villagers chanted, and the rhythm and the tone of their chanting was disturbing somehow, undoubtedly because I was worn out and edgy.

What was happening there behind the huts had been so absorbing that the sight of two figures coming slowly toward "my" fire startled me. Drawing to one side, into the screening shadow of the bushes, I tried desperately to put back on my wet shirt, under which I wasn't wearing even a bra. The more I tried the worse it got. Did the men see me? I could already imagine the interminable stories dear, sweet Madame Van

Derveer would be circulating about the shameless wife of their doctor who was running around half-naked in a village. But a sudden gust of wind, rekindling the dying fire, brought into clear view the two men who were coming toward me. They felt their way with the aid of sticks, and when they came closer and their wizened faces were spotlighted by the leaping flames, I recognized the meaningless and fixed stare of the blind. They halted, turning their backs to the village and giving me an opportunity to study them at leisure. Both of them wore leopard-skin hats, the *lukusu,* that I had seen before, a headdress reserved for notables and very old men in the Ngombe. One of them had the prominent coxcomb tattoo down the middle of his forehead and nose. This, too, was characteristic of the Ngombe. They both wore scanty loincloths hanging loosely from underneath their leopard belts, and necklaces of leopards' teeth. While I was examining them and struggling to get my shirt back on, two more shadows appeared and joined the others. One of the newcomers, an old man, was also blind. He was led by a small boy of eight or nine who was not blind, but seemed so extremely agitated that he, too, gave the impression of being unable to see. He kept turning his head toward the distant celebration. It was obvious that he longed to be there.

"*Losako,*" the old man who had just arrived, apparently certain of the presence of the two others at this spot, greeted them.

"Old wood does not bend," replied one of the oldsters now squatting by the fire.

"Nothing escapes Djakomba," answered the other, and the newcomer took his place among them, evidently according to prescribed custom.

Surprisingly, the conversation was carried on in a dialect similar to Bangala which, after the intensive course in Brussels, I understood reasonably well. But it took me a moment to recollect that Djakomba was the name of their legendary god.

All three old men sat smoking their *potongo* (horn pipes) and said nothing. Finally, the little boy, who was loitering by the fire, spoke, seemingly addressing no one in particular.

"Why am I not with the others?" the little boy said petulantly. "Bokumi, Boboka, Mosebe, and others, no older than I, are at the feast."

No one replied. The child sighed deeply.

At this point I had at last struggled back into my shirt sleeves and had nearly stepped forward. But before I could move, the little boy addressed the old man whom he had escorted.

"Why aren't you at the celebration, Grandfather? The grandfathers of Bokula and Ekomila are there. Boboka told me," he went on, "that he heard the *monganga* say that they would bury half of the meat with the dead mother of Aluo, eating only the other half. Boboka thinks that they will bury even less, only a small part. There are many people at the celebration." He sighed regretfully and added, evidently as a weighty argument, "And they are going to boil the head separately."

I had just finished reading a book of adventures of an early settler of this territory, full of hair-raising tales about vicious *minganga* (witch doctors). "Boil the head separately" was the cannibalistic custom of the Ngombe tribe at the turn of the century. My imagination began to run wild, and I could almost hear the whooping of the warriors as they closed in on me. But I instantly felt foolish, of course. Those years were a thing of the long gone past, and I was fairly close to the "civilized" government post. I shook with silent laughter and a dry twig cracked underfoot. One of the old men, the Ngombe, turned his ear in my direction. He listened for a moment but heard nothing more, since I stood still.

The only eyes that could have seen me, those of the child, were still turned toward the village.

"*Kokolo, kokolo* (take it easy), Molali Moke," said the

boy's grandfather. "When I was your age all the Bangala belonged to our people. At Lulonga, where your great-grandfather was a great chief, there was plenty of *nyama* to eat, but I would not be given the tiniest morsel. That is the law of your tribe, Molali Moke. You shall not taste any meat until you are old enough to hunt and provide meat yourself."

The old man was visibly exhausted by the effort of his speech. He breathed heavily and coughed. "And when you are as old as I am," he added, "and you have lost your father as I lost mine, you will make a vow never to eat meat again, as I made mine and Ngombe Bokoi and Ndinga made theirs. Not because the meat got tougher. There is no such thing as tough meat. For if it seems to be, it's only because the teeth are not good enough."

The two other old people nodded agreement.

"And when you are as old as I am," said the oldster who, I decided, was Ngombe Bokoi, "you will eat nothing at all, for your belly will ache after each celebration!" He cackled, his toothless mouth twitching mirthfully.

"Boboka told me—" began the boy.

"Hold your tongue," his grandfather commanded. "Boboka is a little liar who respects nothing. Was it not you, Ndinga," he addressed the other old man by his side, "who told me that Boboka was saying everywhere that his grandmother would never go to Ibanza, the god of the rich, despite all the food that would be buried with her?"

"He says," said Ndinga, "that she will have to work like a common slave all the way to join Nsungu, the god of the poor, and go on working forever, even after reaching Nsungu."

There followed a brief, reproving silence.

"Grandfather," the boy broke in, "you told me that all people become white after death. But Boboka's grandmother is dead and she's as black as ever. She is not even as light as Bokula."

"Stop asking so many questions," the old man rejoined impatiently. "*Kokolo, kokolo* (take it easy)."

Again several seconds were spent in silence. The three old men refilled their pipes and the boy passed around a burning twig to light them. The celebration in the village was reaching its peak. The wind carried waves of sounds in our direction.

I finally came out from behind the concealing bush. The little boy stood there fascinated, his bulging eyes not leaving me for a second.

"Am I not the *mwasi na monganga mokonji* (the wife of the chief doctor) from Busu Melo?" I told them in Bangala, speaking interrogatively to make an affirmative statement.

But the boy was already running away, and presently his shrill voice was echoing from somewhere behind the huts. It was very quiet here, and to break the silence I said, "*Losako* (greetings)," the way the old man who was the last to arrive had done.

"Old wood does not bend," answered the Ngombe.

"Nothing escapes Djakomba," replied Ndinga.

"I defy *moloki*," said the boy's grandfather

Only much later did I realize that in addressing that greeting to the three old men, a greeting reserved only for equals or superiors, I had honored them and, then and there, had acquired three good friends.

I was still reflecting on the enchantingly quaint manner of the oldsters' acknowledgment of my "*Losako*," with their references to Djakomba, a legendary god, and *moloki* (the devil), when the silence was abruptly shattered. People yelled, voices that sounded weird grew into the uproar of an excited crowd. The noise swelled with each passing second and before long an inflow of bodies and light from many torches flooded the small clearing where the old men and I were. Some Africans squatted, some sat down, their legs crossed under them, some knelt, with puzzled faces lifted toward me. They all gazed at me, nudging one another with delight. Then they whirled wildly around me.

This was *Isongo*, the dance of joy and mourning. They danced it in my honor and the whole village participated in the tribute. Some of the women were practically naked, their bodies painted bright red. A few wore brass necklaces and bracelets on arms and ankles, and short raffia skirts at the hipline. None among them had on *pagnes*—the unmistakable badge of the inroads of civilization, let alone regular dresses, generally indicating the proximity of a mission. The men wore brief loincloths. I smiled at two women squatting beside me and they grinned back, showing their triangularly filed teeth. One of them, instead of red, was coated with *mpembe* (white clay) that had dried in uneven streaks on her thin, shriveled body. Her hairdo also differed from that of the other women. Her short hair was tortured into what looked like dozens of tiny pigtails that pranced on her head like little wires. The *mpembe* and the hairdo were emblems of mourning. A small boy of eight or ten stood alongside the woman. Although he eyed me inquisitively there was no fear in his face, fear that was in the eyes of the other children.

The curious villagers pressed in on me from all sides, because those in the back were pushing and shoving in order to get a better look at me. Anyway, with me inching away, and the throng following me like a rippling wave, in minutes the whole crowd, with me in its midst, was slowly shifting toward the center of the *mboka*. It was hard to tell how many people there were. Perhaps fifty, it seemed offhand. We were moving toward the big fire which was still throwing up bright sparks above the thatch of the huts.

"*Mwasi na monganga mokonji te?*" (Is she not the wife of the chief doctor?) they exclaimed on all sides.

As the men and women walked, they whirled to the explosive beat of tom-toms. By this time I was so exhausted that the flames of the torches and the leaping bodies around me made me giddy. I rubbed my eyes which smarted unbearably.

It had probably taken us no more than five minutes to

CHAPTER IV

There were several large fires blazing in the square and the dancing continued within their glaring confines. Spectators watched from outside the ring of fire, but I could not see them at first because of the people surrounding me. When this human wall finally split, I beheld an odd gathering. Squatting on the ground or sitting on low stools and chairs were the village elders. When the oldsters saw me, they rose with difficulty, nudging their slower neighbors who also got to their feet.

Only one man remained seated. He had tried to rise from the low chair that was too small for his overflowing bulk but was unable to manage it. He stuck out his tongue from one corner of his thick lips, breathed heavily, sweated and combed the earth with his short, pudgy fingers. He slipped to the ground and, obviously giving up the idea of rising, burst into happy laughter. His enormous Buddha-like belly heaved and bounced like a balloon in the wind. He was drunk, as were many others. Drunk or sober, however, he was apparently an important personage for not only had no one dared to laugh at his antics but he was hastily helped up and was being addressed as *mokonji* (chief). On his feet he proved even shorter and fatter than while sitting down. And he was a midget compared to the man by his side who had commanded my attention from the first moment.

This man was huge, over six feet tall. It was hard to determine his age because his face was painted red, white, and yellow. His head was crowned with an edifice of hair, clay, and feathers. His powerful body was clad only in a raffia skirt, the rest of it painted like his face, with red and white predominating. He wore a variety of ornaments, with a brass doorknob among them. From beneath bushy brows his eyes stared at me suspiciously. The little chief looked as though he meant to say something, but he could only negotiate repeated and sonorous hiccoughs.

"*Losako,*" said one of the old men.

Frantically I tried to think of a figure of speech that might capture their imagination, one worthy of the wife of the important *monganga mokonji,* but my weary head refused to cooperate. I had to make some reply nevertheless, so I finally said, "All are equals in the eyes of Djakomba." Although not very original, it apparently pleased the people, because it was repeated with approval all around me.

A man standing behind the chief slapped his meager thighs with both hands and cackled, his toothless mouth a gaping hole. He looked like one of those poor, discussed by the blind old men earlier, to whom my words had brought that hope which was refused him even after death. The fearsome giant, unmistakably disapproving of this manifestation, shook his great body like a wet dog shaking off water, to the accompaniment of the jingling of the collection of miscellaneous objects that dangled from his arms and ankles. But he said nothing and controlled himself, for presently his face had again frozen into a grim mask.

"*Nsamba,*" the little chief yelled, calling for the palm wine.

He had apparently still not quenched his thirst, nor it seemed had many of the others. They drank with their heads thrown back, pouring the wine from gourds held at some distance from their wide-open mouths and spilling not a single drop. They made room for me among the chieftains, fortunately seating me in a comfortable low wooden chair with a high back. The fat little chief was at my right and one of the old men at my left. The gourd was being passed around and I was so tired that when my turn arrived I threw back my head, imitating the villagers, and drank avidly, spilling some of the wine on my face and shirt. My stomach was empty. The *nsamba* was strong. It was not the fresh juice of the palm tree, but one that had fermented in the jug for a day or two. It tickled my dry throat soothingly, clung comfortably to my ribs, and put lead in my feet.

My head swam a little but my weariness was gone and there was a pleasant glow around my eyes. Curiously watching the dancing still going on and on in the center of the circle, I did not think much of the female soloist, for she was neither young nor beautiful. She moved clumsily back and forth, contracting her thin belly, her pendulous old breasts swaying like a pair of socks drying on a clothesline on a windy day.

"*Djibola*," said one of the notables, evidently admiring the dancer.

"*Djibola*," echoed the little chief, but with audible disgust.

Djibola, which means "to open" in Bangala, obviously was also the name of the solo female dance.

"*Djibola*," repeated the chief, contemptuously squirting a long jet of saliva that barely missed the woman. She stopped abruptly. The tom-toms waited.

Another mouthful of the toddy made me think of the banned dance Michael had mentioned to me. "*Etumba, etumba!* (War, war!)," somebody was loudly clamoring for the dance.

It took me some seconds to realize with amusement that it was I shouting the request.

The result was instantaneous. All the young men rushed toward the open space, brandishing spears and wooden shields. The tom-toms resumed their characteristic rhythm and one big *mbonda* (a buffalo-skin drum) was pushed forward.

"Yaha-ha-ha! Ya Bangala! Yaha-ha-ha!" chanted the crowd.

I had heard this rousing cheer before. That's what the muscular young paddlers chanted when, at my arrival on the Congo riverboat, Michael had picked me up in a large dugout to ferry us through a navigable *chenal* to Busu Kwanga, where Michael's car was waiting. This was the proud chant of the riverine people proclaiming their prowess at work and play.

Presently the dance began. Once more the frenzied throbbing of tom-toms, combined with the chanting, made me dizzy, but the feeling vanished after still another reckless draft from the friendly gourd. The men formed two compact groups, facing each other. Their legs widely spread, their knees bent stiffly outward, they advanced from opposite sides toward the middle of the circle, swaying rhythmically. Each challenged his opponent by shouting into his sweaty, glistening face his own, most likely purely fictional, glorious feats in battle, accompanied by the onlookers who roared "*Etumba, etumba.*" In spite of the seeming confusion, as if by unspoken agreement, the men took orderly turns in boasting loudly about their imaginary personal exploits. But at one moment one of the participants yelled out of turn and this infringement of the rules nearly started a real battle. (More than once such innocent dancing festivals had degenerated into bloody fights, even in administered regions. This had forced the authorities in certain territories to forbid the war dance and even the carrying of shields, as they symbolize war.)

Momentarily I lost all sense of reality. I was onstage, but the chorus was singing an unfamiliar melody, and the corps de ballet was performing an exotic dance. But what opera was it? I couldn't remember either the score or when I must rise and sing my aria. What *was* my cue? Panic froze my body, like the night of my debut in a small Italian town, when I had such stage fright that all at once I seemed to have forgotten every word and every note of Musetta's waltz from *La Bohème* I knew so well. . . .

One of the men called in Ngombe to the lilliputian chief who was snoring peacefully, his head bobbing on his fat chest, and my neighbor translated it for me into Bangala: "The water is half gone in the pots."

I was back at the *mboka,* and breathed deeply, recovering from my aberration. A soft breeze carried to me a faint odor of *nyama.* Perfectly sober now, the alcoholic stimulation evaporated, I was uneasy, wondering what was in the big sooty pots. One of the notables sitting nearby had caught my stare.

"Is there not plenty of *nyama?*" he shouted to me, misunderstanding my curiosity. "Were they not the biggest goats I have ever seen?"

"'Plenty of meat'!" scoffed the giant. "Three goats for the whole village! Lately, all we can eat is our own goats! What's happened to our hunters?"

But I was no longer listening to them. Blushing, I mentally swore I would never tell anybody about my overworked imagination, not even Michael. There wasn't any cannibalism in the Congo any more, of course, and I felt even sillier than when half-naked I had tried to pull on a wet shirt under the unseeing stare of the blind old men.

Suddenly the befeathered giant took the initiative. Towering over the crowd, he yelled, his guttural voice rising above the tumult. He had evidently realized that the goodnatured frolic was about to turn into a real fight between the two overstimulated "warriors."

"The *nyama,* is it not ready?" the giant bellowed.

And, as usual, the word "meat," of which they had so very little, had a magic effect on the villagers. The dancing, singing, fighting were forgotten. All the people scurried toward the fires and the huge, sooty clay pots. As soon as the large banana leaves covering them had been lifted up, steam curled skyward in long ribbons.

The little chief, slumped beside me, was snoring rapturously. Exhausted and uncomfortable, I stared at the dark mass of the villagers' backs. It was then that I noticed at the edge of the main path one of the blind old men with his hand on his grandson's shoulder. The familiar face of the old patriarch now seemed to belong to somebody I had known all my life. With great effort I dragged myself toward him.

"Grandfather," I said in a small voice, "I am tired. I need somebody to take me back to my house."

The old man tried to put his hand on my head, but did not dare or could not find it. I took him by the arm and, led by a blind old man who was in turn guided by a child, I staggered for the second time through the narrow village paths between the silent huts. Mysterious shadows seemed to lurk and eerie sounds to come from the dark openings of the huts.

In a little while we were outside the village. It was hard to tell how long we walked through thin jungle on a narrow, spongy path into which my tired, dragging feet sank deeply. Probably close to two hours. The moon was still up, but lower, nearer the treetops of the forest edge, and appeared brighter away from the village fires. But we walked slowly, at a blind man's pace.

Presently we were out on a relatively wide road lined with thick palm trees, and in another minute we were standing in front of my bungalow.

I don't recall what I had told the old man after the long, exhausting walk through the dark jungle. Only when he and Molali Moke were gone, with the return trek still ahead of them, did it occur to me what an effort—verging on sacrifice —the elderly grandfather had made to escort me personally safely back to my home. I was in such a state of dazed fatigue I did not even think of offering him or the small boy a token of appreciation. Perhaps I did not even thank them, although no thanks could repay this gesture of the grand blind oldster who had acquired new stature in my eyes.

Slowly I climbed up the few brick steps leading to the outside *baraza* and before entering the door glanced around at the familiar picture. A sentry stood motionless by a small fire built near the crooked and now naked flagpole in front of the administration "building." All the bungalows were dark. Except for an occasional bat gliding by on its nocturnal mission, nothing stirred.

The shutters of our bungalow were still closed, as I had left them, and in the dark living room I stubbed my toe against the termite mound that had already grown inches high, and did not grumble at it.

CHAPTER V

Awakening the next morning, I was not certain at first whether my adventure of the previous evening had been real or nothing but a dream. The smarting and itching from innumerable mosquito bites, and a touch of an unmistakable hangover, however, were definitely real.

I sat up within the cage of my mosquito net, and remained still for a little while. I relished only moderately the idea of having been drinking with the villagers, which was guaranteed to bring upon my head the hellfire of the local set's censure. There was no way I could justify my behavior. My long-suffering husband was a government functionary. Although there was no law against it, socializing with the African villagers, and most positively drinking with them, was frowned upon by colonials. Even after only a few weeks in this territory, it was clear to me that it would not be easy to get along with Monsieur Van Derveer, who had no designation for the Africans other than "dog-faced monkeys," and his wife, who extended her contempt to all of us residing in Busu Melo. It was Madame Van Derveer and her trigger-happy tongue that I dreaded more than all the other unpleasantness that my unscheduled escapade was unavoidably bound to stir. Unless, of course, nobody had heard about it. I dismissed that highly wishful thought. Everybody would know it; most likely knew it already. With the swiftness with which news traveled over the grapevine, probably Michael, now in Pimu, over a hundred kilometers away, had also already heard about his *mwasi* stuffing herself on goat meat and washing it down with aged palm wine at the *mboka*. Maybe they were even saying that the wife of the *monganga mokonji* had joined the villagers in the outlawed war dance. Yaha-ha-ha! Ya Bangala! Oh, swell. . . .

The clatter of china in the adjoining dining room reminded me that I had not stuffed myself on that old goat. I was hungry. I visualized Albert, our clumsy houseboy, carefully setting the breakfast table and handling the cups and saucers as if they were made out of soap bubbles. There was nothing sophisticated about this eighteen-year-old African except his name, which actually had not been his until he had taken the elevating position of a white man's servant. He had been selected by our cook, Jafke, who, for reasons of his own, had insisted on hiring a local boy who had never been in service before, instead of one of the old hands who were commonly bequeathed to the newly arrived functionaries by their predecessors as they left the territory to return to Europe or moved on to a larger center. "He's honest. He's not corrupted," had insisted Jafke, who probably was himself the champion petty thief of the Congo. Jafke (a nickname he must have inherited from a Flemish employer) had followed Michael from Léopoldville, where Michael had singled him out from among a group of applicants who had clustered at the entrance of the government stopover house on Michael's arrival in the Congo. He picked Jafke because he had stood quietly in the background, instead of pushing his way toward Michael like the rest, and he looked sad and forlorn—an underdog contending in a contest for a plum of a job sought by a dozen formidable competitors. But soon after Michael had hired Jafke, he began to suspect that Jafke's attitude had been a calculated pose, a clever bit of applied psychology, following his having shrewdly and accurately sized up his prospective employer. He proved to be a far cry from that first impression of a modest and quiet boy he had created that day in Léopoldville. But he was an excellent cook, had good manners, and stole in moderation, always in proportion to what supplies happened to be on hand in the pantry.

Jafke was the envy of the rest of the Congolese help at the post, because of his popularity with the village "glamor girls" who invariably swooned at his marimba playing. (The old Congolese marimba is a sort of fan-shaped bit of board, inches long and wide, with a few crude metal rods fastened to the wood at only one end. The tiny "harp" is held in one hand while the fingers of the other strike or pluck the free end of the bars, producing a primitive, oriental sort of sound.) Since Jafke was a bandy-legged runt of a fellow who seemed poor competition for some of the other Busu Melo boys, his attraction for the village women was somewhat of a mystery to everybody. The riddle was solved one day by Michael's assistant, Leport (who else!), who had sneaked close to the marimba-strumming Jafke behind the kitchen quarters one night, and had overheard him whispering softly and amorously to the rapturously listening woman at his side: "I'll give you some of *mondele*'s (white man's) sugar . . . some flour . . . a tin of *nyama* . . . a bar of soap. . . ."

I felt a little giddy when I got on my feet and, after slipping on a light robe, started for the adjoining bathroom. I had to wait a few minutes before I could use it, because, standing on a wooden ladder propped against the open window, was a pair of dark muscular legs. Thanks to Michael's genius for organization and ever-present resourcefulness, we had a running-water system. While the rest of the local officials were still using the jug-and-basin system, and had their portable bathtubs filled by the chained prisoners of the "Water Brigade" transporting the water directly from the creek, Michael had an empty oil drum installed on our roof, connected to the washbowl and tub with pipe fittings painstakingly collected piece by piece from all over the territory. The source of the water remained the same, of course, but after the water tank had been filled and the two bare legs had disappeared from in front of the window, one had the luxury of running water. It was hot and cold running water. It was hot during the day, when the sun brought it close to boiling, and cold during the night.

It was Jafke, and not Albert, who was waiting for me in the dining room, a pot of steaming hot coffee in his hands. As usual, he was impeccable in a clean, stiffly starched white uniform, which the Congolese menservants wore in the large centers, and which I insisted that my domestics also wear in the interior. Jafke's black face seemed to be less fresh, however, and he appeared even shorter than his five feet, probably because he was not carrying himself as studiedly erect as usual.

"Albert is sick," he announced. "He must have eaten too much at Busu Kwanga last night."

Jafke's Bangala had the polish of mission schooling. The first time I asked him if he knew Bangala, he had proudly replied, "I speak Lingala."

"Albert must have had too much to drink," I said, and instantly bit my tongue.

"He did," said Jafke. "The palm wine can be *makasi mingi* (very strong)."

I gave Jafke a suspicious sidelong glance. Was he alluding to my drinking *nsamba* in the village last night?

"We have very little sugar left," he changed the subject. "I don't know where it all goes."

"I know," I could not resist remarking.

"Stealing from the white man a little is not really stealing, Madame," (he pronounced "Madame" something like "madamu" or "madama," Congolese fashion) he remarked, without bothering to deny the implication.

"That's an interesting approach," I said.

"The white man has so much of everything," he explained. "When you fill a glass with water from a river, it does not make the river drier."

"Sugar isn't water from the river," I objected meekly.

To an African manservant who followed a European into the bush, the never-ending supply of provisions arriving month after month at the white man's house appeared like an interminably flowing river of riches. He worked hard on measly pay, counting on the real payoff at the end of the three years marking the termination of the government functionary's regular Congolese term. Then, at his employer's departure, he might inherit lots of old junk, like a couple of pots and pans; maybe some kitchen utensils; maybe a folding cot or his *mondele's* cast-off tropical clothes. And it was only natural that while waiting for that distant, happy day he should help himself a little to the white man's seemingly inexhaustible supplies. Madame Van Derveer would probably vehemently disapprove of my ideas. She spent a great deal of time and ingenuity trying to catch her boys stealing. She went to considerable lengths, such as building intricate patterns out of sugar lumps in her sugar bowl, and was proud of herself when she succeeded in trapping one of the "baboons."

"There was a big celebration in the old *mboka* last night," Jafke interrupted my thoughts. "A very big celebration," he repeated.

Was he staring at me? "Yes?" I did my best to sound indifferent.

"Mmmm," he went on. "*Mondele* Van Derveer and *mondele* Fallet were not here last night, they had both gone to Lisala. And our own *monganga mokonji* is in Pimu. And the *monganga moke* has only come back this morning, and, with no government men around, the village went crazy, and they drank a lot and they even danced the war dance. And the *mwasi na mondele* Van Derveer was awfully angry and wanted to send the sentry to stop it all, but he was scared to go so far alone at night and she said when *mondele* Van Derveer came back he would arrest lots of people for it, and—"

"Was any outsider there?"

"There was nobody but the villagers. Busu Kwanga had its own celebration. Only the local *basenji*," he said contemptuously.

He would not call me a peasant, so he didn't know yet I had been there, too. And Michael's *agent sanitaire*, Monsieur Leport—the *monganga moke* (junior doctor) to the Africans —who had been on inspection down the river, was back. I would have a chance to learn from him all the local news, maybe even including that about myself.

"You forgot to eat your papaya," said Jafke. "Would you like me to get you some mangoes from your tree?"

He was talking about the mango tree that spread its lush, fruit-laden branches over the kitchen quarters in the backyard. It was "my" tree because I was its principal user. Not that I ate that many mangoes. But I sampled half a dozen or so before selecting one to my liking—for each seemed to have its own distinctive fragrance and flavor. It made me feel quite luxurious.

I shook my head and got up from the table.

"There are some village *bana* (children) waiting for you outside," he said, pointing to the back door.

CHAPTER VI

The first thing I saw outside were the breeches and shirt I had worn yesterday and had abandoned in a heap on the cement of the bathroom floor. They were washed clean and drying on a clothesline stretched between two of the many brick columns that supported the thatched awning of the roof on all four sides. Five pairs of eyes furtively watched my every movement. The eyes belonged to five kids, two of whom I already knew. I smiled at the children, and they grinned back at me. They all were about eight or ten and looked healthy. One boy, the one I had decided last night was Boboka, had one of his front teeth missing, and the only girl in the group was timidly hiding behind the boys.

The presence of the children revived in my memory the picturesque village, the exciting folklore, the Africans' songs and dances, their primitive way of dressing that one seldom saw on the traveled government road which ran only a couple of hours' walking from the heart of their *mboka*. Here I had a Congolese community within reach, a people who lived as their forefathers must have lived long ago, they and their ancestral customs unspoiled by destructive contact with tourists.

This was exactly what I had dreamt about. It also came to me that, because of the unusual circumstances, I had a rare opportunity of getting close to the villagers, a chance I would never have had otherwise. And their response was also exceptional. The African was wary and suspicious of outsiders. And, as a rule, the white man, the "superior" white man, at least the old colonial for whom the average villager was nothing but a "baboon" or "ape," did not even try to crack the artificial and superficial front presented to him by the distrustful African. Perhaps a missionary working in a remote region has an opportunity to learn something about authentic African customs. But then he deals with people gradually conditioned to accept him and his teachings and finally willing to abandon the honored old ways and accept the civilizing man's alien ideas. Even in my privileged position I had to be careful in asking any questions of these children, or I would end up getting the same kind of answers the Africans had for all outsiders—information having nothing to do with either fact or truth. Stealing from a white man wasn't stealing, said Jafke. Perhaps neither was lying, I thought.

Suddenly I had an inspiration. "You like to play games, don't you?" I asked the children, hoping they understood my Bangala.

They answered in unison with an affirmative "Mmmm."

"Do you want to play a game with me?"

A second and eloquent "Mmmm" was their reply.

The youngsters waited with shining eyes. They were like all other kids the world over, and I have always gotten along exceptionally well with children and young animals.

"Let's pretend that I'm a very little girl who knows nothing and you are all grown and wise. I'm going to ask you many questions and you are going to answer them. Understood?" I suggested.

"*Malamu, malamu!* (good)" shouted the children, clapping their hands. The little girl hopped merrily on one foot.

All five of my little friends were naked, naturally. The

girl was somewhat older than the boys. Her breasts were already budding, and with her intricately braided hairdo she looked like a miniature woman.

"What are your names?" was my first question.

"Boboka," said Boboka.

"Molali Moke," sang out my own private little Christopher Columbus.

"Bokumi," said the third boy.

". . . he is not even as light as Bokula." The words of Molali Moke, speaking to his grandfather, returned to my mind. I smiled at the fourth boy who was considerably lighter than the rest, and guessed he was the same one mentioned by Molali Moke. He was not a mulatto, but his skin was the color of light chocolate. "And what is your name, Bokula?" I asked.

The boys giggled so much that two toppled over and rolled on the ground, but the little girl was indignant.

"*Mwasi na Monganga Mokonji,* are you not a *mwana moke?* (a little child). You must pay attention and not remember anything!" she chided.

"Mmmm," I agreed, turning to the little girl, "I'm going to be careful. What is your name, young lady?"

"Ekomila," replied the thrilled child.

"Are those your real names?"

"Mmmm," they echoed in unison again.

"*Monganga* Djito ordered us never to give our true names to a white man," said Molali Moke, "or *moloki* (the devil) would get us."

"Then why did you tell me your right names?"

"*Monganga* Djito said white man, and not white woman," Molali Moke explained with conviction.

"Don't some of your names sound like those of villages or rivers?"

"Mmmm," Molali Moke confirmed. "They're the names of places whence our grandfathers came."

"But not all our names are like those of villages," added

Bokumi. "The chief's name is not really a name. It is a *nkombo* (a nickname). He's called Mafuta because he is so fat."

"And Djito is not the real name of the *monganga*, either. He is called *djito* because he is so big and heavy."

"Which one is *Monganga* Djito? Is he the tall man with the feathers who was next to the chief last night?" I asked the children.

"Mmmm," they chorused, somewhat uneasy at the mention of the medicine man, which, having met the *monganga* myself, didn't surprise me.

"It is he who took your gun," added Molali Moke.

I was dumbfounded. Of course, my gun and ammunition —I did not remember bringing them back home with me last night. I recalled leaning my gun against my chair, with the ammunition belt hung on its muzzle. Now the witch doctor had both. This was another and still more embarrassing complication. The Africans were not permitted to have modern firearms in their possession. Now not only Madame Van Derveer would have something to talk about, but her husband, too, as chief of territory, would have plenty to say. Should I report the whole thing immediately, try to recover my gun myself, or maybe through Michael? The Africans seemed to have a deep regard for him.

"How do you know *Monganga* Djito has it?" I asked.

"After I had brought Grandfather home last night," Molali Moke explained, "I ran to the spot where I had seen your gun, but it was gone. Then, early this morning, I wanted to ask Grandfather what I ought to do, and my sister Baloki told me that he was with *Monganga* Djito and I ran over to his house to look for Grandfather. I looked inside. The room was empty, but I saw your gun. It was hidden under a *lomposo na nkoi* (a leopard skin) with only a little end of it showing, but it was your gun, I am sure."

"Why didn't you take it and bring it back to me?" I asked, realizing the futility of asking him such a question. No village child would ever enter the hut of a *monganga* who had the power to chase away *likundu* (bad luck), who knew how to elude the designs of the devil, but who, when he so desired, could also bring down a horrible fate upon the head of his enemy. In any event, not the hut of the fearsome Djito. "Then you left without having seen *Monganga* Djito?" I went on questioning the child.

"He did not see me," he replied gleefully, "but I saw him, all right. When I returned to the main square I heard the sound of voices coming from the House of the Council. Djito was there and he was very angry. Grandfather, Ndinga, and many other old ones were there speaking together. Chief Mafuta was there, too, but he said nothing; he slept."

"Go on, tell me everything you heard," I urged the boy, interested and curious.

"I did not understand what *Monganga* Djito wished to say," he continued. "He shouted that if the poor thought that they would become like the rich after death, soon they would begin thinking that they were like the rich before they died, and that there were no separate gods for the rich and the poor."

"What else did he say?" I was getting more and more interested, for the witch doctor had evidently referred to my answer to the *"Losako"* (greeting).

"He did not say anything more," said Molali Moke. "It was the chief who did. He woke up, said that he was thirsty and that the Council had met to discuss his business and not that of the gods. He said that when somebody sleeps with somebody else's wife he ought to pay for it."

For a little while Molali Moke went on telling us about the chief's outrage at a man by the name of Ngele, who had been caught sleeping with one of the chief's wives. But I only half-listened to him, even though his discussing the whole matter so knowingly, like an adult, was amazing in itself.

"I'd like to walk over to your *mboka*," I said.

Jafke came out of the house carrying the breakfast dishes to the kitchen quarters, built separately as usual a few yards behind the bungalow, and stared with undisguised disapproval at the children's muddy feet.

"They'll leave lots of chigoes all over the place," he remarked.

"While I'm dressing," I replied, "give them a jar of preserves."

"A whole jar!" Jafke was indignant.

The jar was gone a few minutes later when I reappeared.

"I gave them only half a jar," announced Jafke, emerging from the kitchen. "Half a jar is plenty, why should one waste all that good stuff on little *basenji?*"

"Did you put the other half back in the pantry?" I asked, more to tease him than anything else. But he wasn't in the least embarrassed.

"Didn't you say to give them a whole jar?" he replied. "You didn't tell me anything about putting half of it back in the pantry."

Maybe half a jar was enough. They had probably never eaten anything like that before. Their eyes shone and they did not stop licking their lips and fingers all the way to the old village.

Walking between rows of mud huts bordering the main road, it took us only about twenty minutes to reach the boggy trail by which the blind old grandfather and Molali Moke had brought me back home. How different it appeared now in the sunlit early morning. The marbly design of sparkling light filtering through the high canopy of trees, and the small gemlike birds on the wing above wild hibiscus bushes dispelled the gloomy loneliness of the path. And a bunch of playful monkeys swinging from tree to tree, one carrying a tiny baby on its back, momentarily made me forget the object of my hike.

After an almost two-hour walk the hairpin trail winding through thick jungle opened on the small community, and before long we found ourselves in the main circular area, where alone the smoldering fires were a reminder of the previous night's festivities. This ancient hamlet with all the earmarks of a community of riverside people—with fishermen's nets drying out in the sun, the people's hairdos, the Bangala they spoke—was surprising in its relative nearness to the typical new Ngombe village of Busu Melo, that had sprung up on both sides of the government road, with its small cassava and corn patches, the villagers' characteristic coxcomb tattoos and Ngombe dialect. To be sure, I was not a trained anthropologist, and my idea about the history of the territory and its people was quite sketchy.

When we approached the meetinghouse, the largest hut in the village, the crowd was already dispersing. Boboka, who had hopped away for a few minutes, returned with an explanation:

"They gave Ngele a few days to find somebody to speak for him."

"Nobody will speak for him," opined Molali Moke. "He has nothing with which to pay a good man to speak for him."

Evidently a good lawyer is as expensive in the jungle as in the civilized world, I thought absently, at the moment not a bit interested in Ngele's problem. I had a problem of my own, and should I not recover my gun, perhaps I would need a lawyer myself. But my problem was solved with greater ease than I had anticipated.

When I walked up to the giant witch doctor towering above a small crowd surrounding him he did not appear as fierce-looking in broad daylight as he had the night before.

"You have something belonging to me, Djito; you have my gun," I told him, with casual firmness.

"How could I have it," he retorted. "Did you give it to me?"

"If you have forgotten where you put it, look under the leopard skin in the corner of your room," I rejoined.

When the hubbub of the crowd died away, the arrogant Djito said humbly, "I meant to do the right thing by keeping it for you, *Mwasi na Monganga Mokonji*. I shall bring it to you directly."

He disappeared behind the nearest row of huts and before long—while the crowd was curiously examining me, giggling delightedly, some of the women touching first the flowery print of my blouse, then my bare arms—Djito came back and, with a grin that unveiled his yellow teeth, handed me my gun and ammunition belt. The relief at avoiding complications made me hastily take them and allow him to leave without a word. My gun and nine remaining cartridges seemed like dear friends lost and found again.

"My sister thinks we had better go and play by the stream," Bokumi said timidly.

"Mmmm," the children and I agreed eagerly.

My business completed, I was free to enjoy myself with my little friends. Michael wouldn't be back before noon, and after all that poking by all those inquisitive hands, the stream seemed like a wonderful idea.

The ever brighter sun made me squint, and remembering my sunglasses in the ammunition belt pocket I put them on. The effect on the kids was remarkable. They gaped at me incredulously, evidently never having seen sunglasses before. Impatient to start for the stream, I removed the glasses and put them back into the belt pocket. Had I removed my eyes and tucked them away the effect could not have been more striking.

Glancing about me on our way to the stream I recognized certain features of the landscape. I noticed the small pile of cold ashes, the skeleton of last night's fire where I had met the old men and Molali Moke. Gaily I followed the children who, skipping like a herd of *mboloko* (tiny antelopes), rushed toward the forest.

We were at the small creek in no time at all. The sun shone on the red sandy bottom of the stream. Swarms of small yellow butterflies were struggling against being carried away by the breeze. It was hot. I sat on my haunches at the edge of the stream, washing my hands that obstinately refused to yield very much dirt without the help of soap. The children were in the water, splashing like ducklings. They called out to me to join them. My clothes all at once seemed infinitely more immodest and out of place here than nakedness, and stripping down to my brief panties I quickly waded into the stream.

Had I been black I would have in no way attracted their attention. But the sight of my pale body enchanted them. They called out in amazement and ecstatically rolled their eyes. I attempted vainly to hide in the shallow water, but it came only to my knees.

"Your breasts are round like those of Baloki," remarked Ekomila.

"Is she the sister of Molaki Moke?" I laughed self-consciously.

"Mmmm, she is Molali Moke's *nkaja mpomba* (elder sister)," said Ekomila. Then she added dreamily, "When I grow up, mine will be round also and not long like those of my mother."

The whole group of kids was examining me. But I suddenly was certain that they looked at me the way they might examine an uncommon butterfly or lizard, and the uncomfortable sense of false modesty drained away. We played in the water, throwing handfuls of it at each other. It splashed against our bodies, sparkling on the smooth dark velvet of the children's skin. We had a truly wonderful time. Later we sat on the edge of a partly submerged old dugout, swinging our legs in the water, and the youngsters no longer paid any attention to my pale skin.

When I got back home a few hours later, I felt rested and refreshed, despite the long hike. I knew now that I would have no idle hours on my hands from this moment on, for I would be going back to the *mboka* and the children as often as possible—Madame Van Derveer or not.

CHAPTER VII

For the next two weeks I was unable to return to the old *mboka*. Not because of Madame Van Derveer. To my relief and amazement, nobody had learned of that eventful first evening I had spent at the old village, or about my lost and found gun.

"The Africans are very good about keeping their secrets," Michael told me when I shared my experiences with him. "In all likelihood the whole 'civilized' population was asleep, all the servants were at the Busu Kwanga wedding celebration, and none of the villagers themselves would talk about what goes on in their midst."

What was really keeping me from revisiting the *mboka* was that Michael was staying at the post, and naturally I wanted to spend every available moment with him. I owed this unexpected pleasure to the car, which had broken down just as he was starting out on one of his inspection swings. Now, in between his work at the hospital across the road, where he was organizing a territorial clinical laboratory and treating his patients at the dispensary, he was trying to repair his jalopy with the aid of Carlos, the Portuguese trader. Carlos ran the best general store in Busu Melo for both Europeans and Africans. He also happened to be the only man within a hundred kilometers who knew a little something about motors. Although probably even a qualified mechanic would have had trouble putting back in shape Michael's beat-up Chevy.

The dilapidated car looked from the front somewhat like a convertible, for it sported a locally made canvas top over the driver's seat. From the rear it had the appearance of a small truck, because of a wagonlike contraption that had replaced the back seat. It was resold by each departing functionary to his successor, with hardly any reduction in the original price, although Busu Melo possessed only one road of about three hundred kilometers spanning the length of the territory. And the only way of going beyond that was loading the car onto a boat privately owned by a large palm-oil exporting company of Mongana. Mongana, with its lush tropical fruit orchard, profusion of flowers, and modern conveniences, was a self-contained community at one end of the road from where their small craft regularly crossed the Congo River to Lisala. No new cars were ever brought into the territory, and the four cars already in it were there for good.

Finally, one bright morning, after dismantling the motor part by part, Carlos made his final diagnosis.

"Nothing doing," he declared, showing us a few corroded pieces that had been a piston, "you'll have to write to Léo, although I doubt they have spare parts for this old model. Maybe you'd better write directly to America."

Michael and I only glanced at each other in dejected silence. This was the end of our well-mapped plans for the rest of the year. Now, without his jalopy, his work sometimes kilometers away, he would either have to leave me alone for a few weeks—at which I balked—or expose me to the hardships of constantly being on the road. This meant transportation by bone-marrow-jolting *tipoye* (a seat strapped between long bamboo poles slung over the bearers' shoulders). It also meant dirty, hot, and often crumbling stopover houses, all sorts of insects and vermin, a steady diet of monotonous canned food and drinking water from questionable creeks, an idea that Michael had ruled out from the start. I wanted to plead with Carlos. Wasn't there anything that could be done? Maybe one could put this thing together with glue or something? But Michael signaled to me to keep out of this.

"Well, that's that, thanks, Carlos," he said. "I'm sure you would help me if you could."

"You know I would, Doctor. I haven't forgotten the favor you did me once," said Carlos, scratching his curly dark head, never protected by a pith helmet or even an ordinary hat.

Carlos was a big, muscular fellow, at one time a prize-fighter in his native Portugal, his burnished copper skin of the mulatto darkened by the ten-year-old Congolese suntan.

"Forget it, Carlos," Michael said a little too quickly. "Come, let's have an early drink."

"All right," Carlos said absently. "All right," he repeated, as we walked up the front *baraza* steps.

We waited patiently in our morris chairs for Albert to serve us our drinks, while the houseboy was desperately making an effort not to knock over any of the bottles.

Monsieur Leport, who had had time to leave Busu Melo and come back again from another brief tour of duty, dropped in for a moment, wearing his usual khaki shorts (the only shorts worn by a European in the territory), and stretching his long, thin legs across the *baraza,* flashed all his gold-capped teeth in a convivial smile.

"Leport, I understand that you and some other fellows have played a trick on Richot," remarked Carlos, making Leport guffaw with delight.

"Who is this Richot, and what sort of trick did you play on him?" I asked Leport.

He guffawed a little more before explaining, "We celebrated Richot's son's birthday when we all met in Gunji.

Richot runs a small trading post there—he buys palm oil from the natives and sells it to Mongana. His son is a mulatto."

"They all got drunk—Richot, Silva, and Almeida. And he, too," said Carlos, pointing to Leport. "You know the other two, they're always pickled."

"Actually, Richot was the drunkest that time," said Leport. "That's why the trick was played on him."

"What trick?" asked Michael, who had evidently not listened to the exchange.

"When Richot passed out and fell on his face, we put his whole left leg in a plaster cast. I had my surgical trunk with me, as usual, so we had all we needed. Almeida, who had remained in Gunji for a day or two, promised to keep Richot in the cast for at least twenty-four hours before telling him that it was only a gag and that his leg wasn't really broken."

"I hope he won't be too sore at you," remarked Carlos. "Richot is a mighty big fellow to have to fight." He shot a disdainful glance at Leport's spindly legs.

"I won't be back in Gunji for the next month or so," laughed Leport, "and by that time Richot will have cooled off. By the way, Carlos, the Sisters at the Busu Modanda Catholic Mission have asked me to ask you when you'd take a look at their car as you've promised them."

"*Sacré bleu,* so I did," Carlos swore, jumping to his feet as though he had been attacked by the cannibalistic red ants.

A strange expression crossed his face, and somehow I thought it was reflected on Michael's face, too.

"I'm sure you'd do for me anything you could," he repeated as Carlos was leaving, a bit irrelevantly, it seemed.

"A nice chap that Carlos," said Leport. "He went all the way to Lisala the other day just to get something for me."

The "something" Leport was so mysteriously referring to was a sewing machine he had ordered for his African *ménagère,* and he was the only one who thought it a secret. People said that he was sincerely in love with her. These local women, often not even pleasing to the eye, had a great attraction for European men. A legend had it that the women from Lake Kisale region in the distant Katanga used special herbs to attract men. But, of course, Mariette, Leport's *ménagère*, who had rather fine features and a truly beautiful body, had no need to rely on any magic herbs, or the powerful ally of all women everywhere: the loneliness of the long nights that imprisons men in some heaven-forsaken place, when a spoken word, laughter, and an illusion of companionship meant more perhaps than sexual gratification.

"He had quite a fight with his Mariette last night," Michael told me, after Leport had gone.

I knew about it already, and I also knew that it was not Leport who had come out the winner. Paulette Fallet had told me that Mariette had used on Leport the maneuver that enabled the local village women to hold their own in scuffles with their drunken males. It consisted in grabbing the male by the skin of his testicles and twisting it until he gave up. For the first few seconds the woman had to protect her face with her other arm from her man's blows. But as a rule the man gave in instantly. Michael had once told me that the tough and rugged Carlos had not lost the contest he had had with his *ménagère* when she had taken hold of him one day, but had required six stitches on his scrotum. Maybe that was the favor for which Carlos was still grateful to Michael—the stitches.

The following day Carlos's motorcycle came roaring into our front yard, and triumphantly he showed us a shining cylinder for Michael's car.

"The Sister's car is about the same year as yours," he explained. "It will fit."

"How sweet of the good Sisters," I said. "I must thank them the first time I see them."

"I wouldn't do that," grinned Carlos. "They don't know they have done you this little favor."

"Don't tell me you took one of the parts from their car

without telling them?" I was astounded. But glancing at Michael I had a sudden suspicion that he had known all along what Carlos had meant to do.

"So I did," Carlos confessed breezily. "The Sisters' car needs new tires anyway. The old ones are falling apart. Their car has been immobilized for more than a year now. Don't order the piston," he told Michael, "the Sisters will order it together with the tires and a couple of other parts they need."

"You'll go straight to hell when you die," I chaffed Carlos.

"No, I won't, Madame," he grinned, showing off his strong white teeth. "The good Sisters told me they pray for me all the time. They're very grateful."

The next day, trying to make up for lost time, Michael left earlier than usual, his overloaded "gypsy wagon" swaying dangerously as he turned into the beautiful palm-lined Busu Melo road. The loud roar of his ancient Chevy, unchecked by the hopelessly rusted muffler, had scarcely died away, when, singing the first-act aria from *La Traviata*, I was leisurely heading along the narrow path toward the hub of the old *mboka*.

CHAPTER VIII

The early morning mist clinging to the ground lent an eerie quality to the forms of the women busily carrying out of their mud huts the shallow clay pots with the embers of the fires that had as usual served to keep them warm during the chilly and humid night. Some of them, as was the custom, had their babies straddled across one hip as across a saddle, as always making me wonder how they could go about their chores at the same time. A few men, stretching lazily and yawning noisily, joined the women at the starting fires.

My official call on the parents of Molali Moke at this sunrise hour was a bit unconventional perhaps, but the only time one could find the whole Congolese village family "at home" was either at the crack of dawn, before they had scattered on their daily chores, or at their late evening gatherings.

Molali Moke's family received me outside their hut, around a small, smoking fire, and offered me a low hand-carved ebony stool. It was hard not to stare admiringly at Molali Moke's sister. What an odd whim of nature it was to have had such a delightful creature born to such insignificant parents as that aging woman, mashing manioc in a huge wooden mortar at the entrance to their hut, and that hunched man, crouching by the fire. So flawless were the proportions of Baloki's almost naked body that it evoked a work of art created by a great artist.

Once again it was pleasantly surprising to find that like those of the children, young Baloki's face and body were unmarred by the tattoos on which the Ngombe tribe prided itself, acquiring the keloid scars through a series of painful pricks and incisions from early childhood. The elders' faces and bodies in the Ngombe were all ornamented with a variety of prominent scars. Baloki's young body was freshly coated with *ngola*. Nearly all the local village women used it. That coat of finely powdered red bark blended with oil probably protects more efficiently against sun and insects than clothes, and it looks attractive, too. The *ngola* covering Baloki's mother, however, was blotted out and smeared in several spots and its color had faded, making the woman appear to be wearing dirty, torn tights. She was one of the few among the villagers who did not speak Bangala. In fact, one wondered if she could speak at all, since she never once opened her mouth.

"You are a beautiful *ngondo*, Baloki," I told her, "you must be the most beautiful unmarried girl in the *mboka*."

"You would be the most beautiful," replied Baloki, "if your long lashes did not hide your eyes."

Baloki was having makeup trouble, she told me. The night before she had painted her eyelids with *mpembe* (white clay) in honor of her sweetheart's visit. Now she was trying to remove the *mpembe* by applying a black paste and rinsing it off her face with water. The dark stuff lathered almost like soap.

"Do you know how to prepare this, Baloki?" I pointed to the paste.

"Mmmm, it's quite simple," she replied. "I char some banana skins and mix the ashes with palm oil. But I prepare very little of it at a time, for I'm the only one in our house who uses it. Molali Moke is too small to be dirty; my mother changes her *ngola* only once every moon, and my father has himself scraped with an iron blade."

"With what?"

"With an iron blade," repeated Baloki. "Every new moon my mother scrapes him with it."

They offered me some food. Even had I been starving to death, there was little for me to eat. The smell of the *nsongo* (cassava) paste that had fermented for days in swampy water (the usual local procedure for destroying the prussic acid in its roots) was indescribably horrid. The eggs, which were rotten, were not edible, either, since most villagers in the interior ate only the spoiled eggs, because they considered it impractical to consume fresh eggs that might eventually turn into chickens. The only things fit to eat, to my way of thinking, were the delicious *bitabi* (midget bananas). Not wanting to hurt their feelings by refusing their hospitality, I accepted a banana, to Baloki's visible delight.

Baloki disappeared for a short while, leaving me to chat with her father, who told me that he was in the sugarcane beer business, brewing *masanga na nkoko*. He had started to tell me how hard he had to toil to compete with other palm wine dealers and that he could not even take time out to go to the meetinghouse, when Baloki reappeared, accompanied by her *ndeko* (bethrothed), Lisengo. He was a tall lad with the broad chest of an athlete. He and Baloki, who were unmistakably in love, made a handsome couple.

"He knows how to make anything he wishes out of a piece of iron," said Molali Moke, and Lisengo preened himself, gazing proudly at a two-pronged spear he had evidently made.

"Where is your grandfather?" I asked Molali Moke, glancing at the dark entrance of the family hut.

"He's at the meetinghouse," said Boboka, who, along with my other little friends, had just joined us. "The old ones will decide about Ngele, you know, the man who slept with one of the chief's wives without paying for it."

"Some of Ngele's friends have collected a few things to get him a man who'll speak for him. Ngele is poor, he has nothing of his own," remarked Baloki, who was already making up her eyelids with fresh *mpembe*.

I jumped eagerly to my feet. "May I go the meetinghouse and listen to the palaver?"

They all stared at me with surprise.

"Is not everybody going to be there?" said Lisengo. "Maybe Ngele will be beaten up," he added; wishfully, I thought.

"Is it not too early yet?" Molali Moke's father said indifferently.

But apparently it was not too early, for the village "street" was by now jammed with people heading for the main square, and I noted again the exceptionally fine posture of these African men and women, which they owed to carrying everything on their heads. In spite of the nakedness of the women, their freshly applied *ngola*, their intricate hairdos, and their slow and silent barefoot shuffle, the throng reminded me of a leisurely Sunday crowd in any small community in the world.

When we had finally made it to the meetinghouse, there were so many people milling in front of it that getting closer seemed hopeless. But Lisengo, putting his broad shoulders to work, cleared the way for me through the throng. The meetinghouse was actually nothing but a square thatched roof supported by poles driven into the ground and surrounded by a waist-high bamboo wall to enable the whole *mboka* to have a good view of the interior from the outside and to hear the palaver conducted by the village elders.

The village council was composed of many more men than I had expected. They squatted in a tight circle, smoking their *potongo*, and among them was Molali Moke's grandfather. In addition to the leopard-skin sashes and *lukusu* worn by the notables, a cheerful touch was contributed by Chief Mafuta in a red velvet waistcoat, a large door key dangling from his fat neck. But first prize should have been awarded Djito who, in a medley of feathers, bright paint, and jingling cat-bells, seemed to fill the whole space. Alongside the chief stood a man with an enormous fagot of short sticks in his arms. There was a similar bundle in the arms of another man who stood beside the accused Ngele, whom the children had pointed out to me as his defense counsel, and a woman who laid down her burden of sticks at his feet. The significance of all those sticks became clear to me only after the proceedings had begun.

Each time that one or the other party scored in the argu-ment, conducted in rapid-fire Ngombe that Lisengo translated for me into Bangala with amazing ease, the man tossed a few sticks into the center of the ring. The elders either approved, or made the speaker take back a stick or two. The debate was brief. Ngele's defense consisted of denials of his illicit rela-tions with one of Chief Mafuta's wives. She was a tall woman with tremendous breasts. Unfortunately for Ngele he could not deny that he had been in the woman's hut. It was there that Mafuta had surprised him, and the argument went more or less as follows:

"Why did you not ask the chief for permission to sleep with his wife?"

"Because I had no desire to make love with his wife."

"But you were found asleep in her house?"

"Is it necessary to get the chief's permission to sleep?"

This was a point in favor of the accused, and no one pro-tested when Ngele's defender cast several little sticks into the middle of the meetinghouse.

But just as things seemed to be going so well for Ngele, the woman herself suddenly betrayed her lover.

"He was not asleep all the time," she said complacently, and went on graphically to describe to the assembly the mi-nute details of that night of love. At each of her disclosures the chief's lawyer cast a stick. Sometimes the sticks were hurled by Mafuta himself as he contentedly guzzled *nsamba* and scratched away at his fat belly.

Ngele's eyes did not leave the convicting lips of his mistress. There was neither fear nor indignation on his face; he visibly savored once more the memory of the pleasures of that night as the woman revealed them to the assemblage.

When her voluntary confession was finished, the chief's representative victoriously tossed several handfuls of sticks into the arena. Before the sentence of guilty was pronounced, however, Ngele was offered another opportunity. If he still persisted in pleading innocent, perhaps he would prefer to submit to a *n'ka* test?

This barbaric test was inflicted occasionally by witch doctors, even in administered territories, upon some unfortunate accused of a real or imaginary crime. It had been described to me on a riverboat by an administrator returning to his headquarters from an investigation of just such a case in the bush. The test was outlawed and had almost disappeared from the Congo. It was the ordeal by poison. The one subjected to it was forced to drink a brew of a plant containing tetanic poison concocted by a witch doctor.

Ngele, a small stick in his hand, did not hesitate long. "No, I do not want the *n'ka* test," he said, tossing away his last symbol of defense.

Some minutes later the judges pronounced their verdict: the man was guilty. Was he prepared to pay? So many spears, so much of this and that?

Ngele was unable to pay, of course, and the jury adjudged him Chief Mafuta's slave until the price imposed should be paid or the guilty man should have worked for an equivalent period. Ngele did not flinch. He did not seem stunned or dejected by the sudden change in his fortunes, although the price for a single night of love was staggering. It would have to be paid for with months or years of hard labor. He stared at the beefy woman who was walking away swinging her elephantine rump. There was nothing in his eyes except the desire the confession had rekindled. Poor Ngele was apparently going to be a *moumbu* (a slave) for the remainder of his life.

Just as I had often been amazed by, say, an audience giggling in all the wrong places at a serious play, or other such instances of strange reactions in my own "civilized world," so was I now puzzled by the reaction of the villagers following the verdict. The tension of the crowd abruptly gave way to a loud explosion of laughter. Many men, seemingly unable to stop laughing, held their sides; others rolled on the ground. When this collective paroxysm had finally subsided, several people, completely exhausted, were stretched on the ground, and the *ngola*-painted faces of the women were streaked with laughter-induced tears. As I was preparing to leave, the crowd began to disperse boisterously, the hum of their voices filling the square. And it became clear why Molali, who claimed that he was so busy, had come with us, after all. Throughout the palaver he had appeared totally uninterested in the final outcome, and had wandered discreetly around the square, animatedly discussing something with several other men. Finally he had evidently reached a satisfactory agreement with one of them, for a smug grin had spread over his sour face. Now this man Molali had been talking to suddenly drew general attention by loudly yelling: "I have unsuccessfully tried many expensive drugs to relieve my bellyaches, and yet a single gourd of Molali's *masanga na nkoko* has cured me. What a pleasant treatment, huh?"

Molali had obviously hired a publicity agent for his sugarcane beer factory.

"Chief Mafuta didn't seem very angry at his wife," I remarked to Molali Moke's grandfather, failing to understand the fat chief's reaction to the evidence at the trial. I had been prepared for a scene of jealousy and recriminations, perhaps even bloodshed, when the woman's guilt was established. Baloki had told me that years ago the outraged husband used to pierce one of the calves of the unfaithful woman with his spear.

"Why should he have been angered?" interjected Molali. "Is he not going to be paid?"

Little Boboka, who was trotting alongside us to visit Molali Moke, was again more familiar with the behind-the-scene details of the scandal than any of the grownups.

"A few days ago," he said, "I heard Mafuta's wife telling him that Ngele was coming to see her at night. Chief Mafuta laughed and laughed. I think that he did not understand it well."

Naive little Boboka, I thought. The chief had understood only too well. It was poor Ngele who still did not see the trap into which he had so willingly fallen.

CHAPTER IX

Back home at the post a few palavers had also flared up, but we had no meetinghouse with wise old men puffing away on their *potongo* to settle our differences.

To begin with a small war had erupted among the Portuguese traders. There was nothing new about it, and nothing personal. Each time the traders made ready to attend a public auction, arranged for them periodically by the administration at various points of the territory to allow them to buy raw materials from the Africans in open competition, the merchants went into a huddle to agree among themselves on the top bid for the products: so much for palm oil, so much for copal, so much for palm-oil fruit or copra. They would slap one another on the back, laugh at the "baboons" they were going to outwit this time, and seal their shrewd financial deal with bottlefuls of warm imported beer. Then they would go to the auction. Before long, they would all get worked up and, forgetting their clever agreements, would outbid one another until they had all bought everything the villagers had to sell at prices higher than their retail value, hating each other's insides.

As a rule, the traders would gradually recover from their financial fiasco by raising their store prices, and eventually the money would trickle from the villagers back into their own tills.

This time, however, after the usual competition at an auction where they had bought a great deal of copra and copal at a loss, they were not given the opportunity of recouping their money. Some of their friends, the Portuguese traders from neighboring Busu Kwanga, had dropped their store prices to lure the people, and Busu Melo had to follow suit. Then Busu Kwanga dropped the prices still a little lower, and again Busu Melo had to follow, with the result that local stores were now underselling to the villagers. And it looked as if the "baboons" had better common sense than the astute European traders. Now Almeida blamed Silva, and Silva blamed Almeida, and Carlos blamed them both, and all three blamed the administration for not imposing fixed, low prices on native products.

And the local administrators had started a little war of their own. Actually, it was the same old one-sided war, with the chief of the territory persecuting his helpless assistant. At least that's how Madame Fallet represented it to me when we ran into one another near the vegetable garden.

"This morning my poor Gaston was doubled up with stomach cramps at the office," Paulette Fallet complained poutingly, "but he wouldn't go home. He knows that *Alembi te?* would report him to the District if he did."

She flushed, making me wonder if it was because of her indignation or the mention of her husband's stomach cramps. Paulette, who talked freely and with relish about all sexual matters, was prudish when it came to discussing other bodily functions. In fact, she had nearly died of dysentery rather than consult Michael when he first arrived in Busu Melo.

Later that day, I found out that Gaston did not dare leave his desk even when far more serious matters than a simple bellyache were involved. Roaming aimlessly about the post, I happened to pass the Fallet house and suddenly heard Paulette's high-pitched screams.

"Drop that knife, drop it, I tell you!" she shouted.

Rushing up the three brick steps leading to their *baraza,* I saw, through the open dining-room window, Madame Fallet standing on one side of their table and Kutu, their houseboy, on the other. Kutu was wielding a long kitchen knife.

"He's gone completely crazy!" she shrieked in my direction. "You, do you hear me?" she screamed at the boy, "drop that knife!"

I ran down the steps and toward the Administration Office, where I found Monsieur Fallet sitting behind his desk by the window, looking dejected, but not doubled up with stomach cramps. At the sight of me, he cheered up instantly.

"What's the matter? Do you have the *mafumba*—" he started, baring his rather dirty teeth, blackened by his chain-smoking of Gauloise cigarettes.

"Kutu's gone berserk, and he's waving a knife," I said breathlessly, ignoring his stale crack about the red ants, that he probably meant might be in my pants.

His smirk vanished. "Sentry! Sentry!" he yelled.

The sentry standing guard out front came running, and saluted smartly, striking together his bare feet.

"Where is your rifle, you idiot?! Go get it and run to my house. Kutu's gone *elema!*" Fallet stormed at the sentry.

The soldier, after picking up his rifle which he had left at the office entrance, was already galloping toward the Fallets' house, closely followed by the sergeant, a *chicotte* (a whip made out of hippopotamus hide) in his hand.

"*Mon Dieu,*" whimpered Fallet, leaning out the window to listen to what was happening across the road at his own bungalow.

"Aren't you going with them?" I shrilled at him, before running after the soldiers.

"I can't," whimpered *Nkoi* (Leopard) whom all the villagers feared, "Van Derveer is just waiting for me to leave the office. The cheat is himself home developing his lousy films, but he would get me if I left the office . . . *Mon Dieu* . . ." Then abruptly he added in a firmer tone, "But they'll get Kutu, Kutu wouldn't dare."

They got Kutu, all right.

When I looked toward the Fallets' bungalow, the sentry was shoving Kutu in front of him toward the local jail. The sergeant was following them, Kutu's knife in his hand. Kutu was bleeding profusely from a few cuts on his bare arms. Instead of Madame Fallet, he had finally turned the knife on himself.

easy at the village. There, just as the *nyama* had first to be hunted and killed before it could be eaten, since except for a few goats there were no domestic animals in this region, so had the strong beverages first to be made before they could be drunk.

Although there were hundreds of oil palms cultivated by the local population in and around the *mboka*, there was always a shortage of palm oil for preparing their food, toiletries, and body-anointing, because all the trees were exploited to produce *nsamba*, that excellent wine made of fermented palm-tree sap that I had drunk on my first visit to the village. Even palm trees felled accidentally were sapped dry to provide *ekwabu* (a lower grade wine).

Besides hunting and fishing, the only work that appealed to the men was the manufacture of *masanga na nkoko* (fermented sugarcane beer). That was Molali's only occupation, and most of the time it was a lucrative one. He had a real beer factory and was its president. The manpower consisted of that silent creature in streaked *ngola* who was his wife and the mother of his children, Baloki and Molali Moke. I had watched the woman at work. For hours on end she ground with a heavy wooden pestle bits of pared sugarcane. Then she spread it on tightly woven nets (that she also had made in her "leisure" time), placing under these empty gourds to catch the syrupy mash trickling into them from the nets. Molali, who usually napped in the shade of a tree, occasionally dragged himself over to inspect the operation. Finally, when the last drop of juice had dripped into the gourds, it was his job to measure out into the liquid a certain quantity of good *masanga* that would cause fermentation. Two days later, the beer would be ready for consumption and profitable trade.

Molali's business was not well organized, however. There were days when customers had to be turned away disappointed, because as soon as it was ready, the supply of *masanga* was sold out to early comers. On such occasions Molali, who was a miser, bitterly reproached his wife with being nothing but an old lazybones and hinting broadly at seriously considering getting himself a second wife who would bear him more children and make more *masanga*. The poor woman only bent lower over her wooden mortar and pounded incredible quantities of sugarcane. Then everyone saw a contented Molaki sticking his greedy nose into the gourds, after which he would go back to napping, satisfied that his wife was working hard enough to please him. But, on the other hand, sometimes when the beer was ready, there were no customers. When that happened, Molali made the rounds trying to convince his neighbors that his beer was the best in the world, excellent for one's health. It was effective against constipation as well as for curing diarrhea and it also possessed other remarkable properties, such as attracting fish and driving away fleas. The fickle neighbors, however, did not always feel like drinking *masanga*. They sometimes favored the *nsamba*, or even its poor relative, the sour *ekwabu*. That would leave Molali overstocked with quantities of beer. Since he would not offer even a drop to anyone for fear that this might jeopardize future business and he was too stingy to let it go to waste, he drank it all himself. And when he was drunk, he beat his wife, who silently accepted the punishment for having prepared too much beer. This happened practically every other day, but I no longer attempted to interfere. When I stepped in the first time, Molali's wife had been most indigant.

"Is he not my husband?" she said, putting me in my place in rapid Ngombe, obligingly translated for me into Bangala by Baloki. "Did he not pay a good price to my father? Can he not teach me to do what is right?"

Trying not to show my embarrassment, I withdrew, and drunken Molali's "lesson" to his wife was picked up where it had been left off as if nothing had happened.

The way alcohol affected these men and those of some other tribes was curiously different. For instance, Michael said that he had never seen the Mongo fight, but that whenever the Bobo (individuals of uncertain origin in the Bomboma

Territory) were drunk, they invariably ended their celebrations by lashing out at one another with sharp knives. Since the intoxicated men were barely able to keep on their feet and stumbled into each other's arms, the knives cut into their backs above the shoulders. Then, when they had had enough of this, they all gathered to apply certain leaves with medicinal powers—a treatment that speeded the healing of the gashes and left prominent and permanent scars.

Another pastime at the *mboka* was sharing of wives. This was common practice among the Mongo in the Yakata Territory, Michael had once told me. But I was surprised to observe it in my *mboka*. The villagers used their wives as they saw fit. They passed them on to friends or neighbors and the affair was perfectly in order as long as it was supervised by the husband. If a *mobali* happened to catch a man making love with his wife without his consent, however, the man was brought to trial.

One morning, strolling down the main village "street" escorted by my usual companions Molali Moke and Boboka, plus at least a dozen other kids, my other good friends among them, I noticed that only the very old women were squatting in front of their huts as we passed. This was because all the young and able ones had gone fishing, Molali Moke explained to me. It was the height of the fishing season, since it was a relatively dry period and the water was low in the flooded plains. Molali Moke suggested we go over to the creek. As we came to the end of the village street, we turned to the left, crossed a narrow stretch of jungle, and wound up at a fairly wide watercourse. Several small pirogues were waiting on its soggy, muddy shore, explaining the deserted little stream at the other end of the *mboka*. It was here that the villagers congregated to wash and fish. Two or three men were leaving in small dugouts, propelling them rapidly by pushing long poles vigorously against the muddy bottom; others returned, appearing unexpectedly from beyond a sharp twist in the stream.

Abruptly, as usual in Africa before a tornado, it became quite dark and the wind rose brusquely.

A man in a brief loincloth began to blow into a *njeka* (a hollow wooden tube). He gesticulated wildly, bucking hard the onrushing wind as though to prevent the tornado, but his frantic efforts had no effect.

"Maybe his *njeka* is only powerful enough to scare a lover away from his wife's arms," one of the other men snickered.

Meanwhile my little friends and I, along with the rest, had scurried for refuge under a giant tree. I had seen a tornado once before, on the riverboat sailing up the Congo River on my trip from Léopoldville to the Busu Melo Territory. While the paddlewheel Mississippi-type boat was loading firewood at a small riverside station, the abrupt twilight had blanketed everything and heavy clouds gathering seemingly out of nowhere had obscured the clear skies. The wind had blown so violently that birds flying across the river had been kept at a standstill, unable to move an inch. In spite of their flapping wings they had appeared to be held back by invisible strings, and finally had been carried backward to the shore from which they had just taken off.

The local population was on familiar terms with the lightning abruptness of a tornado and with its force. The riverside people would never consent to cross the Congo River in a straight course, even in a large pirogue. They would zigzag from islet to islet, paddling furiously to avoid being caught in a wide expanse of water that could in a matter of seconds be transformed into a boiling sea. The African tornado has been described hundreds of times, but I doubt if any who have written about it have had the experience of being caught by it in the jungle, wearing scarcely anything more than a light dress that was nearly torn to shreds by the wind that swept before it everything in its path.

Now, to keep the wind from carrying me off, I hugged

the treetrunk for dear life. The rain fell almost horizontally and the branches afforded us slim protection. The raindrops were so huge that my body felt as though it were being lashed. In such a deluge, we were all bound to be washed clean in spite of ourselves.

The tornado passed as abruptly as it had come. The villagers all shook like wet animals and, drenched and sneezing, I shook with them, regretting that the *njeka* had proved ineffectual against the elements. The children had resumed their games in the water. All the kids were quite adept at keeping afloat in the unsteady dugouts that tipped at the slightest movement.

It reminded me of my first lesson in one of those pirogues on the Congo River, near Léopoldville, before embarking for Busu Melo. "Don't move. Don't sneeze. Don't even wink an eye," were my instructor's words. And without moving, sneezing, or winking, I had held out in the tricky canoe only a few seconds.

On my way home, still flanked by my faithful lieutenants, Molali Moke and Boboka, and a couple of other kids, I came across a most arresting scene.

A small, low wooden hurdle had been erected in front of one of the village huts and miscellaneous objects hung all over it. A witch doctor in working clothes (not my friend Djito), befeathered and liberally painted, was circling around the hurdle with short dance steps, lifting his head and arms rhythmically skyward and making incantations. All at once, at a sign from the *monganga's* hand, a young woman, clutching her breasts with both hands as though to soothe her labored breathing, jumped over the hurdle.

"She has tried the *mokandu* twice already," Molali Moke explained to me, pointing to the barrier, "but still she has not had a *mwana*."

"In spite of Mokolo's being a very good *monganga*," added Boboka.

The children and I resumed our stroll, for the fertility rites of the *mokandu* were finished. The woman, escorted by her husband, had reentered their hut, the thatched mat serving as its door was lowered over the entrance; the ritual was to be completed within the privacy of its clay walls.

It crossed my mind that somebody ought to tell the Fallets about the *mokandu*. And, picturing Madame Fallet painted in *ngola* and jumping over a low hurdle in front of the Administration Office, I startled the children by laughing out loud. But most likely, if the villagers could see Paulette Fallet, who desperately wanted a baby, burning candles to the Virgin every Sunday in the chapel of the Catholic mission of Busu Modanda, they would feel as I felt about the *mokandu*. The only thing they would understand was Madame Fallet's rushing right from the chapel to join her husband in their shuttered bedroom for the final act, which was the same.

CHAPTER XI

The following morning, expecting a runner from Michael, I did not go to the *mboka*. A policeman, who had convoyed a few prisoners from Busu Djanoa to Busu Melo, reported that the medical expedition was still fighting to stem the spread of the typhoid epidemic, and this meant that Michael's return home would probably be delayed. Immediately, even though realizing that it would do neither my reputation nor my standing among the local "socialites" any good, I thought of asking Carlos if he would take me to Michael on the back seat of his motorcycle.

In the early afternoon, while still wondering whether there might be a chance of getting a message from Michael or if I should walk over to the village for an hour or so, the village, as it were, came to me.

"Some *basenji* are waiting to see you in front of the back porch," Jafke announced snobbishly, as usual.

"What are they selling? If it's a chicken you can buy one without me," I said. I knew that my going to the back door would not change much. The chicken would be the invariable small all skin-and-bones tough local chicken, and Jafke would manage to put a few *centimes* in his own pocket, anyway.

"No," he said, "they don't want to sell anything. They wish to buy a *mono*."

"To buy a medicine from me?" I said, more amused than annoyed. "Let them go to the hospital. The dispenser will give them whatever they need."

"They want your *mono*," Jafke insisted, and it was hard to tell whether he was in earnest or not.

Intrigued, I stepped out onto the back *baraza*. A small group of men was waiting for me at the back steps. They were *basenji* in breechcloths, all right—not a single pair of trousers among them. Some of the men did not speak any Bangala at all, and I even had trouble understanding the halting dialect of those who, representing the others and themselves, spoke it. They inquired humbly whether I would consider helping them. One of them wished to rid himself of the bad luck that had clung to his home for many days. An owl came every day to perch on his thatched roof, an owl under whose guise hid *moloki* (the devil). Another wished to purchase a charm that would punish with a big, bad *likuku* (scrotal elephantiasis) any unsuspecting thief who might be planning to steal his corn. Still others desired favorable charms possessing various powers. They wanted charms of all sizes and kinds, cheap and expensive, effective over long periods of time and for a few days only. They were prepared to pay me, and since they were there anyhow, they said they wished to receive news from their deceased relatives. And while they kept on enumerating their wishes, utterly bewildered, I tried to figure out what was behind all this.

"I'm not a *monganga*," I finally interrupted them.

"Mmmm, but is not your *mobali* (husband) a witch doctor? A great witch doctor?" said the one who wished for a *likuku* for a potential thief of his corn. His scanty loincloth was inadequate to cover up his own advanced case of elephantiasis.

It was impossible to explain to them that my husband was not a witch doctor, that he was a medical doctor, since in Bangala there do not exist two separate terms distinguishing a witch doctor from a physician. The word for both is *monganga*.

"Did not the *monganga mokonji* bring back to life a *mwana* that was already dead?" said another one.

He was obviously referring to a timely administration of adrenalin to a sick baby—after it had collapsed in shock following an injection by a local *infirmier*—that had boosted to new heights Michael's already well-established reputation of a great *monganga* among the African population in the territory.

"And did not the *monganga mokonji* chase the devil out of the body of another *mwana* that was burning up with heat?" put in a third man. "And doesn't his *ntonga* (needle) make vanish the sores of yaws?"

Surely, it was written all over their faces, the wife of such a great *monganga* must have picked up quite a few tricks of her husband's trade, so how about it?

"Why not see Mokolo about these problems?" I finally suggested, remembering Boboka's praise of the witch doctor performing the fertility rites, after trying to think of a fitting answer that would rid me of my uninvited guests without having either to lose face or undermine their confidence in Michael. "I'm here today and may be gone tomorrow. But your *minganga* (witch doctors) will remain with you always."

They had evidently not thought about that. They shifted uneasily from foot to foot, considering what to do next. They agreed that it would indeed be ill-advised to antagonize the *likundu* practitioners.

"You wouldn't care to have the dead come back and learn your secrets, would you?" I added, putting an end to their hesitancy. "They will, if you insist upon learning theirs!"

"Mmmm," chorused my awed visitors.

I reentered the bungalow for a minute, giving them a

chance to leave. When I reappeared, the crowd was gone, leaving on the back *baraza* offerings of gourds, palm-oil fruit, and banana clusters for favors they had not received.

There were screams coming from in front of the Administration Office. It was probably a prisoner being lashed by the African sergeant. The *chicotte*, perhaps no longer administered in the large centers, was still in use here in the remote jungle post of Busu Melo. One could tell, without being there, the exact moment of the *chicotte*'s contact with the man's buttocks by the louder screams, followed by a continuous wailing. The screams did not stop at the count of six—the maximum lawful number of lashes. In the absence of both Van Derveer and Fallet, the sergeant in charge was giving himself a treat.

Although realizing I could do nothing to prevent this brutality, and disregarding my promise to Michael never to interfere on such occasions, I rushed toward the office, hoping that in the presence of the wife of an official, the sergeant would count more carefully.

My illusions disintegrated as soon as I approached the scene, for the hulking figure of Madame Van Derveer, in a blindingly bright red dress, stood out against the whitewashed front of the Administration Office. She had modestly turned away her head while the punished man was pulling up his shorts. I left before she could spot me.

About to enter our front garden, I noticed Jafke standing outside on the edge of the road, waiting for me, a note in his hand. It was a word from Michael, which Silva's man had brought from Pimu. Michael would not be back that evening; they were all trying to complete the vaccinations. Everybody was pitching in. And even *"Alembi te?,"* Monsieur Van Derveer, had learned how to handle a syringe and was working long hours helping out. Jafke had another bit of local news he had just heard to tell me. The man who had received the *chicotte* a few moments before was the government gardener who had once or twice taken some radishes to present to his *mwasi*. But somehow, the thought of "Is he not tired?" standing for many hours in the broiling sun, helping to stem the spreading epidemic, did not dispel the mental picture of his wife, watching the lashing of the gardener, not even after it had occurred to me that she might have come to the office on some other business and just happened to be there at the time of the horrible *chicotte* punishment.

Now there was nothing to wait around for, unless perhaps a neighborly visit from one of the two ladies, and after a brief consultation with Jafke about the dinner menu, I decided to go to the *mboka*, after all.

When I got there, I set out looking for the kids, but they were nowhere in sight. Baloki told me I might find them at *mboka moke* (the little village). I looked at random right and left of the main "street." After nearly an hour's search, I finally found the little village behind a cornfield. It was a miniature community, with tiny shacks built of branches. A fire burned in front of each hut, where little girls aged nine to twelve prepared meals, wove fishing nets, and performed various other chores of the African woman for their partners, boys of approximately their own age.

It was apparently a husband-and-wife game, and I wondered where it stopped, and soon learned that it did not stop at all. Ekomila, who greeted me beside her fire, introduced me to her *mobali* ("husband"), a timid boy with the bloated belly of a rickety child, who squinted at me from beneath a protruding brow. I also met her neighbor, a girl her own age who, like Ekomila, wore an elaborate hairdo and had a miniature woman's body, stained red with *ngola*. This neighbor child was visibly pregnant. She was going to be married, the kids told me, at the beginning of the new moon. This marriage was to have taken place many moons later, when she had grown up somewhat, but because of the baby she was expecting, her betrothed desired an immediate marriage, to make certain that the baby, which was not his, would legally belong to him. Up to that time he had not even bothered to take a good look at her, since he was a middle-aged man who already had two other wives.

This was not in the least surprising. For any family at any *mboka* a baby represented wealth. If it was a boy, he did not require too much care. When he grew up a little, he accompanied his father, giving him a hand. If it was a girl, she kept house until the day when her betrothed or his family paid the dowry to her father.

The pregnant little girl did not appear frightened at the prospect of joining a real *mobali*. She did not regret leaving her present playmate, the father of her child. This relationship was not meant in earnest; it was only a game.

A stroll among the huts of the *mboka moke,* swarming with the activities of the small couples, suggested that it was in many ways similar to those of the adults in the real village. There were jealousies and petty quarrels, clans and gossip. Only one striking difference existed: whereas the women in the adult village were absolutely subjugated by their men, here the girls dominated the boys. The cause was clear to me. In the real *mboka* the women did all the work. It was much the same in this little village, but since there was a minimum of real work to be done, there was more time left for lovemaking, and obviously the girls were in charge of that part of life. I searched among the tiny huts for that of Molali Moke. But he was not there. No one had seen him, not even his "wife" who, for the past few days, according to her neighbors' gossip, was sharing her hut with another boy. All the children seemed absorbed in their games and I decided to return home.

Approaching the end of the adult *mboka* I heard Molali Moke from a distance. Evidently he was getting a spanking. He was yelling wildly, and I hastened to his rescue. When he saw me coming, Molali hit his son as fast as possible, apparently to get in a few more smacks before I could intervene.

"What did he do?" I inquired angrily.

"If he had brought shame upon your house," replied Molali, "you, too, would punish him." And, taking advantage of my momentary inattention, Molali succeeded in placing another blow on junior's bottom.

Molali Moke squealed like a butchered suckling pig. "It is because I would not go to *mboka moke* to play husband-and-wife," he whimpered.

"He never does, and soon people will start saying that he is not a male. Look at what he does while the girls laugh at him!" grumbled his father, shoving a piece of carved wood under my nose.

It was a rough figure of a woman. Long nicks around the eyes, probably meant to represent eyelashes, aroused my suspicion that the carving portrayed me. I winked at Molali Moke, and the boy, evidently understanding me, laughed and winked back.

Molali Moke's grandfather and his equally blind friend, Ndinga, who had just returned and were settling down near the hut, wanted to know what all the commotion was about. But before Molali could put in a word, I placed the carved wood into the grandfather's unsteady hands, asking him what he thought of his grandson's carving talents. To my amazement, the blind old man instantly knew that it represented a woman.

"Who knows, perhaps there is a mysterious power in the body of this wooden woman," he said. "In the village of Boyange, whence my mother came as a *mwana*, lived a woman whose yelling and swearing had no equals in the whole world. One day her cursing angered Djakomba, the god of the universe, and he transformed her into a wooden statue. Although the lower part of her body had instantly changed to wood, her tongue remained as agile as ever and she continued her cursing. Gradually, however, the rigidity spread to the rest of her body, finally stilling her tongue, which protruded like a long wooden peg. Only a blade run through her heart could change the wood back into living flesh again. Such was Djakomba's verdict. Years passed—"

"Why did no one do it?" interrupted Molali Moke.

"Tut tut, child. Nobody did for a very obvious reason," his grandfather chuckled, showing no displeasure at having been interrupted. "Everybody was happy that this *monoko makasi* (loudmouth) had finally been silenced. Furthermore, the example had frightened all other women into silence and submission also. In those days everyone dreaded the invaders from the north who made a practice of hacking off the arms and legs of their victims so as quicker to remove and steal their brass and copper bracelets. One night, those beasts, who pillaged and murdered and set on fire whole communities, sneaked up to the very edge of the village. One of their warriors noticed Yahiwa's wooden statue on the outskirts and, mistaking it for a sentry, threw his spear into her chest. Instantaneously, the woman came alive and resumed her cursing, picking it up where she had left off years before on the day of divine punishment. Her loud swearing roused everybody and, following a memorable battle, the village was saved. Unfortunately, from that time on their women went back to bickering and cursing. In no other village in the world do women swear as expertly as they do in Boyange."

The legend impressed us all, but Molali was a skeptic. Still holding the cudgel with which he had punished his son, he dispelled the impression created by the story. "Our women, too, know how to yell and swear when they are being beaten," he said.

I was thinking that grandfather's story reminded me of something I seemed to have heard before. Perhaps it was reminiscent of a legend Michael had been told in Mbinga, a large palm-oil plantation west of Lisala. That legend had it that the village of Mbinga had at one time been saved by the piercing screams of *"Mwasi na Balui."* But that *mwasi* was not really a woman at all, but a small clay pot whose oaths had turned back the attacking Ngiri (fierce warriors who had kept their independence up to the early 1920s).

Other stories followed. These probably referred to the early rubber rush at the turn of the century when many Africans had suffered injustices at the hands of the conquering white man. Many storytellers tried to speak Ngombe, but Molali Moke's grandfather sternly insisted that they speak nothing but Bangala in my presence. People told unbelievable stories—a veritable saga of the founders of the village. According to their accounts, this village, many, many years ago, long before the white man came to these shores, was founded by men from more than one tribe. They had all fled the white man's menace, and the invading African tribes from the north and east, only to die by the score in the endless swamps and be devoured by wild animals, be captured and eaten by enemy tribes. Finally, a small contingent of survivors found a haven and settled down in this forest, protected by isolation and oblivion. The original settlers came from the coastal regions and the surrounding inland country, bringing with them into the interior the language and customs of the Bangala. Other fugitives joined them, and since they came from all parts, many dialects, such as Lusengo, Motembo, Bangombe, and Iboko, were spoken, and to create a better understanding among those original settlers and the newcomers, Bangala had been adopted for general communication. There still was a pronounced difference between my modern Bangala and that of the villagers. Many words had a local flavor, but despite all these variations, it was a kind of Bangala. Naturally, the influence of the Ngombe people was now strongly felt in this territory. Many of the descendants of the riverside people, more often than not, spoke the Ngombe dialect even among themselves. As to their customs, although the villagers were still organized in individual families enjoying their private movable property, there was communal sharing of some belongings, like the large fishing nets, the meetinghouse, and definitely all land.

While the oldsters were reminiscing and reviving memories of the past, a crowd had gathered behind us. Other narrators came forward with new stories, more and more fantastic, since some of the incidents in them sounded recent. A

middle-aged man with hard features told of tortures he had suffered at the hands of an administrator named *Nyoka.*

At least a hundred Europeans had been nicknamed
"Snake" by the Africans, but despite the many improbabilities
of the story, it was likely that the man was actually referring
to an administrator in the Budjala region, a sadist who had
tortured many people before ending up in an insane asylum.
This villager might have been one of the deranged administrator's victims. The man told how he had been forced to stare at
the blinding sun for long minutes, that might have been
hours. A hail of *chicotte* lashes fell upon him when, unable to
endure it a second longer, he turned away his face. Then his
hands were tied together with a length of leather strap, with a
stick inserted between them, a stick which was given a little
extra twist every hour, until his hands swelled and blood trickled from beneath his nails. He told about the agony of being
tied for what had seemed an eternity in the path of carnivo-
rous ants that tore away at his flesh, and of countless other
horrors. And the expression on the faces of his listeners made
me think that the penalty for the criminal inhumanity of one
irresponsible man would someday have to be paid by all
white-skinned people of Africa.

The evening was nearly spent when the small group
separated and melted into the darkness. Escorted by Baloki and
her Lisengo who led the way on the narrow, now familiar,
path, I left the smoky fire. Alone the two old men, grandfather and Ndinga, staring with their unseeing eyes at the
smoldering charcoals, were probably still dreaming about the
tumultuous past in the cherished days of their youth.

CHAPTER XII

When I dragged myself out of bed the next morning, a touch of fever that had kept me awake during the night was gone, leaving me tired and edgy. I really had only myself to blame, since for the past three days I had not been taking my daily quinine. I was aware of the importance—in a region where one hundred percent of the population had it—of keeping malaria under control at all times. As a rule, I always kept in mind the popular Congolese saying that "one had the malaria one deserved."

Actually, my neglecting to take the capsules was all Albert's fault, I thought with mounting irritation. A well-trained Congo houseboy never forgets, along with the salt and pepper shakers, to set the all-important bottle of quinine capsules on the table. But then, Albert was not a well-trained houseboy; he was not a houseboy, period. I even suspected him of the far greater crime of the jungle—that of refilling our large regulation Berkefeld filter (the European's insurance against intestinal infection in the African bush) with unboiled water. I would have to start training him a little harder, I thought idly while he was serving me lunch, as clumsily as ever, but I had no way of knowing that in an hour or two he would undergo the most intensive training any houseboy has ever had.

It all came about a little later, while I was resting and trying not to go to sleep before getting word from Michael (I even hoped he might return). Carlos came roaring into our front garden on his souped-up motorcycle, the bearer of an electrifying message.

"Where is *mwasi na monganga mokonji?*" I heard his ringing voice outside.

I was out on the *baraza* before the slow Albert had answered Carlos.

"*Kokolo, kokolo,*" Carlos said, taking one look at my face, mixing up the Bangala with the French, probably out of habit, since he spoke Bangala with his customers most of the day, with his *ménagère* most of the night, and spoke French only occasionally with us, the "High Society Set." "Take it easy," he repeated in French, "everything's all right. I have good news."

The good news was that Michael was coming home for dinner, together with Van Derveer, Fallet, and Leport. And he was also bringing with him the district commissioner from Lisala, who happened to be around on an unscheduled inspection tour. Oh, yes, *le commissaire de district* was with his wife. They intended to return back to Mongana right after dinner. Everyone was invited to have dinner at our house, including himself, Carlos added, exhibiting his strong white teeth.

Dinner? My temperature had most likely jumped several degrees. It was about two in the afternoon. "Do you know what time they all will be here?" I asked, hoping for a miracle.

"Around five," he said.

Splendid! I had all of three hours to prepare for the reception. Perhaps I should ask the sergeant to send a soldier to bag me a water buffalo; or maybe I ought to send word to my village friends to fetch me a potful of dried fish. My larder was depleted, and so were the Busu Melo stores, including Carlos's, following their financial war with Busu Kwanga. Of course, there always were the skinny Busu Melo chickens, and Jafke was a veritable Escoffier when it came to turning out the national Congolese dish—the spicy *moamba* (quartered chicken stewed in the ground pulp of fresh palm-oil fruits and a quantity of *pili-pili*, the hot little red peppercorns). But naturally this would hardly do at a "formal" dinner for a visiting dignitary.

"I nearly forgot," said Carlos, unstrapping a large parcel from the back seat of his motorcycle, "the *monganga* is sending you a roast beef he got from Lisala. Eight kilos. I rode like crazy to keep it from spoiling en route."

I felt my temperature drop back to normal. The roast beef was fresh, all right. Carlos, who always rode his *motuka* like a lunatic, even without having any perishable *nyama* to deliver, had evidently covered the distance in record time. While Jafke took possession of the *nyama*, I ran across to Mesdames Van Derveer and Fallet.

"I really don't see why you should entertain them at your house," Madame Van Derveer said by way of "thank you" for the invitation. "After all, I'm the chief . . . I mean, the wife of the chief of the territory."

I almost succumbed to the temptation of surrendering the honor without a fight. My head was splitting, and I could still picture my houseboy, Albert, standing there bent forward, the pants of his starched white uniform unbuttoned as usual, as I left the house a few moments before. But Madame Van Derveer was wearing the same red dress she had on while her gardener was getting the lash, and the recollection made me stand my ground.

"My husband, as a physician, has the same rank of Captain Commander as your husband," I said.

"But my husband is in charge of this territory," she rejoined.

"Yes, but I've got the roast beef," I parried with what I knew was a clincher.

After that, like all people isolated in strange places under stress conditions, like our husbands jointly vaccinating the population during an epidemic, we three women pooled our resources. Madame Van Derveer would contribute the hors d'oeuvres—the invariable deviled eggs; Madame Fallet offered to have her cook bake fresh bread; I was to make a cake, my famous cake that was always a hit with the men here. It was no wonder, since I poured a whole pint of Scotch between the cake's chocolate-filled layers. Jafke was taking care of the roast. (Months later I wished that Jafke had also been in charge of the deviled eggs, for I had learned that Madame Van Derveer had caught her cook slicking the hard-boiled eggs in his mouth to make them glisten before serving them.)

Most of my day was spent not on the cake, however, but on training Albert. This was one satisfaction I would not give either of the two ladies: having to borrow one of their boys. And with a determination born of necessity, I rehearsed my *mosenji* (peasant) in the art of formal serving at table. Again and again and again I had him go through all the motions, until I heard the approaching sounds of the motorcade, heralded by its rusted-away mufflers, behind the wide bend of the Busu Melo road.

It seemed to be one of those days when everything goes well. Everybody, except me, that is, felt wonderful. The commissioner enjoyed the trip and was quite complimentary on the work done in the territory in general, and the spectacular teamwork of our husbands during the sudden threat of an epidemic in particular. He had heard about my interest in Congolese customs, and Madame Van Derveer, who had started sneering a little at the beginning of his remark on the subject, made herself smile and said that, yes, wasn't it nice of me to go so often to a remote native hamlet and look after the pickaninnies. And my barefoot but white-capped-and-gloved Albert, in his freshly starched white uniform, did not knock over a single glass, and his pants had remained buttoned throughout the preliminaries. And after a few highballs, the khaki field uniform of the commissioner did not clash with the naphthalene-reeking black dinner jacket Carlos was heroically sweating in. And the *moke* (the little helper) Jafke had hired himself for the grand occasion had brought me word from the kitchen that the *nyama* was coming just beautifully: rare in the center and well done on the outside.

The whole crowd was already very gay when we went in to dinner, and Leport's gold-capped teeth had never shone more dazzlingly. We weathered the deviled eggs nicely, and Albert was as impeccable as any well-broken-in houseboy could be, not looking at me even once for our prearranged signals to remind him in what order to serve our protocol-minded guests. He poured the wine without spilling any, and removed the empty plates from the right—a detail that had seemed particularly difficult for him to remember during our last-minute rehearsal.

I had almost allowed myself to relax as Albert had ceremoniously carried in the pièce de résistance, the precious *nyama,* when abruptly something went wrong. Evidently suffering a sudden mental block, Albert planted himself firmly in front of Michael, at the other end of the table across from me, blissfully ignoring my desperate glances. At first discreetly, Michael jerked his head eloquently in the direction of the commissioner's wife, at Michael's right, but Albert, anchored in front of him, ignored him completely.

"Aren't you going to serve the *nyama* to the *mwasi na mondele mokonji?* (the wife of the white chief) Michael finally whispered in Bangala.

But Albert did not yield ground. Not Albert. "*Te,*" he said, shaking his head from side to side, "*te.*"

"I don't understand," Michael said in French, obviously taken aback, forgetting to whisper by then.

"*I* do," said the commissioner, and started to laugh. "I was told of a similar circumstance in which a houseboy had refused to serve a guest first because, the boy insisted, it was the host's house, and his *nyama,* and that it was his prerogative to choose the best piece."

Perhaps the *nyama* lost a little of its goodness after this, for it was slightly cold when everybody had stopped laughing. We laughed almost as hard as the villagers at Ngele's trial, and Albert, who was the only one who did not comprehend what had happened, at last obeying Michael's desperate gestures, slowly walked toward the district commissioner's wife.

"That wasn't the end of my story," added the commissioner. "When the boy had finally approached the guest and instead of presenting the platter to him had set it down on the table and the exasperated host had inquired if he wasn't going to serve the meat with his hands, the rattled boy did just that!"

And while we laughed some more, Albert planted himself in front of the commissioner's wife, holding the platter out of her reach, and Michael called jokingly in Bangala, giving rise to a new wave of hilarity, "Aren't you going to serve the *nyama* with your hands?"

And as if reenacting the story just told—a story he was not supposed to have understood—suddenly flustered, Albert, the always impassive and slow Albert, grabbed a thick slice of roast beef in his gloved hand and slapped it down on the plate of the commissioner's wife. And for a second I imagined a spark of derisive mischief in his usually sleepy eyes.

CHAPTER XIII

It looked as if a rare period of serenity had descended upon Busu Melo. Perhaps it was the aftereffect of the few days our husbands had spent together, united in the common cause of vaccinating the population; or we women joining forces in receiving the *commissaire de district* and his wife; or maybe our laughing off our accumulated pent-up tensions during the *nyama* incident (that had already started to circulate around the Congo as a good joke), but everybody seemed friendlier to one another. Van Derveer appeared to be working harder at the office, and one could again see Monsieur Fallet sneaking out during working hours for a "glass of lemonade" at home. Madame Van Derveer had us all to dinner, and we again ate her deviled eggs. Carlos, still flushed with his social success, sent each of us ladies apples imported from Belgium, that is, an apple apiece, and kept wearing a tie for three days following the dinner party. And Leport, who had finally given his Mariette the long-ago promised sewing machine, had not had a single fight with her and went about looking like a man on his honeymoon. Even the three local traders had stopped call-

ing one another names in Portuguese and reached a new
agreement designed to "fix the baboons" for good.

Michael worked at his temporary hospital-laboratory-
dispensary, coming home regularly for lunch, and I thought
he was starting to regain some of that weight he had lost during his emergency expeditions. But I should have known it
was too good to last. And, sure enough, on the fourth day I
found Michael's hastily scribbled note on the breakfast table,
telling me that he had rushed off to visit the riverside people
on the right bank of the Congo River. There had been rumors
of some kind of epidemic, so it could be a real emergency, or
maybe Michael had planned to sneak out before dawn to
avoid having to give in to my insistence that I accompany him
on a rough dugout trip through a tsetse-infested region. He
was sure he'd be back by tomorrow noon. And he was sorry
we would be unable to drive up to the Catholic mission of
Busu Modanda as we had scheduled for that day. Wasn't it
disgusting that a physician could never make any definite personal plans in this wilderness?

After simmering down, I rejected the idea of perhaps following Michael in another dugout, which my village friends
would have surely provided, or packing up and returning to
Europe. Michael was away, but his jalopy was there, so why
should I have to change my plans for the day? *I* wasn't a doctor, was I? Perhaps I might drive over to the far end of the
territory, where I had once seen extraordinarily vivid butterflies, and stop along the way whenever I fancied.

My intended leisurely drive was thwarted from the start.
It took Jafke all morning to fill the tank with gas from the
large new drum he had trouble opening without a helping
hand from Albert, who had left with Michael. Preparing and
serving lunch took Jafke another couple of hours, and the
shadows had begun lengthening when he and I had finally set
out on our way. By the time I had made the first stop just
before the Catholic mission, it was practically the moment to
turn round to make it back home before nightfall.

I glanced at the rapidly darkening African dirt road winding between two rows of palm trees, then at the shabby *gîte d'étape* (stopover shelter) whose wooden piles supporting the thatched roof were decorated with intricately plastered termite passageways, and finally at Jafke, decked out in his brightest silk shirt. Leaning nonchalantly against the open car door, he was waiting for my decision.

"It will be dark soon, and the car batteries are nearly shot," I said.

"Mmmm," Jafke agreed, looking skeptical.

"And the *monganga* won't be back before noon tomorrow."

"Mmmm."

"Maybe I might as well spend the night at this stopover house. We could start for home first thing in the morning. You know some people in this *mboka*, don't you, Jafke?"

"I know Father Gabriel," he replied, making it plain that he knew the true reason for my willingness to spend the evening at this crumbling hut in the mosquito-plagued jungle hamlet, less than two hours' driving from the relative comfort of my own Busu Melo house. And he was right, since the chance to visit Father Gabriel had a great deal to do with my staying overnight.

Father Gabriel did not live at the imposing Catholic mission a few kilometers farther up the road from his own tiny church at the far end of the village. Almost from the moment of his arrival in this isolated equatorial region, he had chosen to settle here to convert the people of this remote community.

Even before meeting him on Michael's and my previous swing through this region, I had heard about this soft-spoken missionary often seen trudging up the road like an African *mosenji*, without porters or servants. However, unlike a villager, who would have his wife carry his possessions behind him, or else take along only a light spear, Father Gabriel was always weighted down with a supply of food, blankets, and remedies for the sick and the needy.

What others told about Father Gabriel, and his own accounts, made me envision the hardship-filled years he had spent here after abandoning his comfortable existence at the old mission with its neat cells, ample meals, the companionship of other priests, and the large red-brick church whose dome was filled with chants and whose altar reflected the flame of candles.

At first, in his voluntary seclusion, his church had been the tropical forest, and his prayers rose lightheartedly to the choir of birds and the whispering of a jungle stream. Neither the tom-toms nor the shouting at the nearby village had disturbed his meditation, for to him it all testified to the presence of people who needed him. There were so many sick to care for, so many souls to save. Then, sometime later on, with the aid of a handful of followers, he had built his shrine.

The church exterior was that of an unassuming clay structure squatting beneath a bristling umbrella of thatch. But the interior, thanks to Father Gabriel's genius, was an artistic masterpiece. With cheap paints, good at best only for coating the rusting metal of colonial trunks, he had transformed his tiny low-ceilinged sanctuary, making it appear vast and alive, like the forest in whose lap it rested, peopling it with images of saints who seemed to add their prayers to those of the handful of African villagers.

I found Father Gabriel seated atop an empty crate behind his bamboo hut, engrossed in his painting. A group of gawking kids surrounded him as usual. Holding their breath, their white teeth gleaming in broad smiles, the youngsters followed each stroke of his brush. Once in a while, when a detail took shape, giving birth to a familiar object, a child gasped, as at the sight of a miracle, and the kids' joy reflected in Father Gabriel's own happy eyes.

All at once he noticed me standing beside him gazing at the canvas, and embarrassment, rushing a wave of blood to his head, darkened his already sun-baked face.

"I'd really meant to paint only the solitary road with this

motionless palm," he said, after we had exchanged hellos, "but I thought the kids might enjoy more this nest and the birds and the monkey . . . Of course, the picture is ruined." He laughed, suddenly relaxed, and the children replied with delighted giggles. "Oh, my," he added seriously, noticing a group of approaching villagers. "This is the hour set aside to-day for discussion and mediation of village problems. Would you care to stay and listen to our palaver?"

I nodded appreciatively. This wouldn't be the first time that I was present at one of Father Gabriel's "town meetings."

But somehow this didn't turn out to be one of the missionary's good days. The purpose of the meeting became clear from the first words Father Gabriel spoke to one of his recent converts.

"Otungu, are you not a good *mokristu?*" the missionary began solemnly in his polished Lingala. "A good Christian does not take a second wife into his home."

"She was my brother's wife," Otungu replied matter-of-factly. "I inherited her upon his death."

This was a common complication. Otungu was a fine young man. He was proud of his *kuluse*, the small, shiny cross that hung from his neck, but his attitude indicated that he was not prepared to give up without a struggle a robust woman who represented a negotiable asset.

Father Gabriel, after surveying the crowd of villagers, had apparently decided on a short sermon. When it was finished, Otungu, evidently won over, again looked him straight in the eye, but was not allowed time to repent.

Chief Bulukulu, who had arrived unobserved and had listened from his *tipoye*, carried by a team of four husky Africans, broke the spell.

"Father," he puffed amiably, "you have said that all men on earth who are good will be rewarded in heaven. Will there be some happier than others?"

"There is no favoritism in the Kingdom of Heaven," the missionary said. But his eyes, as he looked at the chief, betrayed uneasiness, as though he were anticipating trouble.

The chief guffawed and went on, "If, as you claim, all men are equal in the land of your God, why are all the *santu na Ndako Nzambe* white? There isn't a single black saint in your House of God. Does then a black man never have hope of becoming a saint?"

Father Gabriel must have mentally reviewed all the images of saints gracing the walls of his chapel. Then he evidently had a brainstorm.

"Don't you think that all black people turn white after death?" he asked, referring to the local belief.

But the crowd appeared unimpressed, and Chief Bulukulu challenged Father Gabriel again:

"When I repeated to *Monoko Makasi* what you had once said about all men being brothers, he told me that I was a dirty no-good, and not his brother." The chief burst into laughter, and concluded, "*Monoko Makasi* thinks he is better than I, the great Chief Bulukulu, because his skin is white. Me, I think that black skin is far more beautiful both before and after death. If your God considers that *Monoko Makasi* is right, then your God is good only for white people."

Father Gabriel sighed heavily. There was little he could say, and I realized his predicament. I knew the Territorial Agent, Van Ditsen, nicknamed "Loudmouth" because of the virtuosity of his cursing. He was the last person on earth to whom a villager might advance the idea of the brotherhood of man. . . .

The palaver ended without solving anything.

Presently, Father Gabriel and I were slowly walking toward the road, and when I glanced at his face it appeared worn and old, the face of a defeated man.

"Father," I said, "would you do me the pleasure of dining with me at the stopover house? I have a few tins . . ."

But he shook his head and paused under the palm tree he had been painting earlier.

"I'm sure you'll find the right words to convince these good people, Father, that you'll find the inspiration to do the right thing."

His bitterness suddenly broke through. Maybe he didn't even realize that he was talking to me; maybe he was thinking aloud. "How does one fight bigotry?" he said. "Is it possible that violence should be fought with force, and lies with subterfuge?"

Visibly trying to shake off his thoughts, and still oblivious of me, Father Gabriel slowly walked away. And in the rising mist of the abrupt African night, I could see him entering his church.

The next morning, while Jafke waited for me in the rested-up jalopy, I strolled over to Father Gabriel's hut to say goodbye. But there was no reply to my soft knocking. Perhaps the good Father was asleep, or maybe he was already out on an errand of mercy.

The tiny church was also empty, but it was still filled with acrid smoke from the old rusty lantern hanging at the door. Again I visualized Father Gabriel as I had left him the previous night, defeated and miserable. But as my eyes wandered along the still shadowy walls, I felt elated and reassured, and knew that Father Gabriel had found the answer.

For among the saints keeping their eternal vigil, there now was one whose benevolent face was the shade of deep black velvet . . . .

Jafke and I returned to Busu Melo just a jump ahead of Michael, and I was too eager to tell him about my marvelous experience to stay mad at him for his running off on this short trip. Besides, the uncommonly idyllic mood of Busu Melo seemed to continue on its serene course.

It was nice and peaceful all around—nice weather, never more than 100° Fahrenheit in the shade, not a single case of typhoid, not a single palaver, African or European. In fact, it got so nice and peaceful that my nerves began to tauten by the minute in anticipation of an inevitable thunderclap that I felt would unavoidably follow this uncommon pre-tornadic calm.

Things began to happen one afternoon as I was sitting on

the back *baraza,* chatting with one of Michael's patients just discharged from the hospital, and as always endeavoring to gain a better understanding of a bush African's psychology. The young villager of about eighteen was elated not because he had been cured of a serious attack of malaria, but because Michael had thrown in the little extra favor of circumcising the lad. It was actually a big favor from a local viewpoint, for in this region where all males were circumcised very early in life, the one who was not was regarded as almost an outcast, a freak no woman would sleep with. Now he was expressing his unreserved gratitude to Michael and me.

"Am I not a man now?" he said. "Am I not a happy man, and was not *Monganga Mokonji* the one who made me happy?"

"Mmmm," I acquiesced. I unfailingly enjoyed hearing Michael's patients praise him.

"And did not the *Monganga Mokonji* do more for me than my own father?"

"Mmmm," I agreed.

"Now," he added very solemnly, "*Monganga Mokonji* must give me a new loincloth to wear."

"Why must the *Monganga Mokonji* give you a new loincloth?" I wanted to know, trying to keep a straight face. Of course I actually knew the answer, for I had once been told of a similar situation, except that it was a pair of pants in that instance.

"Is he not more than a father to me?" he asked with immovable logic, "and does not a good father provide his son with everything he needs?"

The tornado broke loose before I had a chance to react. It appeared in the shape of Baloki, who came running toward me, sobbing wretchedly, her beautiful face streaked with the white of the *mpembe* on her eyelids. Her misery was infinite, she told me. It had been bad luck to go to the meetinghouse that morning. Her misfortune was that, as she was chatting there with the neighbors, her radiant young beauty had caught the eye of the lustful Chief Mafuta. Soberer than he had been in a long time, he noticed her and loved her. At this very moment, two men sent by the chief were discussing the question of Baloki's dowry with her father, Molali. There was no doubting the outcome of the parley, for in the Congo the dowry must be paid by the prospective bridegroom to the girl's father. The bargaining might last for days or weeks, but the result was certain. No one in the *mboka* would be able to top Chief Mafuta's price, and this was a genuine threat to my little friend's happiness. Her sweetheart, Lisengo, was not rich and could never pay the price customary for a beautiful girl such as she. The dowry would be especially high in her case because of her social standing, since she was the granddaughter of Lulango, the blind grandfather, who belonged to the small group of still living founders of the village. A new flood of tears spurted from Baloki's eyes at this point of her account, when it dawned on her that there was in reality no hope whatsoever for her and Lisengo.

This sort of thing was common tragedy in the Congo where a girl seldom married the man of her choice. It would have been wiser perhaps to leave Baloki to her fate, governed by centuries-old customs, and forget the whole thing. But I was quite fond of Baloki and disliked Mafuta who, among his other unpleasant traits, had spots on his back reminiscent of those of lepers. The idea of allowing Baloki's father to hand her over to that drunken satyr who prostituted his wives revolted me.

"Don't fret," I told the girl, "no one will give you to Mafuta, I promise. Go find Lisengo and tell him I wish to speak to him. It is he who shall be your *mobali*."

Baloki's beautiful young face radiated happiness. But after she had left, I got to wondering how I should be able to keep my rash promise. Since the price had to be paid, it was necessary to get for Lisengo more than what was offered to Molali by the chief.

"Michael, do you happen to know how much a local girl is worth in this region?" I asked him as he was walking past me on his way to the car.

"Plan to buy yourself a slave?" he teased me.

"No, I'm serious," I said. "I'd like to marry off Baloki to her boyfriend. Chief Mafuta—"

Michael was no longer smiling. "Look, darling," he said, "this is something I won't let you get mixed up in."

"If it's because people are talking—"

"No, not because of others, because of you yourself. You'll get in trouble. From what I've heard from my local aides, Mafuta is a vicious little schemer and he has his witch doctors behind him. He is the real ruler of the village, he's not like one of those phony officially appointed chiefs who are running around with the government badge of chiefdom that Van Derveer has hung around their necks. I simply won't stand for your getting involved in this, that's final. You must give me your word that you won't offer to pay Baloki's dowry."

For some time, Michael had been showing greater interest in the people of my *mboka*. He said he'd go down there with me as soon as he could spare the time, and often inquired about my village friends.

"All right," I said reluctantly, "I give you my word. I shan't try to overbid Mafuta."

Michael reached the carport—a thatched roof on four wooden posts—and I remained standing for a little while, steaming quietly. Michael was probably right as usual, but I was not afraid of drunken little Mafuta. However, if I could not help my friends financially, what else could I do to prevent the ruin of Baloki's and Lisengo's lives? What and how?

"Coming to play in the creek?" asked Molali Moke who, along with Boboka, had escorted Baloki to see me and had stayed behind, probably hoping for some preserves.

"*Te*," I said, "it will rain soon."

"*Te*, it won't," said Boboka.

"Yes, it will," I insisted. "Maybe we'd better stay here and have some jam?"

"Maybe it will rain," said Boboka quickly.

While the boys were devouring orange jam and Jafke kept mumbling something about *basenji* who ought to be subsisting on dried fish, I went on thinking about Baloki and of my pledge to her.

"Who is the wealthiest man in your *mboka*?" I asked the boys.

"Chief Mafuta," said Molali Moke.

"It used to be Djito," said Boboka, "But today it is Mokolo, the *monganga* whom you have recommended to the village. He works all day long and has even increased his fees."

This was news to me. I did not recall recommending anyone by that name to the villagers. Then I remembered having used the name of Mokolo in speaking to the *likundu*-seeking visitors I wanted to rid myself of. Boboka's words gave me an idea of how I might save the enamored couple.

While I was walking with Molali Moke and Boboka, who never stopped licking their lips all the way on the road leading to the mboka trail, I was trying to map out a future strategy. But my barely shaping ideas were abruptly interrupted as we approached Carlos's establishment. From somewhere in the back loud voices were shouting something that made it clear that the short-lived idyll in Busu Melo had already come to an end. Presently Leport, Carlos, Almeida, and Silva appeared from behind the *potopoto* combination store and living quarters that Carlos called home.

"How could you do it to me?" Leport shouted, throwing up his hands.

"I forgot, it slipped my mind." Almeida sounded deeply apologetic. "Anyhow, we are all in this together."

"All in this together!" shouted Leport. "Whose plaster was it? And who did the actual putting his leg in the cast? All in this together—" He choked on his words and started to cough.

"Richot is a mighty big fellow to have to fight," remarked Carlos. "Did you ever get a good look at his fists?"

"If he's gone to Lisala, his leg must have been in awful shape," lamented Leport.

"It should," said Carlos, "after three weeks in a plaster cast—a bad plaster cast."

Leport looked like a man about to pick a fight, but he was apparently too deflated. In a gesture of exasperation, he grabbed his head, knocking his pith helmet to his nose, and walked away.

"Almeida was supposed to tell Richot before he left that the plaster cast was only a practical joke, but he forgot all about it," Carlos explained to me.

"And Richot had to go to the Lisala hospital. Maybe he had gangrene," said Silva. "The cast was rather tight."

"It slipped my mind, I left before he woke up, he'll understand," Almeida said wishfully.

"We'll find that out when he gets here," said Carlos. "He's coming here tomorrow," he told me.

Why doesn't Leport send his bosomy Mariette to do his fighting for him? I wanted to suggest.

My houseboy, Albert, came walking up to me to report smartly that "Monganga Mokonji has gone back to the hospital to operate. He said to let you know he would be late."

On the night of the district commissioner's visit, Albert had gotten a good beating from the smaller but authoritative Jafke, and seemed to have profited from that lesson. He stood erect, his pants were always buttoned now, and he made periodically sure of it by passing his hand over the strategic area.

It was my turn to explode. So Michael had sneaked back to the hospital. Naturally he would be late. Michael was a research man more than a surgeon. The least little operation took him hours. Maybe this very instant he was making another youth happy with the coveted circumcision, while I was left alone. It would serve Michael right if I gave away a pair of his trousers to his grateful patient.

"Go tell *Monganga Mokonji* that I'll be late myself," I said. "I'm off to the *mboka*."

"Mmmm," said Albert.

"Mmmm," I echoed, and turning about, followed the children on the narrow path leading to the village.

CHAPTER XIV

At Molali's house the bargaining was at its peak, but it was practically certain that it would not be concluded that day. Molali was elated: he savored the good fortune of being the father of a lovely and enviably lucky girl who appealed to the most important man in the *mboka*. He would not consider any dowry offered and at each new proposal feigned surprise. A sarcastic smile would play on his face, that he then screwed up into a mask of sadness, as though the ridiculous price offered him insulted the beauty of his daughter and the nobility of his family and ancestry.

This was what he told the go-betweens, but his eyes twinkled with happiness, since this, his highest ambition, was being realized. He evidently knew the *mokonji's* appetite and was sure of his game, for he was not disturbed when the callers had finished smoking their *potongo* and departed expressing disappointment because the transaction had not been concluded. He knew that the envoys would return with other and better offers, and the go-betweens knew it also. Everybody knew it, but many words of regret were spoken, as if this were a definite breaking off of negotiations.

Molali, who was fully aware of Lisengo's courtship and who therefore no doubt expected a scene, tears, or perhaps Baloki's flight to the forest for a day or two, appeared agreeably surprised and delighted with his daughter's contented air and conduct. In addition to avoiding useless complications, that in the end would change nothing, he was proud of his daughter, for he told me, "When a beautiful girl is sensible, she is worth double the price."

Knowing why Baloki was being so reasonable, I smiled at her, and to my amused surprise she winked at me. Molali Moke had evidently taught her the trick.

It was too late in the afternoon to start looking for Mokolo—the witch doctor the villagers credited me with recommending to them. Besides, because of the delayed negotiations between Chief Mafuta's envoys and Molali, I had a little more time to think out my vague plan to ensure the witch doctor's assistance to help Baloki.

Before sundown, in spite of the interrupted bargaining, Molali gave a feast. A large group of villagers gathered around his fire, which was bigger and brighter than usual. After many *losako* (greetings) and several rounds of endless figures of speech that precede all assemblies in which notables participate, the guests finally settled around the fire, smoked their *potongo,* ate and, most of all, drank. It happened to be one of those days on which Molali's wife had prepared a great supply of *masanga.* But even so, because of the special occasion, there was not enough of it after all. And when there was nothing more left to eat or drink, they began telling stories of the past. And although thinking that by now Michael had probably finished circumcising his patient, I stayed on, fascinated by those stories. Tactfully, they said little about the impending nuptials, since it was not as yet official, but there was a tendency to tell stories in which love, marriage, and women played an important part. As usual, Grandfather Lulango's story was the most fantastic. He told us about a day of long ago, when he was a small child. That day the sun abruptly hid in a perfectly cloudless blue sky. No one knew where it had disappeared to. Only a tiny speck of sunlight had remained visible and it grew as dark right in the middle of the day as it would on the gloomiest night. The nocturnal birds flew about, but the forest stayed still and silent in that weird combination of night and day. The sky had turned black and the stars appeared. The panic-stricken people thought that this was surely the end of the world.

Alone Lulango's father, the great-grandfather of Molali Moke, who was the wisest and most learned *mokonji* of the whole region, knew what had caused it all and explained it to his people. The sudden darkness enshrouded the earth because the sun, that since time immemorial had been in love with the moon who until then had been cool toward the sun and stinting in bestowing her favors, had finally been admitted into the moon's hut and had concentrated all his light and warmth on his beloved mistress, forgetting all about the rest of the world. So everything grew dark until the sun had recovered his senses.

"And the stars, Grandfather?" Molaki Moke inquired eagerly.

"The stars are the moon's children," his grandfather explained.

But this opinion was not shared by all. One old man said that he had heard about a Mongo tribesman who must have known what he was talking about, for he was the grandson of Bakakoto's slave whose wife was the last one to have gone up to the heavens and to have come back down again. The Mongo claimed that the sun that glided above the earth had a long black tail, like the tail of the Mongo women's brief below-the-waist apronlike raffia garment. And it was that long tail in the sun's wake as it went by that obscured the daytime sky and brought on the night.

"Mmmm, but what about the stars, the stars?" Molali

Moke's grandfather, who resented that his interpretation should not have been unanimously accepted, insisted impatiently.

"The stars are nothing but daylight showing through the sun's tail," the old man replied calmly. "The Mongo said that his grandfather had told him that Bakakoto had told him that his wife had told him that the sun's tail is quite old and has many little holes through which the day shows."

They all looked up at the "little holes" blinking down at them from the dark sky. They must all have thought about the passionate desire of the ardent sun for the cold and beautiful moon. The word "love" in the Bangala vocabulary stands for "desire." When a man says to a woman, *"Nalingi,"* it means both "I love you" and "I want you."

Everybody was interested to hear more about Bakakoto's wife Lotito who had been in the sky, but the old one who had mentioned her name did not know much more than he already had told us. They asked Molali Moke's grandfather, who knew all the old legends, but he was too offended.

"Why not ask the Mongo who is the grandson of Bakakoto's slave?" he pouted.

However, the blind old man was finally cajoled with a drink and a freshly lit *potongo.* And when a diplomatic masculine voice remarked, "Look at how many children the moon has out tonight," the oldster began his story. "Everybody knows that there are people who live in the sky just as they do on earth. But the people of the sky who can see Djakomba, the god of the world, invisible to us, are immortal and know not the miseries of our existence. Long ago, nevertheless, earth people could visit those of the sky to beseech various blessings from its more fortunate inhabitants. In order to reach the sky they had to climb a great stone bridge that joined it and the earth. They returned bringing back with them sight to the eyes of the blind, strength for young men wounded in combat, and even youth to the worn bodies of the aged. Only two conditions were imposed upon those visiting the sky. They had to come back to earth the same day and never once so much as glance back on their way down the bridge. The gifts from the sky people were so numerous then that all infirmities had nearly vanished from the earth, and many had begun dreaming of eternal life, the same as that granted to the sky people.

"One day, however, Bakakoto's wife Lotito journeyed to the sky to seek a favor. There she met a young sky man with whom she was instantly smitten. Since she was young and beautiful, the lad returned her desire. She failed to return to earth that same day, or even the following night. When at last she walked down the span, she constantly kept turning around to signal amorously to her sky lover. Djakomba heard of this and he wrathfully destroyed the bridge that spanned the sky and the earth. And this is why the people of the earth must suffer and die."

He appeared lost in meditation for a moment, then added: "There still remains a heap of crumbled rocks on the Congo River, near Upoto. That is where the bridge commenced."

Before leaving Brussels to join Michael, I had read a Congolese legend about an immortal "Sky People," but it was quite different. In it, the earthling in search of immortality for his own people had been admitted to the sky on condition that he stay awake a full seven days and nights. He failed because he had succumbed to sleep. I preferred grandfather's version.

I looked about for Baloki to see what impression her grandparent's legendary love story had made upon her, but she was gone. She was living her own love story, and it was certain that she could be found behind her parents' hut. Barging in on the couple wasn't exactly to my liking, but I had to have a word with Lisengo, so I slipped away from the gathering around the fire. To my surprise Baloki was alone. She was absentminded, smiled vaguely, and when I inquired of the whereabouts of Lisengo, she said with quiet pride:

"He went to kill *Mokonji* Mafuta."

A distant uproar of shouting voices, the beat of tom-

toms, and the gallop of men's bare feet running toward the center of the *mboka* did not allow me a chance to react.

"He did it, he did it!" Baloki murmured excitedly.

"And what if they catch him?" I said. "Will they not kill him for this?"

Baloki had apparently not considered such an eventuality. She had thought of nothing but the love of her hero who was going to deliver her from a loathed prospective husband. Presently she trembled with dread. She wanted to run to the place where things were happening.

Rapid footfalls approaching Molali's house, where the celebration continued, promised news. Forcing Baloki to stay put, I went back to the fire where everybody was in a state of agitation, for the news was stunning: someone had made an attempt on the life of *Mokonji* Mafuta, and the *mokonji's* men had nearly seized the assailant. There had been a brief but furious skirmish, but the unknown aggressor had escaped.

Carrying a torch taken from the hand of one of the men, I rushed home. Multitudes of insects danced around me, sizzling as they fell into the suddenly brighter flame of my torch, while I almost ran on the narrow trail that had lost its familiarity in the dark. A couple of times somber shadows with flickering greenish eyes melted behind the bushes. I wasn't really scared, since I knew that no animal would come near the flame. But I was certainly glad finally to bound up the steps of our bungalow.

The assailant was squatting on my back *baraza*. One of Lisengo's eyes was completely shut, his left arm hung limply and blood trickled from a long cut in his chest. He regretted only that Mafuta was still alive.

"I shall kill him tomorrow," he said coldly.

"If you do," I warned him, "you will never have Baloki for a wife."

"But if I do not kill him, will he not have her for a wife?" he rejoined.

"Didn't I guarantee Baloki that you'll be her *mobali*?" I

said, and was surprised to learn that Baloki had not said a word about this to him. "Go to the hospital now. *Monganga Mokonji* will take care of your wounds," I added.

But he shook his head. "*Monganga Mokonji,* is he not a man of the white man's king? He will send me to jail," he said.

"You're not afraid of me," I said, "and am I not the wife of *Monganga Mokonji,* a man of the white man's king?"

"*Te,*" he said solemnly, "I am not afraid of you. Are you not just a *mwana* (a child)?" Then he corrected himself. "Anyway, are you not our friend?"

His athletic figure disappeared into the night just as Jafke came out of the kitchen quarters, and almost immediately Baloki materialized on the road, running toward our bungalow.

"Where is Lisengo?" she whispered.

I ignored her question. "Why didn't you tell Lisengo I had promised to help you two get married?"

"If you could only have seen him when he left me to kill the *mokonji!*" Baloki explained, gazing at me with eyes brimming with ecstasy for her brave sweetheart.

The moon had made its glittering entrance.

"Is she not beautiful?" Baloki whispered admiringly, looking up at the moon. Perhaps she had heard the ardent love story told by her grandfather after all.

But I did not share her enthusiasm, for that cold lover paled in the presence of this warm-blooded girl. And thinking of the recklessly bold Lisengo brought to my mind another man who did not dare rush to his wife's rescue for fear of displeasing his superior.

Baloki left, armed with my flashlight that I had forced into her hand, and city slicker Jafke followed her semi-nude figure with covetous eyes.

"Mmmm, *kitoko mingi* (very beautiful)," he said appreciatively.

Michael was still at the hospital. It was not a circumcision this time, Jafke informed me. A man from Busu Kwanga had been gored in the belly by a water buffalo; the *monganga* had to operate on him without delay.

As I sat there lounging in one of my living-room morris chairs, waiting for my *monganga* to come home. I could envision how the operation went. I was once present at such an emergency intervention Michael had to perform a week after my arrival in Busu Melo. With no immediate transportation available, sending the patient to Lisala, the nearest hospital with adequate facilities, which was a day's drive away, would have meant the man's certain death. It was a strangulated hernia in that instance. Michael was operating in a makeshift operating room at his "hospital," by the light of a Coleman lamp and with the assistance of three African aides. And their assistance was not of the kind a surgeon receives from qualified personnel in a well-equipped operating room. One of the aides was pouring ether onto a wad of gauze over the patient's nose, but without watching the patient; he kept his eyes on Michael. And Michael would glance up from the open wound at the patient's face and say, *"Lisusu"* (some more), and the aide would then let a few more drops of ether fall onto the gauze. And the second aide was standing by, turning the pages of a surgery book that Michael kept consulting every so often as he was operating. And the third attendant, armed with a towel, was stationed behind Michael, mopping his brow, to prevent the sweat from dripping into the open wound.

It was growing late. The moon had slid behind the dense jungle wall, and the sky over the village had taken on a red glow. Sitting quietly, listening to the weakening hissing of our Coleman lamp on its high wooden stand, to the chorus of sounds of the equatorial bush night, punctuated by the tireless tom-toms at "my" *mboka,* I imagined hearing the excited voices of the villagers celebrating the saving of their obese *mokonji.*

When would Michael come out of his operating room, 113 with its whitewashed clay walls and a strip of tarpaulin sus-pended above the table, designed to prevent the dirt from showering his patients as it dropped from the ceilingless thatched roof? A major abdominal operation takes such a long time—particularly when it is performed by a specialist in tropical diseases.

CHAPTER XV

A few days later Busu Melo relapsed into its old pattern of existence. Michael had again "hit the road" on a new public-health mission. And, as in the past, he returned home late at night, to start out again at dawn the next day, in an attempt to carry out his scheduled program before the beginning of the rainy season, although it looked as if the rain would win the race after all.

My little friends brought me the latest news from the *mboka*. Molali Moke said that everything was at a standstill and that his father worried himself sick because Mafuta's envoys had not returned as he had expected. So perhaps the chief had given up the notion of marrying Baloki, which was wonderful news, of course, and I relaxed, since I really still hadn't a clear-cut idea of how to save her.

Michael's patient, on whom he had so painstakingly operated a few day ago, was doing fine, and apparently would survive. It gave Michael added prestige among the local population, although it appeared that such feats did not impress the administration. A letter from Coquilhatville, the capital of the Equatorial Province, sent as usual through channels, had arrived from Lisala, requesting an explanation why the doctor in Busu Melo was performing major surgery, which was authorized in well-equipped urban hospitals only. The letter was of course not in reference to the last, still convalescent case, but to an earlier one—the strangulated hernia operation I had witnessed. That patient, who was a prisoner in our Busu Melo jail at the time of the emergency operation, had landed in Coquilhatville a few months later, and, while being treated for malaria at the Hospital for Blacks, had explained the origin of his post-operative scar.

"So help me, I'll send back the trunkful of surgical instruments I was supplied with in Brussels!" Michael threatened. But he almost instantly asked Jafke to send a message to the *infirmier* at the "hospital" across the road, not to forget to load the heavy trunk on the car early tomorrow morning for the next trip.

For the past forty-eight hours thunder had been rolling over the tropical forest and lightning had been zigzagging across the dark, threatening sky. The nerves of the Busu Melo residents also seemed to tighten in an alarming crescendo, with already practically nothing remaining of the brief period of harmony that had rendered life tolerable at our isolated post. The torrential rain that came down abruptly one morning, turning the main road into a regular mountain stream, and that in the next few days changed into a continuous drizzle, did nothing toward easing the accumulating tension. Perhaps it even contributed to complicating somewhat the relationship among European Busu Melo residents. At any rate, there was a new clash between the Portuguese traders and, this time, the government administration.

It started one morning on the *baraza* of Carlos's store. I was the only customer present, and shortly after my arrival Monsieur Fallet dropped in to see Carlos on some official business. We had scarcely said hello, when a sudden cloudburst pouring tons of water on Busu Melo trapped us both at the store. Sitting on the *baraza* floor, under Carlos's overseeing eye, a lone small village boy—one of Carlos's cheap-labor squad—was cleaning a huge stack of copal. After the customary remarks about the rain, humid heat, and other such exciting local topics had been exhausted, we silently watched, through the torrents of rain, a large banana tree being torn to shreds by the gale. It was then that Carlos decided to inspect the small pile of copal the child had just finished scraping with a knife to reveal its gem-like sparkle.

"Look at this!" Carlos shouted at the visibly terrified boy who sprang to his feet. "Look at this, you dirty little baboon!" He was pointing to a dark spot on one side of a piece of copal. "Is this the way you do your work, is this what I'm paying you good wages for?" he continued shouting. "Put out your hands!"

Before Fallet or I knew it, Carlos was punishing the child, who was holding his hands palms up, by striking them with a small flat board, reminiscent of a long-handled hairbrush, designed for this barbaric purpose. The child did not scream, nor did he attempt to avoid the blows. Tears streaming down his cheeks, he would jerk away his hand after each blow, instantly to put it out for the next one. This was a practice strictly forbidden by law, and as a rule no trader would allow himself to resort to this inhuman punishment in the presence of a government functionary. Not that either Van Derveer or Fallet was unaware of the practice, but it was one thing to tolerate something done behind their backs, another to witness the law flouted. Perhaps after dining at our house with the district commissioner and our local administrators, Carlos had gotten the idea that he now belonged to the "inner circle" and could get away with practically anything. Or maybe he had just acted without thinking.

"Stop it!" I screamed after the first blow.

But Carlos only grinned in my direction. Fallet glanced helplessly at the deluge outside.

"Stop it, Carlos," he echoed meekly.

"The little *macaque* (the dog-faced little monkey) will

uin me if I don't watch out," Carlos said, dealing the boy another blow. "This is supposed to be top-grade copal."

"Monsieur Fallet, make him stop it at once!" I screamed again.

"Stop it," said Monsieur Fallet, moving toward Carlos.

They eyed each other, and for a moment I thought they would come to blows.

"I'll have to report you, Carlos," said Fallet, with some authority this time.

Carlos's bovine neck, suddenly swelled by his bulging veins, grew even thicker. Fortunately for him, a thunderclap drowned out his answer. Then he threw down his mean little board, and a moment later the Fallets' houseboy appeared with Fallet's raincoat and, wading across Carlos's flooded front yard, Fallet left, most likely to referee another village palaver at his office.

At "my" *mboka* things were also more complicated than ever, as I discovered one morning, when it looked as if the thin drizzle was the best weather we might hope for in the next two months and, in spite of feeling wretchedly tired after a virtually sleepless night, I went to visit my village friends. The rumbling thunder of a distant storm was accompanied by the incessant beating of tom-toms celebrating the little *mokonji*'s narrow escape from an assailant.

Baloki's red eyes made it instantly plain to me that Molali Moke's news about Mafuta's giving up the idea of marrying Baloki must have been wishful thinking. Indeed, the chief's representatives were scheduled to return the following day.

The village paths were empty, probably because the menfolk were sleeping off hangovers from festivities of the night before, and the women, taking advantage of this, lingered on in their huts beside their sleeping husbands. Only a few aged women, who had not attended the celebration, now, as always, busied themselves near their rekindled fires. I walked along the deserted main path, on which the huts emerged one by one out of the milky fog that possibly might not lift for days, looking for Mokolo.

Molali Moke, Boboka, and the other kids who came to my marmalade parties had told me that the chief witch doctor, Djito, was away from the *mboka*, a fortunate coincidence that would make my plan easier to carry out. Now, having heard that Mafuta's go-betweens were returning to Molali's house to renew negotiations over Baloki's purchase price, I was afraid that they might be concluded sooner than I had expected.

It took quite a while to find Mokolo, whom I finally spotted on one of the side paths. He was performing the dance of *lela*, intended to cure a stricken man who was stretched across the threshold of his hut. I regretted having missed the beginning of the rites of this shrewd witch doctor, who was garbed in a multicolored costume that would have made Djito green with envy.

My attention focused on the sick man. He had trypanosomiasis (the awful Congolese sleeping sickness) in an advanced stage, and had been getting regular injections for it in Michael's hospital dispensary. The realization that the cachectic old fellow was dead gave me quite a shock. Mokolo, engrossed in his *lela*, gazing alternately at the ground and then skyward, appeared unaware of the man's death. Then he abruptly stopped dancing.

Now he turned to the wife of the dead man. She had wasted no time and was already coated with the *mpembe* and had braided her hair into the *mansundu* (the mourning hairdo).

"If you will provide your *mobali* with enough food and drink for his long journey, he will go to Ibanza. If you do not and let him go without anything, he will join Nsungu," Mokolo said to the woman. "Despite his dishonorable end, however, he will not return in the shape of a big ape to eternally roam the forest, for my *lela* has purified his *elili* (his spirit)."

So it was not to heal the man's body, but to save his immortal soul that Mokolo had performed the sacred dance of *lela.* Quite conceivably sleeping sickness had not been the sole cause of the man's premature death. Boboka had said some days earlier that the man had squandered his daughter's purchase price so that when the girl had returned home to her parents, there was nothing left to give back to the deserted husband. What's more, the girl had aggravated matters by running away from the *mboka,* and her father was left with neither daughter nor her dowry. As a result, the poor man had been savagely beaten by his son-in-law and the latter's family. And now, since he died without repaying his debt, he was considered a crook by his fellow villagers. There was not a man, woman, or child in the whole little community who doubted but what after his death the embezzler would be turned into a huge ape that would forever roam the forests of the western Congo.

Mokolo tried to sneak away, but I didn't let him. "There's something of the utmost importance we must discuss," I told him.

"Would I not be the most honored man to discuss a matter of importance with you, *Mwasi na Monganga Mokonji?*" he replied, "Walk with me to my hut, and let us discuss it there."

Regardless of how interested in discussing the matter, I was hesitant about going to his hut, over whose entranceway hung a repulsive mask. But Baloki's dejected expression made me overcome my reluctance. There was another brief delay, for Mokolo had one more call to make. He went to see again the woman who had jumped over the *mokandu* (the fertility hurdle). Evidently the last *mokandu* had proved no more effective than the ones before, since the woman was not yet with young.

Everything was in readiness for the new rite in the back of the woman's hut, where there was a small grave of her firstborn, who had died because Moeka, who according to the children had been an evil man, had conjured a bad *likundu* on the baby.

Presently the woman placed herself in front of the grave and wailed:

"Have I not given birth to one *mwana?* Why can I not have another child?"

Mokolo said nothing, but gesticulated so violently that his *njekele,* the assortment of charms dangling from his arms and legs, filled the air with a peculiar jingling. All this was now becoming nerve-racking, but fortunately the ceremony was finished at last, and Mokolo and I were again on our way. The drizzle had stopped, and it was good to be able to unbotton my raincoat, which was steamed up on the inside.

When we finally reached Mokolo's hut he offered me a hand-carved ebony chair standing under a low thatched awning in the backyard. His place was like a laboratory of a medieval chemist. There were countless gourds and jars suspended over glowing charcoals. Several bamboo stems were cut to allow the liquids to run from one gourd into another. Judging from the quantity of medicines he was concocting, my "protégé" was not only a quack but perhaps something of a physician as well. In a nasal monotone he went into a detailed description of the various drugs he was preparing. He seemed to caress his gourds with gentle fingers, and lingered over one, apparently his favorite.

"It is the red root of *nkasa,* and the one over there has the bark of *mukungu* in it," he explained.

Mokolo was not trying to conceal his passion for those two gourds, one of which contained *nkasa* used in the ordeal by poison that killed, and the other one *mukungu* used in the test that blinded. His prestige and his power were born here. I made a mental note to mention to Michael that the witch doctor was brewing these two ghastly drugs, and Mokolo had no doubt noticed the expression on my face, for he went into a description of his other medicines, showing me a gourd that he said contained small live frogs.

"These frogs should be eaten by persons who spit blood and cough. Do you cough, *Mwasi na Monganga Mokonji?*" he inquired.

"I do not cough," I replied emphatically. "I do not need any frogs."

"Did I offer you any frogs?" he countered.

Then, after we had agreed that I did not need his frogs, I told him what I did want from him:

"I want you to help a girl from your *mboka* to marry the man she loves and who loves her. The man is poor, the girl is *kitoko mingi.*"

"A beautiful girl is beautiful today and an old hag to-morrow," remarked Mokolo. "It is the family that counts. Who is the girl?"

"It is Baloki, the daughter of Molali."

Scowling, Mokolo considered what I had told him for a moment. "The man who takes away a girl coveted by Chief Mafuta should have more than her purchase price," he replied. "Otherwise his marriage will not last long, not longer than his life, which will be very short indeed."

"Not if he is helped by a *monganga* as powerful as Mokolo," I flattered him. "I've always thought you were the best *monganga* in the *mboka*. That's what people say, and that's what I, too, say when people ask my opinion."

"I am the best *monganga*," Mokolo decided. "I shall try to arrange all this, but leave everything to me. The chief shall not desire the daughter of Molali any longer."

On my way to Molali's house, I wondered how Mokolo was going to persuade little Mafuta to give up the idea of marrying Baloki.

While I was walking by the hut of the dead man for whom Mokolo had performed the *lela*, my eyes were drawn to a hypnotizing sight. When I came closer, I saw that the man's naked body was coated with *mpembe*, and the neighbors were gravely plugging his ears with red clay. I hurried away, trying to put out of my mind the sight of this white-painted head that was being decorated for the man's final journey, but the image kept returning with the sounds of the mournful chants the villagers had intoned.

At Molali's house I found Molali Moke in tears. Despite his grandfather's admonitions, he had accepted a chunk of goat meat at the celebration, and grandfather Lulango had learned about it through a dream he had had as he was slumbering by the fire. A marabou had stopped by his son's house and had tried to swallow Molali Moke. "It is not he that I really want to eat, but the *nyama* of the goat which he ate," the bird had explained apologetically. As a result of this dream, Molali Moke had received a good dose of pili-pili, the hot peppercorns, to purify him of the forbidden *nyama*. It was his blind old grandfather himself who had administered it to him, since Molali, Molali Moke's father, was a materialist who did not believe that one should turn down a piece of meat when it could be had for free. He himself ate rats, bats, ravens, insects, and other creatures, which he regarded as being *nyama*. Still, he did not dare to oppose his old father whom he respected, particularly since the old man's social standing would make it possible to demand a higher dowry for his daughter Baloki.

Molali Moke's mouth was all red from the *pili-pili*, his eyes red from crying, and his buttocks were probably sore from the spanking he had received. He felt guilty, for he did not even attempt to wink at me. Boboka, who as usual was standing on one foot, like a stork, watching all that was going on, told me that Molali Moke had, a short time before, received still another dose of *pili-pili*, but not by mouth. None of them had any doubt whatsoever that the red peppercorns would burn up all the forbidden *nyama* he had eaten the other day. It had been another less important witch doctor of the neighborhood who had blown the fiery infusion, with which he had filled his mouth, through a hollow straw into Molali Moke's bowels. Molali, who had to pay for the "medication" with a whole gourd of *masanga*, was unable to calm down, even though he had already beaten his wife.

"I've just seen a dead man," I told Molali Moke, trying to take his mind off his punishment. "Why did they plug his ears with red clay and paint his head with the *mpembe*?"

Instantly, the little boy perked up and, aping the attitude of his learned grandparent, explained solemnly:

"They have plugged his ears so he would not hear that his *mwasi* had immediately stopped weeping for him, and they have painted him with the mourning *mpembe* since his *mwasi* had refused to wear it for longer than one day, and so the dead man had to wear his own mourning."

Taking Baloki to one side to let her in on the cheering news, I assured her, "Chief Mafuta will never desire you again."

CHAPTER XVI

I could not return to the *mboka* the next day to find out if Mokolo had done anything about his pledge to me. Michael was home, and we decided finally to drive over to the Catholic mission at Busu Modanda, as we had intended the day he had dashed off on his short inspection tour. Michael had two matters to attend to. The first was official business: one of the nuns attached to the mission had at one time taken nursing courses and had offered her services to give weekly intramuscular injections to a few villagers living within walking distance of the mission. It was time, Michael felt, to see for himself how this program was working out. If we hurried it up a little, we would be there during the injection period. The other matter was of a personal nature: to offer the nuns a small donation—about the price of a piston of a Chevrolet car. Monsieur Leport, who had also returned to the post, asked to come with us. He was rather nervous, because Richot, the man he and his companions had put in a cast as a gag, was going to pass through Busu Melo that day, and had been inquiring about Leport's whereabouts.

I was at the wheel that morning, unable to concentrate on my driving. This trip was taking me away from my village, where important events sealing Baloki's fate were about to happen, but we were approaching the hamlet where I had seen Father Gabriel such a short time ago. If only I could have known then that I'd never see him again and that his inspired transformation of the gallery of saints adorning his chapel would be the last work of his magic brush. For Father Gabriel was found dead of a heart attack in his hut on the night following my visit, and as if his remarkable church could not survive without him, it had gone up in flames shortly after his death. . . .

When we drove by the village that stood silent and appeared deserted, I thought that the jungle had already started to reclaim the ground where the tiny church had once been. I was scarcely aware of the rest of the drive, and as we were nearing the red-brick mission, I bore down on the accelerator on the long smooth red clay driveway that was such luxury after the bumpy main Busu Melo road.

"Darling, will you please slow down," Michael asked me. "Do you see what I see?" he turned to Leport.

Slowing down almost to a crawl I, too, looked up from the wheel, but noticed nothing to get worked up about.

"Incredible!" said Leport. "Such ignorance! How can she do a thing like that!"

"Do what?" I asked.

By now we had pulled up in front of the mission's bungalow-dispensary, and watched Sister Madeleine at work. She sat facing us on the *baraza* at a table laden with medical supplies. Fully clothed villagers approached the table one by one, turned their back to her, and she gave each an injection.

Michael jumped out of the car and, running up the red-brick steps two at a time, rushed toward her.

"*Ma Sœur,*" he addressed her breathlessly, forgetting to greet her first, "how can you inject these people this way? I mean, what about asepsis, injecting them like this through their trousers?"

"But *Monsieur le Docteur,* I don't," she said quietly, and smiled disarmingly.

"I'm sorry, *Ma Sœur,*" Michael persisted, quite ill-at-ease, "but I saw it with my own eyes . . . All these men are fully dressed."

It was not easy for poor Michael to practically accuse a nun of lying—a nun who had volunteered her services to aid the sick. But *Sœur* Madeleine did not appear in the least disturbed by Michael's remark.

"Indeed they are fully dressed, *Monsieur le Docteur,* except for a small hole cut out in the seat of their trousers. I'm most careful to move the trousers each time, to shift the hole a little, so as not to inject in the same spot. And I always swab them with iodine through the hole in their trousers." She showed poor, embarrassed Michael a swab dipped in iodine.

Throughout our visit, we tried to keep from betraying our amusement, but as soon as we were out of the good nuns' earshot, on our way home, both Michael and I couldn't stop laughing about this new medical technique that combined the strict hygienic requirements with the chaste dignity of a nun turned nurse.

Leport did not share our amusement, and we soon learned the cause for his extraordinary preoccupation.

"If you don't mind, *Monsieur le Docteur,* and *Madame,*" he said presently, "I'd like to stick close to you for the rest of the day. Maybe Richot won't dare to attack me in your presence."

"Sure thing," said Michael.

"Why don't you have lunch with us," I offered. "You're welcome to stay with us until Monsieur Richot leaves the post."

"He won't leave until he's seen me," wailed Leport, "but I accept with a thousand thanks, Madame. At least that way there will be someone to come between us."

Our bungalow, as we found out, was the last place Leport should have sought sanctuary, for when we pulled up at our *baraza* and started to get out of the car, Richot himself emerged from our living room, towering over everyone and everything from the front porch.

"I've been waiting for you," he told Leport, after saying hello to us. "Jafke told me you were coming back with the *monganga*. I didn't want to leave here without seeing you."

"Take it easy," said Michael, trying to get between Leport and Richot.

Both Michael and Leport looked surprisingly small beside the husky trader. Leport raised his right arm, probably to shield his face, and a second later we were standing there, watching Richot pumping Leport's hand, which he had grabbed in mid-air.

"It was a perfect job," Richot was saying. "Doctor Bolotinha, at Lisala, said that a fracture like mine is not easy to reduce, but that you did it just right. He showed me the X-ray where the bone mended."

"You mean . . . you mean there *was* a fracture?" stammered Leport.

"He's a riot," said Richot, chuckling. "He was so drunk that he cannot remember why and how he set my leg in a cast. You should give him a promotion, *Monsieur le Docteur*," he suggested.

But Leport, who was still mopping his brow, but now grinning his gold-toothed smile for the first time in two days, did not need any other reward.

"Well, let me tell you something—" he began.

"Let me first tell you," Richot interrupted him, "that I left a case of whiskey on your *baraza*. Now what did you want to say?"

"Nothing," said Leport, "nothing at all."

After Richot left I went to the back door to give Jafke instructions for lunch, and found two messengers from the *mboka* waiting for me there.

"Baloki said to tell you to come right away," said Molali Moke.

"Mmmm," echoed Boboka.

The kids did not give me a chance to ask any questions and were already skipping away like two playful chipmunks. Something important was happening at the village, something the two little eavesdroppers did not want to miss, for they had rushed away without even as much as a glance in the direction of my pantry.

All through lunch—which started with deviled eggs Jafke had learned how to prepare from Madame Van Derveer's cook, fried chicken (mostly skin and bones, as usual), and a can of pears, a delicacy in the interior, for dessert—I was trying to imagine what might have happened at "my" *mboka*. I was only half-listening to Leport's spicy gossip, which he had heard from Almeida who had just come back from Lisala, about *Sœur* Angélique's being madly in love with the chief physician of the hospital for Europeans in Coquilhatville; and about the middle-aged wife of one of the Mongana oil company's European employees having an affair with a young African; and about our own Silva's being a homosexual who raped small village boys he hired to clean his copal.

Lunch dragged on, till coffee was served on the front *baraza*, for another hour, but as soon as Leport and Michael had left for the hospital, I was on my way to the *mboka*.

As I had anticipated, the news was about Baloki, although I had hoped for something entirely different. The sly Mokolo had kept his word, all right. He had made Baloki undesirable, but to all eligible men in the village, not to Mafuta alone, as I had asked him. Now I wished he had rather done nothing.

At Molali's hut I found the whole family squatting in front of it around their fire. Everyone, that is, except Molali himself. Presently he appeared seemingly from nowhere, dashed over to his daughter and, before anyone could realize what was happening, slapped Baloki twice, causing her to lose balance. She fell into the fire, upsetting the large, sooty pot containing the family's evening meal. This made Molali lose his temper completely, for that was a tasty dinner going to waste. Forgetting his rage he tried to salvage with a stick bits of fish that had been simmering in the pot, without any concern for his daughter. Fortunately for Baloki, she did not wear any clothes that might have caught fire. When Molali was satisfied that there was no more fish to be saved, he wailed, holding his head like a man struck with disaster.

"My only daughter, a daughter who ought to be the pride and consolation of my old age is nothing but a no-good, barren female that no one will want for a wife. *Nsoni, nsoni, nsoni* (shame). Shame upon me, shame upon my house, shame—"

"Who said that I am barren!" Baloki jumped to her feet like a feline, with eyes flashing belligerently. "The one who said this is the greatest liar in the village. Tell me who said it so that I might scratch out his evil eyes. If I had not drunk the infusion of *iika* and of papaya roots for three days of the past moon, I would have had a *mwana*. I could have had one; I can have a baby any time, if I want one, and I can prove it!"

Her father was not listening, however. Crushed by his misfortune, he squatted on the ground, swaying from side to side like a mournful pendulum. His eyes stared bitterly into space. He was an outraged father and, most of all, an outwitted trader. It was clear that all this was the result of Mokolo's doings, and I wanted to learn all the details. But it was impossible to wring anything from Molali.

"My grandmother had eleven; my mother had seven; and my daughter cannot have even one. *Nsoni, nsoni, nsoni,*" he had begun muttering under his breath.

When he had finally regained some composure, I learned what that wily but stupid Mokolo had done. A persistent rumor was circulating in the *mboka*. It was being whispered that Baloki could not have a *mwana*, that she was not equipped with the necessary female organs to conceive a child. Many of the men in the village wondered how they had failed noticing this before. Her round breasts alone, which were quite obviously not made for nursing a *mwana* as were the elongated breasts of the other village women, were proof enough of her infecundity. All this gossip would have had little importance, had not Mafuta taken advantage of the opportunity. One of the little chief's representatives had spoken confidentially to Molali, and had hinted to him that Mafuta had not given up his intention of marrying Baloki. He could afford the luxury of getting a beautiful girl, good only for sleeping with. But, of course, in substance, with all these derogatory rumors, he was prepared to pay only half of what had been offered the last time, and this only because of his great regard for old Lulango's family position. And all the time Molali had hoped to get four times as much!

I was seething against Mokolo. Perhaps my resentment was heightened by the realization of my unwitting part in the witch doctor's scheme that instead of setting things right appeared to have aggravated the situation. Lisengo's anger was mounting even faster than mine, or perhaps he didn't try to conceal it as I did. Baloki whispered to me that her beloved was planning another attack on his powerful rival, which of course would amount to suicide, since the little chief was being guarded better than ever before.

"Mafuta will not have his way" had been Lisengo's parting words to Baloki, when she saw him just before he had vanished into the dense bush, she told me.

Naturally, this made me feel even worse, for now I was afraid of what this brave young man driven to despair might do.

I knew that I had to think of something, and without delay. But I couldn't come up with any concrete idea. To begin with, I tried to reason with Molali.

"Since Baloki is sure she can have a *mwana*, why not

give her a chance to prove it? When she's pregnant she will be worth even more than originally," I suggested.

Molali considered it for a moment, and then replied in an unsteady voice, "But supposing she cannot prove it? Then I would not even receive the dowry the chief is offering me to-day." No, he concluded, there was nothing left but to accept the humiliation and the price offered by Mafuta.

Infuriated against myself, against that miser Molali, against Mokolo, and against the "generous" little chief who was allowing himself the luxury of taking his fifth wife for no reason other than lust, I was setting out for Mokolo's hut to have a word with him, when a strange woman arrived to call on Molali. She did not appear very tidy, but it turned out she was the local midwife. It immediately became clear that her unsolicited visit was a direct result of the unfortunate rumors about Baloki. She asked to speak to Molali in private, but taking advantage of the fact that nobody dared to stop me, I followed them into the hut. This woman's name was Mula, that is, it was not her true name but, as in so many other instances, a nickname, which translated meant "a wave." The nickname was extremely appropriate since she was one of the most obese creatures imaginable. She was a veritable mountain of flabby flesh that quivered with her every motion and spread out like the protoplasm of an amoeba or—like a wave.

This woman, so aptly nicknamed, again made me think of how observant the Africans generally were. The Europeans living in the large centers were usually recipients of a series of standard, banal, and casually chosen sobriquets. For instance, a man wearing spectacles might be nicknamed "*Talatala*" (Glasses). One has to have lived in the jungle to have heard truly picturesque nicknames. I thought of our own Monsieur Van Derveer, nicknamed "*Alembi te?*" (Is he not tired?), while another portly administrator, not unlike our own in size and shape, in another small post, had been dubbed "*Njoku alembi*" (Tired elephant). One of the territorial agents in our own

Busu Melo territory, who was a snooper and had the habit of sneaking soundlessly behind the villagers' huts to eavesdrop, had been nicknamed "*Makolo na Nkoi*" (Leopard's paws). Another, who was exhausted by years of life on the equator and who had become completely apathetic, had been re-nicknamed by the bush Africans "*Pamba te?*" (Is he not worthless?) instead of his years-old original nickname of "*Nyoka*" (Snake). And a glutton, whose sole interest was food, and who always made a ritual of each meal, but who despite all that remained skinny, was "*Molimo na Libumu*" (The soul of the belly). His fat wife, on the other hand, who was thought of as romantic, had been nicknamed "*Libumu na Molimo*" (The belly of the soul).

Mula, flooding half of the hut with her quivering flesh, sat down on the hard-earth floor of Molali's house before stating her business. She had come with a proposition. She had no incantations or dances in mind for Baloki, however; she suggested trying a bit of surgery instead.

"It hurts a little when I chase the bad *likundu* out of a woman's body with this iron rod," she said, indicating a short length of iron bar in her hand. "Sometimes the woman loses some blood, which is bad blood, since she bears the evil spirit within her. But afterwards she can have as many *bana* as she desires. Occasionally she can have two at the same time, for did not my last patient have twins?"

Molali thought over Mula's proposition very carefully. The price of the "operation" was not negligible, since it would cost the equivalent of two weeks' intake from the sale of beer. Fortunately, his overwhelming miserliness won over all other considerations and he decided against Mula's intervention.

When, heaving raspingly, the unmistakably disappointed Mula poured herself out through the narrow entrance, I also left. For although it was beginning to dusk, I meant to find Mokolo and give him a good dressing down.

He appeared to be waiting for me in front of his hut and bared all his teeth in a triumphant grin as I approached him.

"Everything is almost achieved, heh?" he said slyly, fueling my annoyance and indignation. As far as I was concerned, nothing had been accomplished. Little Mafuta still desired Baloki, but only for half the original dowry price now, and I wondered who had outwitted whom.

"Another rumor will circulate about Baloki tomorrow that her presence alone brings infecundity into any house," Mokolo hastened to reveal to me the rest of his scheme. "Did not her own mother have only two *bana*? Chief Mafuta will never want to risk his whole fortune on such a girl, even as desirable as Baloki. To tell the truth, nobody will want her, and the man who takes her for a wife shall get her for a very low price."

Mokolo had no need to name the man he had in mind. He reflected for a moment, shaking his head and chewing on his lower lip, a crafty expression on his flat face.

"Is Lisengo not the one who is so clever with iron?" he presently inquired.

"Why?" I asked cautiously.

"Does he not make beautiful two-pronged spears?" he went on knowingly. "Where is he?"

Lisengo had been hiding out in the bush ever since the attack on Mafuta. He and Baloki had met a few times after sundown on my back *baraza*. His eye was much improved, his wound had almost healed, but his left arm was still in bad shape and he could move it only with great difficulty. It was plain what Mokolo was insinuating. He remembered the skillfully made two-pronged spear that had been found near the entrance to the chief's hut, and from this he had drawn the incriminating conclusions involving Lisengo, Baloki, and Mafuta.

"I don't know what you mean," I said, "but if *moloki* has been whispering funny ideas in your big ears, do not forget that Lisengo is a special friend of mine."

Mokolo shook his head in agreement, but the expression of his foxy, shifty eyes belied the gesture.

An unpleasant surprise awaited me at my own house. Lisengo and Baloki were there, and Lisengo was bitterly reproaching Baloki for having concealed from him her infirmity, to which Baloki was replying only with a flood of tears.

"You're nothing but a great big wooden goat," I upbraided Lisengo, "if you don't understand that this rumor about Baloki is false. And if you should hear even worse things, remember that this is only to mislead Mafuta. After you've married Baloki you will have a dozen *bana*, which will prove to everyone that you are smarter than *Mokonji* Mafuta. But all of this will happen only if you stop acting like a goat. Otherwise you will have hairy children with little horns and tails."

They both understood the joke and laughed. However, when I told Lisengo about Mokolo's suspicions, Baloki started crying again, and the alarmed Lisengo decided to hide out for a while longer in the forest. I advised Baloki to try and get some sleep, for tomorrow promised to be a trying day for her. It was easy to foresee that she probably would have another argument with her father and that he undoubtedly would give her a "persuading" beating.

CHAPTER XVII

The following morning was definitely not the beginning of an ordinary day. Jafke, while personally serving me breakfast, brought me up on the latest village news.

Poor little Baloki could no longer show her face anywhere, for the villagers shunned her like the much-feared *moloki* himself. This I thought to myself, was unimportant, for it could serve only to disgust Mafuta forever. But at the second news item my previous night's qualms returned. Chief Mafuta accused Lisengo of an attempt on his life. The accusation had been based on the seriousness of Lisengo's mysterious wounds and his well-known ability to make two-pronged spears, one of which had been found near the scene of the crime. Mafuta did not ask for Lisengo's detention when the villagers found him with Baloki behind Molali's hut, however, and he did not intend to have Lisengo sent to the government prison, either.

It was Baloki who, a little later, filled me in on the chief's intentions. He offered Lisengo an opportunity to defend himself and prove his innocence.

"*Monganga* Mokolo will give Lisengo the test of *n'ka,* poison," she told me, and started to sob.

"They can't do that," I said, "it's against the law."

"But this *is* the law," said Baloki.

It was obvious we were speaking about two different laws, although no matter how backward and isolated the territory we lived in, it was absolutely out of the question that the local authorities would tolerate the ordeal by poison in any village. I wished I might talk to Michael about this, but he had left before sunup and would be back only late that afternoon, and things were happening fast at the *mboka.*

I left Baloki on my back *baraza* sinking her teeth into half a loaf of Jafke's freshly baked bread, and headed for the office. There I had to wait for a while, for the morning post routine that had started with the reveille at six followed by the roll call of prisoners had not yet been completed. The prisoners, shackled two-by-two as usual, stood in a semicircle, watching the daily lashings. They were at the mercy of the tall black sergeant who reported them to the administrator, pointing out those among them who in his opinion ought to be punished for having sat down to rest while at work, or answered rudely, broken a spade, or sometimes, as I learned later, for having refused him a petty bribe.

Monsieur Van Derveer was away on a short inspection trip, and the whipping with the *chicotte* was being carried out under the supervision of Monsieur Fallet who stood on the *baraza* of the office. Carlos was standing alongside him. Evidently they had reconciled since that last incident involving Carlos's little copal boy. It sickened me to have to witness this outrageous *chicotte* business, but Fallet's car, loaded as if for a trip, was waiting in front of the office, and I could not let him go without talking to him about the *n'ka* test Mokolo was planning for Lisengo at Mafuta's instigation.

As the *chicotte* lashed out at the first two prisoners they did not even flinch, as though they did not suffer any physical pain. However, when the third prisoner was stripped to expose his buttocks, the two Congolese soldiers who were holding him down by his head and feet appeared to be in need of all the strength they could muster, for the first whiplash drew blood, and the man started to howl. And when the sixth blow had been struck, cutting away a strip of the man's skin, he no longer was struggling, for he had fainted.

My mouth opened to tell Monsieur Fallet what he had already heard me say on so many other occasions—my opinion of the *chicotte* or any other kind of corporal punishment in general, and of the manner in which it was administered in Busu Melo in particular—when Carlos spoke.

"He's a softy," he remarked disdainfully, while the unconscious prisoner was being carried away.

"I don't know," said Fallet, "I think it takes quite a bit of stamina and guts not to scream under the *chicotte*."

"Did you see the other two? Both of them were smiling as they left," insisted Carlos.

I thought to myself that I knew what silenced their cries, for hatred poured from their eyes, despite their smiling mouths.

"I'll wager you you'd be unable to stand six blows without howling. And you're a tough customer, Carlos," Fallet said, grinning.

"What do you bet?" Carlos asked quickly.

But Fallet had already rushed past him, toward the sergeant in front of the office *baraza*. "Stop, you gang of monkeys! Stop! Since when do we give the *chicotte* to a woman!" I heard the administrator shouting.

"But this is not a woman; it is a man," the sergeant stammered. "He comes from the men's prison."

"And what are those?" raged Fallet, pointing an accusing finger to the full-blown breasts adorning the prisoner's chest.

"And this!" countered the sergeant, pointing to something that left Monsieur Fallet gaping.

Fallet surveyed the hermaphrodite, scratched his head

with an air of perplexity, and mumbled, "There should be a provision for cases like this!"

The hermaphrodite must have been occupying his thoughts even when he was listening to me a little while later, for he was annoyingly vague.

"I don't see how we can do anything before the *n'ka* test has actually been forced on a native, Madame," he finally told me.

"But it will be too late after the *nkasa* has been given," I insisted. "I know that the chief has ordered the test, and I also know that the witch doctor has some *nkasa* on hand."

"Every witch doctor has some," Fallet said, shrugging, "but they wouldn't dare use it. And if they did, we'd go after them. Just think, Madame, what Van Derveer would have done to me had I allowed that thing to get the *chicotte*. He would insist it was a woman!" he concluded our fruitless interview.

There was nothing more I could do for the time being.

While I was walking back home where Baloki was waiting for me, it dawned on me that the idea of Mokolo's deliberately killing Lisengo during the *n'ka* test didn't make any sense. It was logical that Chief Mafuta would want the test and its fatal outcome. It would eliminate his competition, the brave, handsome young man who had attacked him once and who might perhaps try it again. But Mokolo? He was on my side, working in Lisengo's behalf. What would Mokolo stand to gain if Lisengo were to die in this monstrous test by poison? The anger and displeasure of the *mwasi na monganga mokonji* who might send the villagers to another witch doctor? And who could bring about an investigation by the men of the white king? No, the test wasn't in Mokolo's interest, nor would he dare subject Lisengo to it. But, just in case, I sent Baloki back to the *mboka* with a stern message for Mokolo.

"Tell Mokolo that Administrator *Nkoi* knows all about

the *n'ka* test," I said in a voice charged with ominous overtones. "Should Lisengo die, Mokolo would hang for it."

Baloki left somewhat reassured, and accompanying her up to the road, I saw the hermaphrodite, now scot-free, heading in the direction of Busu Kwanga, swaying his heavy breasts as he walked, and tugging on his breechcloth to cover up what had left Fallet gaping at the office. A second later Fallet himself drove by in his car, honking repeatedly and grinning broadly. Evidently the crime the hermaphrodite had committed was not anywhere as serious as the responsibility for jailing him.

I kept thinking about Baloki while returning to the bungalow. Obviously, my optimistic conclusion that Lisengo would not get the *n'ka* test did not solve Baloki's immediate problem. There was only one way to settle the matter, and I alone could help my friends. I took the decision so abruptly that I halted in the middle of the garden, somewhat startled by it. I would have to break my word to Michael, for the first time in our life together, and outbid little Mafuta. Michael would understand, I tried to reassure myself. If I wanted to be absolutely honest with myself, this decision was perhaps not as sudden as all that. For time and again, hearing of Baloki's humiliation, and realizing my share of responsibility for it, I had considered this possibility, but had always instantly dismissed these thoughts while there was still hope to somehow arrange everything. When I had resumed my slow stroll toward the bungalow, I was already figuring out how to go about it. Should I simply give Lisengo some money? Or open an account for him at Manuel's store?

Waiting for me near the back *baraza* was a policeman from Busu Bulu who had come riding a rickety bicycle to deliver a present from Michael—a baby chimp. A hunter had killed its mother, a huge ape that weighed about one hundred fifty pounds, and the baby, which had clung to its mother, had survived the fall from the tree.

Paradoxically, Madame Van Derveer was perhaps indirectly responsible for this marvelous gift, for in the past few weeks she had been needling Michael at every opportunity about how silly one had to be to have chickens as pets in Africa.

The little female chimp's name, said the policeman, was "Lola," "Lobi," or "Loba." The first of these three possibilities was out of the question. Lola was the name of a beautiful girl, one of Michael's many conquests before our marriage—definitely not a name I would have wanted to become a household word. *Lobi,* according to the appropriate gesture accompanying it, means both yesterday and tomorrow in the Bangala dialect, and the baby chimp was very much a creature of here and now. *Loba,* on the other hand, means "to talk," and the lovable animal had not ceased her hoo-hoo'ing from the moment she was set down on the floor of the *baraza.* So I promptly decided on "Loba."

Loba instantly adopted me as her mother. A bottle of canned milk equipped with a nipple fashioned from a rubber-glove finger, snipped off a pair of Michael's surgical gloves, sealed a warm friendship that was to last until our departure from the territory, and an affection that is still alive in my heart today.

It did not take me long to realize that Loba would demote Desdemona and Othello to second-class "pethood." And Jafke must have read my mind, for he readily came up with a suggestion.

"Now that you have an ape to play with, how about having Desdemona (he pronounced it "Desdemwana") for dinner tonight? Is she not the fattest chicken in the whole territory?"

"Don't you ever dare!" I stormed. "Desdemona and Othello are as sacred as the cows of India—better remember that!"

Jafke, who had never seen a cow or heard about one, Hindu or otherwise, could not understand my remark, of course. But his disappointed expression reassured me that he got the message: the fattest chickens in the territory were not for eating.

In the early afternoon, while I was playing with Loba, Baloki, who must have been running all the way, returned with more news from the *mboka*.

At first the look on her face made me imagine that Mafuta had given up the idea of having the ordeal by poison carried out. But chattering wildly Baloki told me that, on the contrary, the *n'ka* test had already taken place and that Lisengo, although quite sick, for he had been vomiting a lot, was still alive. She was so happy that she almost forgot her own ordeal. Gradually, word by word, I got her to recount the whole story.

There had been no trial this time, for the case was too clear-cut. The people all agreed that it was an act of generosity on Chief Mafuta's part to offer Lisengo a chance after his guilt had been established. The test did not take place in the center of the square, as usual, but to one side, near an old tree trunk that had withstood hatchet and fire. That had been Mokolo's idea. He had pushed Lisengo toward it until Lisengo found himself nearly pinned to the dead trunk. Lisengo himself had appeared barely more alive than the tree. He was gray, stooped, and broken, Baloki told me tearfully. He had accepted the large cup-shaped gourd filled with the *nkasa* and had looked around him hesitantly. Then, raising the cup, he had drunk its contents in a single gulp and had thrown it into the crowd, which took this without moving. The tension that had seemed to mount with each passing second gripped the onlookers, who avidly bent forward. Lisengo's body had begun to sweat heavily and he had appeared to have suffered a spell of dizziness, for he staggered, Baloki said. He trembled from head to foot and all the muscles of his strong young body tautened. Instinctively he had seized the tree trunk with his sound arm. At that moment, Baloki said, she had been unable to bear any of it any longer, and shutting her eyes not to see Lisengo fall, had begun to keen, the way all their village women do when their men die.

Listening to Baloki's account I realized that I was absolutely right and that the witch doctor had no intention of killing Lisengo. Even without my warning he probably would not have risked a real *n'ka* test so openly. He must have fed Lisengo a weak solution of poison, or maybe no poison at all, imagination being sufficient to render anybody ill under such circumstances. If a man fell during a *n'ka* test, he was considered guilty even if he survived it, and the fact that Mokolo had led Lisengo toward that tree was, it seemed, proof that Mokolo was not taking any chances. The rest of Baloki's description bore out my speculations.

When she had reopened her eyes, Baloki went on, it was all over. Lisengo had let go of the dead tree, had stepped away from it and, at the moment when everyone had expected him to collapse, had straightened up and, unaided, had stood firmly. Then Lisengo did something that Baloki could not comprehend. First he took one uncertain step forward, and then had suddenly started to laugh, without anyone present joining in his strange mirth. Baloki said she had been badly frightened by this weird, solitary laughter. Then, still laughing, Lisengo had approached Mokolo and had deliberately spat in his face.

I thought I understood why Lisengo had laughed. All his life, with deep-rooted superstition, he had believed in the mysterious power of the witch doctors, in the fairness and justice of their secret rites, and their laws and rules. He had no way of knowing that what he had drunk had been only a diluted or harmless infusion. But he knew that he was guilty and that he ought to have died, but nevertheless there he stood full of life and recovering his strength by the second. He had laughed at all he had feared until then, at all he had respected and had unquestioningly believed in.

Baloki left in an uplifted frame of mind, but a little later Jafke got the very latest news from a villager who had brought a catfish to sell. Chief Mafuta still had his mind set on Baloki.

"Chief Mafuta is *elema* (crazy)," the man had told Jafke. "He intends to marry Baloki in spite of the bad *likundu*. Naturally, the purchase price will be only half of the half that had been offered before. But even so, is it not an extravagance in the case of an accursed girl?"

Of course, Mafuta would change his tune about his offers for Baloki's dowry as soon as his young competitor steps in and also starts bidding for her. Now that Lisengo had survived the *n'ka* test and with my help would have the means necessary to win Baloki, everything would work out fine. It would be up to my dear friends, as I had already told them before, to reestablish Baloki's reputation by having a beautiful baby after they are married. I couldn't help wondering if it would prove as easy to reestablish my own reputation in Michael's eyes for having gone back on my word to him. But this thought did not weaken my resolve.

I would have to go to the *mboka* early tomorrow, to talk to Lisengo about his dowry for Baloki.

CHAPTER XVIII

Old Molali stopped by at our bungalow next morning on his way to the Territorial Office to relate to me the beginning of the events at the *mboka* that were to change so many things. Molali was even more talkative than usual when he handed me half a dozen eggs, which were certain to be rotten.

"This is not for sale," he said, "it is a present."

"Hunh?" I uttered incredulously, knowing how miserly Molali was.

"Mmmm," he confirmed.

"Hunh?" I repeated automatically.

"I am a rich man now," Molali explained grandly, squaring his stooped shoulders. "My elder brother in Bopako died and left me all his possessions, including his slave." He pointed to the road where an old African stood waiting.

"There are no more slaves in the Congo," I said.

"Hunh?" It was his turn to be incredulous.

Molali actually had good reason for skepticism. Even in the administered villages, where law granted equality to all and slavery was neither sanctioned nor tolerated, there always were a few men who voluntarily stayed on with their masters, since they had no place to go. They were not prepared for life in towns; they could not go back to live in their own villages where nobody would know them after years of absence, and they would be rejected as inferiors and not accepted as members of the community by those who had always known them as slaves. So, it was far easier for them to go on living as bondmen without concern about food, a place to sleep, or even a purchase price for a wife, as this would be paid by a kindly master.

"I am going to the office now to see *Nkoi*," Molali said.

"*Nkoi* left yesterday, he is not in Busu Melo," I told him.

"Is he not back? Did he not only go to Busu Kwanga?" Molali replied, confirming the excellence of the tom-tom news service. "My brother's wife did not come with my slave," he continued. "I want to ask *Nkoi* to have a policeman bring her to me from Bopako. I cannot go for her myself, because of the fire that Lisengo has started. It is very valuable."

"What fire?"

"The fire that Lisengo has started and that burned my house," Molali said without the slightest trace of concern, before leaving.

My curiosity aroused, I nearly followed him to the office, but remembering that Albert had Loba's bath ready, I let Molali go.

I decided to catch up with him after Loba was clean. Soon she was clean not only on the outside, but also on the inside, for she had grabbed the cake of soap in her big mouth. It took Albert and me a good while to recover it, and only after she had swallowed quite a bit of the delicious foam. Molali was still on the office *baraza* when I came out, his hands raised skyward, protesting something to Fallet. I crossed over to the office to get an explanation of what Molali had told me about his house burning down and of his puzzlingly elated expression as he was telling me about it. However, Molali was looking anything but happy now.

"*Mondele Nkoi* told him to go," he whined.

"What are you talking about?" I asked. "Whom did he tell to go? And go where?"

"He told my *moumbu* (slave) that he was *nsomi* (free) now and that he could go anywhere he pleased. So he has left!"

"My guess is that the old boob will be working for Ngondo again before the week is out," Fallet remarked yawningly.

"Who's Ngondo?" I nearly asked, realizing just in time that this was the nickname by which Fallet knew Molali instead of by his real name. Practically none of the villagers ever revealed their true names in their dealings with whites, or with strangers. Even Michael and Jafke sometimes referred to my village friends by names entirely different from those by which I knew them.

"I sent word to your husband to come back earlier this afternoon," Fallet changed the subject, "and to pick up Leport on his way. I wonder after how many lashes Carlos will give up. Before six, I'm sure. I don't want anybody to miss it."

So they had made that idiotic wager after all. "What are the stakes?" I asked.

"A case of Johnnie Walker, if Carlos can take six lashes." Fallet licked his lips. He was already savoring the whiskey he would soon win.

"Carlos is a powerfully built fellow, you know, and he's been hardened by ten consecutive years in a region where most of us whites are supposed to be unable to live for longer than three years at a stretch," I remarked.

"*Chère* Madame, the native sergeant who will give Carlos the *chicotte* is a tough number himself, and he's not exactly a friend of Carlos's."

"Are ladies invited?" I asked, without having the slightest intention of watching this barbaric spectacle.

He hesitated briefly. "N-no," he said. "I realize that my little Paulette is exposed to quite a few naked behinds in this accursed paradise, but a European man's . . . that's different. I don't think your *monganga* would care for you to see Carlos's, either. But all you ladies will be invited to the party afterwards, to drink Carlos's whiskey."

Just then, noticing Van Derveer dragging himself from his house toward the office, looking every bit the *"Alembi te?,"* I hastily retreated, without going to the vegetable garden as I had intended, to avoid him and perhaps having to listen to his compulsive criticisms of Fallet. So he, too, was back, probably not to miss the big event starring Carlos.

Back home, Jafke brought me up on some of the latest developments. First, Loba was a no-good ape, a tricky little thief, who had already learned how to open the pantry cupboard and had stuffed herself with a whole loaf of fresh white bread that he, Jafke, had just baked.

"Look at her *libumu*," he said, pointing to Loba's belly.

But Loba looked quite innocent, whereas Jafke did not. Besides, it was Jafke's *libumu* that looked like an inflated balloon.

The second news item was the same I had heard at the office. There was quite a bit of betting on Carlos. Silva was offering good odds to all takers, four to three against Carlos lasting. Incidentally, Jafke remarked, Silva might find himself in trouble, for some villagers from Busu Kwanga, where Silva ran his general store, intended to lodge a complaint against him with *mondele* Van Derveer for molesting and debauching their small sons. But the news that interested me most concerned Lisengo's setting fire to Molali's hut. It was not an ordinary fire, but the fire of the sun that had descended while Lisengo was playing around with a lens from an old camera Almeida had traded him for six fishing spears. The people in the *mboka* said it was a lucky fire; whoever had some of it in their home could expect favorable happenings. But Molali would not allow anyone to get a single glowing charcoal, and Lisengo was there standing guard, armed with his two-pronged spear, over what remained of the fire. These *basenji* were my friends; perhaps I might get some smoldering coals for our own house, Jafke suggested, as I was starting out for the village to see for myself what all this was about.

At the site of what had been Molali's mud hut I came upon an amazing barter scene still in full swing.

"Just by standing near the fire my diarrhea had stopped," an elderly man told me jubilantly, and I thought I recognized in him Molali's "press agent" who had advertised Molali's beer at Ngele's trial.

One by one the villagers approached Molali and, pointing to the glowing coals, asked him something. I surmised that they wished to carry away some of the lovely fire, but their words were drowned out by the general din and I could only see Molali nod in agreement. Dozens of miscellaneous objects were brought to him in exchange for a few embers and burning twigs. For generations the witch doctors had taught the people that nothing could be obtained without some kind of payment, and that magic things were particularly expensive. Before long, a veritable mountain of useful and, in the eyes of the villagers, valuable objects had accumulated at Molali's feet, growing as rapidly as the coals were dwindling. Molali, who was a shrewd businessman, kept bringing fresh supplies of twigs and throwing them onto the dying coals to satisfy every last one of his eager customers. But eventually there was no more fire to sell. There remained only a few glowing coals that Molali desired to keep for his new mud hut whose construction was already under way. Only yesterday Molali was a poor man. But he had unexpectedly come into some inheritance from his well-to-do dead brother, and now he was rich, maybe even wealthier than Chief Mafuta himself.

Such an accumulation of objects in the hands of a member of the *mboka* was contrary to its communal way of life, and I wondered why the villagers let Molali get away with it. But of course the explanation was quite simple. If the villagers could not object to their little chief's openly breaking the communal law by accumulating his personal fortune, how could they possibly challenge the power of the sun?

Lisengo, who was standing by, rearranging the growing heap of riches, erased the blissful expression from Molali's face, by starting to divide the huge pile in two: a spear here, a spear there; a dozen iron rods here, a dozen there.

"What are you doing?" Molali shouted.

"Am I not taking the half that belongs to me?" said Lisengo.

"Belongs to you! Was it not my house that has burned down?" Molali had a coughing spell and nearly choked. He always coughed and cleared his throat as loudly and for as long as he was able to keep it up, and one suspected that this was his way of getting attention and sympathy.

"Mmmm. But was it not I that brought the sun fire on it?" argued Lisengo.

"*Kokolo, kokolo,*" soothed Molali Moke's grandfather who was warming his old bones at the fire.

A circle of curious villagers had formed to listen to the argument, and after briefly appraising the situation, Molali arrived at a quick decision.

"The fire from the sun can bring only good things. It should not cause discord," he proclaimed ceremoniously and loudly. "You shall get your share later, Lisengo."

It was highly doubtful that Molali actually meant what he said, and obviously Lisengo did not think so either as he stood between the two piles he had started to divide. A sudden idea popped into my head, and I wasted no time putting it to work.

"Why don't you give Lisengo the half that belongs to him now," I told Molali, "and why doesn't he give it right back to you as the price of Baloki's dowry? Thus you will keep all of it and Lisengo will marry the girl of his choice." I mentioned nothing about Baloki's own preference, since it would have served no useful purpose.

For the second time, in a day full of the unexpected and unpredictable, a miracle occurred. Molali agreed to my plan almost before I had finished speaking. Surprisingly, though, in spite of his miserliness, he did not want all this wealth. All he wanted was the original purchase price offered by Mafuta, plus a gourd or a small quantity of local tobacco, just a little something that would top Mafuta's bid. Lisengo could keep some of the riches. Was he not one of the family already, or virtually?

I felt myself blinking incredulously. Then, from Molali's rush of words interrupted by coughs, I finally understood the reason for his behaving so quite unlike his usual self. He relished the satisfaction of being in a position to refuse the chief because of an extra gourd. This would make it appear that Mafuta had lost because he could not bid any higher, as though he had reached the rock-bottom of his financial resources. The very idea made Molali guffaw with hellish delight. This show of generosity, this moment of recklessness that had won over his natural miserliness, was probably nothing but the proud blood of great chiefs, I thought. For Molali was a Lulango. When Molali's son was born, he named him Molali after his mother's village. Then the whole family adopted this name as their own, and the newborn boy became known as Molali Moke (Little Molali). Before coming to Busu Melo I had never heard of this practice. Molali Moke's grandfather had once told me that years ago all families were named in this manner. But that was long, long ago, before "father of" had been dropped from all names.

When I finally left Molali and his family, they were a happy group, and Baloki now openly clung to her *ndeko* (betrothed). And I felt very happy, too, not only for them, but also because now I wouldn't have to break my word to Michael.

"Could you not start another big sun fire tomorrow?" were the last words I overheard Molali saying to Lisengo, followed by Molali's pleased neighing at the unexpected return of his good fortune.

The *mboka* was uncommonly tranquil. It was like a small community on a religious holiday. For at this early time of the afternoon, instead of busying themselves at their regular chores, the families were gathered around their fires to eat and drink. But somehow I sensed that these fires held a special meaning for them. They were brighter and shone more than usual because they were born of the sun. An almost religious silence blanketed the serene village.

It was our own government post that looked and sounded like a jungle hamlet just before a *n'ka* test when I returned home. Half of the Busu Kwanga villagers had walked all the way to Busu Melo to see the *Mondele* Silva arrested and maybe put in chains like any other *mosenji* (peasant). Several irate fathers, leading their seduced sons, ranging in age from about eight to twelve, were at the office seeking justice, and clustered around the office were innumerable witnesses, members of their families or simply fellow villagers.

Leport, whom Michael had brought back in his car, and whom I suspected of waiting for me at our front *baraza* to be the first to tell me the news, was all worked up.

"I've known about it for quite a while," he said, "but of course, it was Silva's own affair."

"Where would Van Derveer put Silva should he arrest him?" I asked, thinking that in a place like Busu Melo, jailing a white man would pose a problem even greater than jailing a hermaphrodite who belonged in neither prison—male or female.

"There's nobody to jail, Madame," Leport whispered, leaning confidentially toward me and showing me his array of gold crowns in a close-up "Silva has skipped the territory. He'll make his way through the Giri to French Equatorial Africa and from there on to Portuguese Guinea. His fellow Portuguese will sell his property and belongings and forward the money to him later. Maybe."

One couldn't help feeling sorry for the shy, quiet man, who invariably lowered his dark eyes, framed by long, feminine lashes, whenever they met mine. So the villagers' accusations were not as unfounded as Almeida, Silva's friend, had been telling anyone who cared to listen, or Silva would not have fled, leaving behind all he owned, including his muffler-less auto (one of the few cars in the territory), the product of twenty-odd years of struggling without a day's vacation, in a territory that Leport had called "an accursed paradise." Silva had left behind even the bets he had collected against Carlos —bets that would have paid him off four to three. For that same evening, when the much-heralded stunt finally took place, Carlos gave up after the third *chicotte.*

CHAPTER XIX

I was growing accustomed to being left alone at the post. It was to be for a full week this time, with Michael and Monsieur Leport on a tour of duty at one end of the territory and both administrators with their wives at the other. Even Carlos, who was still nursing the welts on his buttocks, and his only other fellow Portuguese trader at Busu Melo, had left for Busu Kwanga to split between them the extra business windfall that would be coming their way courtesy of the fugitive Silva. Before leaving Busu Melo, Leport and Carlos had quite a fight. Michael told me that one evening, following some heavy tippling, the two men had decided to swap their *ménagères* for a day or two, and since their women had no objection, they had gone through with it. Only, when Leport woke up early the next morning, he recovered, along with his other senses, his alcohol-dulled jealousy, which was the butt of many local jokes. He had rushed to Carlos's house and, after he and Carlos had traded a few insults, had dragged out his generously upholstered Mariette.

Now the post was very quiet. I seized the opportunity of everybody's absence to practice my singing at home instead of on the jungle trail. One evening I became so involved on the natural stage of our front *baraza* that, oblivious of the mosquitoes, I kept on going way after sundown through most of my repertoire of arias, starting with "Caro Nome" from *Rigoletto* and ending with *Madame Butterfly*'s "Un Bel Dì." Only after I had finished and Jafke had brought out a lighted Coleman lamp, did I realize that I had an audience. My voice, unrestrained by fear of disturbing Madame Van Derveer, must have carried up to our roadside Busu Melo village, attracting quite a few of its residents. Squatting in front of the *baraza* steps in the garden, they sat silently through my strange concert, and were now leaving, commenting loudly and approvingly slapping their thighs with the cupped palms of their hands, producing a sound similar to loud applause. And this simple tribute made me feel as good as repeated curtain calls on any stage after a successful operatic performance.

And in the mornings I wandered about the post with little Loba trailing behind me, having fun picking what I wanted in the community vegetable garden without any interference from Madame Van Derveer.

I was spending more and more time with the lovable chimp, which demonstrated such an incredible degree of intelligence that one was inclined to treat her like a human being. There was only one thing the little ape seemed unable to learn —how not to steal. This presented something of a problem: for our bungalow had its windows and doors flung wide open all day long, and Loba was free to roam as she pleased all over the post. I rejected any and all accusations against Loba made not only by Jafke, whom I thought prejudiced, but those made by Albert as well, and, naturally, by Madame Van Derveer whenever she was at the post. As a rule, I believed Loba's denials when I occasionally demanded to know if she had taken the last piece of her favorite cake or other sweet from the dining room table. Her large, innocent eyes looking straight at me, she emitted plaintive little sounds that never failed to mollify me. Michael thought that Loba might every so often swipe something she couldn't resist, but he also said that she simply didn't understand that she was doing anything wrong.

One late afternoon, however, after Michael's return to Busu Melo for the night, while we were relaxing without talking in the morris chairs in our already darkening living room, we both saw hairy little long-fingered hands grabbing the sill of the still open window. Presently Loba jumped up onto the windowsill, then down into the room, and for a second or two sat quietly, her head turning alternately in the direction of the living room's three doors. Evidently without noticing us, she quickly ran toward the small ebony cabinet, and opened with difficulty its sticking doors. In another second she pulled out a bar of candy she had earlier watched me put there, and began peeling off the wrapper.

"Loba!" I cried.

The startled little chimp put the candy back in the cabinet, slammed its doors shut, then, crossing her arms over her chest, began whimpering like a frightened child. And when I came to pick her up, her liquid eyes were as innocent and as touching as ever.

I had attempted only once to take her along to the *mboka*. Maybe she had sensed some wild animals behind the dense vegetation screening the narrow trail, for at one moment she had pricked her ears and had cried in terror, leaping into my arms, wrapping hers around my neck as usual, and refusing to let go of me. Although I hadn't noticed anything out of the ordinary, her fear was so contagious that I ran all the way back home, realizing for the first time how heavy she had become on all that food she was being fed, all the bananas, mangoes, and papayas she was getting herself in our backyard, and all the sweets she had been filching.

So, when I grew tired of the deserted post and decided to call on my village friends, I left Loba behind, and, as always in the past, took the jungle path alone.

At "my" *mboka,* that shrewd financier Molali, who had

evidently not overestimated the commercial potential of the "sacred flame," was still doing flourishing business. When I stopped by his new hut later that day, several people were clustered around him. It appeared that one of them had accidentally thrown a stick of *mokonta* wood into the fire; he feared that its foul odor would offend the sacred flame and preferred to buy a fresh supply of coals from Molali to build a new fire. Another had dreamed that the sun had threatened him with his long fiery finger. Still another awoke that morning to find that his fire had gone out. Most of these people simply wanted to "keep up with the Joneses," as it were, for they imagined that their neighbors' fires were brighter than their own. They hoped, among other things, that their neighbors' respect would grow in proportion to the amount of charcoals acquired from Molali.

One man alone had not expressed any interest in taking home any of Molali's "sacred" flame. He was Chief Mafuta. Defiant, and resenting Lisengo's disconcerting triumph in the *n'ka* test, he had suddenly revolted against the influence of the chief witch doctor Djito and the wise elders. Some of his well-wishers had sent him burning twigs and coals from their own fires, but he had haughtily turned them down. Presently everyone believed that all kinds of calamities would befall the little chief, for he had offended Djakomba. I wondered, however, which of the two—Chief Mafuta, who had refused the fire, or Lisengo, who had started it—was the uneasier. Perhaps the chief, for he did nothing to contest Lisengo's claim to Baloki. Or maybe it was the opportunistic and realistic Molali, who always did his best to be on good terms with everyone, who was fretting most.

"*Mwasi na Monganga Mokonji,* do you think I should send the *Mokonji* Mafuta a few charcoals?" he asked my opinion and, without waiting for it, shouted, "Bopoto!"

Astoundingly, it was the man Molali had inherited, the aged bondman who had been set free by Fallet, who appeared from behind Molali's hut.

"He is back," Molali said, grinning triumphantly.

So Fallet's prediction had been right.

"*Mondele Nkoi* would not send his soldiers to bring my brother's wife I inherited after his death," Molali complained. "Someday I'll go to Bopako to fetch her myself. Or to get back the dowry my brother paid for her," he told me. "Bopoto," he called again to the old man who had once more disappeared behind the hut.

"What if *Mokonji* Mafuta turns down your fire as he did that of others?" I asked Molali, as he was dispatching Bopoto with a potful of glowing charcoals for the little chief.

"He will not," Molali assured me confidently.

It was conceivable that Molali had some undercover information about Chief Mafuta's hidden fears, or maybe his "press agent" had simply weakened the chief's resistance. Anyway, Bopoto trudged off, hugging the pot to his bare chest in spite of its searing heat. Since all news traveled with fantastic speed in this *mboka,* the fact that Molali had sent Mafuta some sacred coals was making the rounds even before Bopoto reached the chief's hut. It was then that through a strange coincidence events took an unexpected turn. Bopoto was progressing slowly toward the chief's house, followed by the villagers' curious eyes, when abruptly a tornado struck. A whirlpool of wind gathered dry leaves, dust, and sand, sweeping them furiously into the village path down which Bopoto was carrying his precious offering. While the old man, unable to move, was rubbing his blinded eyes, a cloudburst followed the gale. When, drenched and frightened, he finally arrived at Chief Mafuta's house the pot was filled with only a muddy paste in which floated a few now-spent coals. This was nobody's fault; it was clear that the sun-bred fire was denied Chief Mafuta; no one in the *mboka* doubted that this was an omen of worse things to come. The villagers waited a full day for something disastrous to happen to their chief. But nothing happened that day or the next. Then, when the bad omen was almost forgotten by the people and blotted out from their memories by their own daily troubles and joys, suddenly, in one single night, an elephant herd trampled all Mafuta's corn and sugarcane fields. Oddly enough, although the pachyderms had also ruined some of the sugarcane fields adjoining Mafuta's, the villagers did not associate the destruction of the other crops with the bad omen. They staunchly believed it to have been aimed at Mafuta alone. And the first villager whom I tried to convince that there could be no possible connection between the "sacred fire" affair and the destruction of the chief's fields only shook his head.

"*Mokonji* did wrong to offend Djakomba," he told me gravely.

Perhaps he enjoyed Chief Mafuta's predicament. He, like most of my village friends, resented Mafuta's exploiting the land as his personal possession, since all the *mboka* land was communal property. So now Mafuta would have to pay for his arrogance.

As on previous occasions, I tried to get a more definite picture of the idea the villagers had of God, but my new friends seemed rather confused on this subject. They had well-formed ideas about Ibanza and Nsungu, and they could also imagine *moloki,* the devil, but not Djakomba, who had no earthly aspect. True, he was a kindly divinity, they said, but they feared him, for the was too remote to know about human suffering.

It was different near large centers, or in the vicinity of Christian missions, where the influence of the missionaries, Protestant and Catholic alike, was quite strong. But even the handful of the baptized villagers in Busu Melo seemed completely mixed up and associated their new religion with the gods of their childhood.

"One thing is certain," Lisengo asserted, when I asked his opinion, "Mafuta has brought misfortune upon himself by turning away from the sun, and he is going to bring it upon others by cursing Djakomba."

Realizing that it would be impossible to break through

this wall of centuries-old superstition, I decided to wait for the outcome without any further interference. Besides, thinking of myself, as well as many of my acquaintances in various parts of the world who went out of their way to avoid a black cat, it seemed presumptuous to indulge in delusions of superiority to these people.

The elephants failed to return the following night, but came back the night after that. The villagers had no firearms. They had only spears, arrows, and knives, that of course proved ridiculously ineffective in combatting the elephants. Noise was another weapon.

One night, fast asleep after an energetic day of gardening, I was abruptly awakened by rumbling drums. Dozens of tom-toms filled the night with their voices. They were neither the large *mbonda* nor the smaller, also skin-covered, *maseke*, but the wooden *mokoto*. These tom-toms produced sonorous sounds resembling the tattoo of rhythmically falling drops of water. It sounded like an endlessly repeated alarm and was new to me. Pumping up the light of the gasoline pressure lamp on my bedside table, I carried it out onto the front *baraza* where the ever greedy mosquitoes instantly pounced upon me. Jafke and Albert stood outside on the front lawn, also listening to the disquieting noises. I did not recognize Albert at once, for instead of his usual starched white uniform he wore nothing but a loincloth. Farther away, on the road to the right of our bungalow, a few local villagers were agitatedly gesticulating and commenting on the noise.

"I have never seen wild elephants," Jafke said, "only plantation elephants in Binga."

"Neither have I," I confessed. So the tom-tom alert was due to the reappearance of the pachyderms.

There were hundreds of elephants in our territory. But as a rule one would come across only their fresh, still steaming dung, without seeing the animals themselves, just as one did not see the hundreds of antelopes, leopards, and other wildlife.

Perhaps tonight was my chance. Hastily getting into my habitual shirt, breeches, and boots, I left Jafke and Albert still standing on the lawn, and armed with a powerful flashlight rushed toward the *mboka*. Actually the flashlight proved unnecessary, because I joined a sizable group of Busu Melo villagers carrying torches who had halted to wait for me. All of us hurried, jostling each other on the trail, too narrow for more than one. At my right ran a young boy who obviously derived tremendous pleasure from the noise. He bared his teeth in a delighted grin and at intervals blew into an antelope horn that bellowed horribly. We had evidently run quite fast, for I had the impression that it had taken us little over an hour to reach the sugarcane fields of the old village. More tom-toms had joined their voices to the wooden alert of the many *mokoto*. Gradually my eyes grew accustomed to the darkness, and by the light of the torches I presently saw the pachyderms grazing placidly, like contented cows, and trampling all they did not eat. There were quite a lot of them and, although the noise was apparently making them nervous, for they pricked up their ears and stumbled into one another, they did not leave. Not until the men with their beating tom-toms and blazing torches began to advance in a tight semicircle toward the huge animals did the "enemy" go into a general retreat, crushing open a large gap in the flank of the thick forest.

It looked like a victory, but the very next night the elephants were back, and even without Molali Moke and Boboka, who came to my house to keep me abreast of all the details, I could tell by the din the villagers kept making that the war was still in progress. Perhaps had the administrators been around, the whole picture would have been considerably different, with a couple of elephants shot. But the sergeant, alone at the post and carrying out received orders, refused either to leave the post or to lend his rifle. And my own twelve-gauge gun was assuredly not nearly powerful enough to tackle an elephant. This struggle of sound against size continued for two more nights, for the pachyderms kept returning, and finally victory definitely leaned in the elephants' favor. Gradually they grew accustomed to the infernal racket and left more and more reluctantly. In the end they completely ignored the villagers even when the men came quite close to them. Then when recklessly pitched spears began to needle the animals they in turn sent their representative, a huge tusker, against the crowd. This scattered the men into a confused flight, all except one who remained flattened on the red soil, reduced to a bloody pulp by the angered elephant. And I learned that at dawn, when the herd had at last cleared the conquered ground and the frightened relatives of the trampled man were preparing to remove his body, the tremendous bull returned and finished crushing his victim to a mangled nothing. I had no idea elephants could be so vindictive. Belligerent, yes; especially after they became drunk eating fermented berries, but not vindictive.

Surely the villagers were going to do something about it. From reading and motion pictures I had learned that there were many different ways of killing elephants. But "my" *mboka* was a village of *basenji* (peasants) who were fishermen, part-time farmers, and small-game stalkers. Unlike the pygmies, they neither knew anything about bows and poisoned arrows, nor employed any of their miniature counterparts' tricky hunting methods. And since they were not equipped with firearms, prohibited them by law, they seemed to be completely helpless. So, from that night when one of their fellow villagers had been crushed to death by the tusker, the struggle ceased. Perhaps the men had given up more easily than they ordinarily might have, for the rumor about divine punishment was still being heard in the *mboka*. Whatever the reason, before the *mindele* (white men) with their modern firearms had returned to Busu Melo on Sunday morning, the struggle had apparently come to an end and the sugarcane fields had been abandoned to the elephants.

CHAPTER XX

Michael returned home earlier than I expected, bringing news of the government decision to move the administrators' head-quarters to Busu Djanoa, located more centrally. Van Derveer and Fallet were already having bricks manufactured for their future homes there. Michael worried that from now on I would be alone at the post more than ever before, although I never saw much of either Paulette Fallet or Madame Van Derveer even while they were in Busu Melo. Now all of them were away most of the time. The vegetable garden was sadly neglected since everybody had lost interest in it, including my-self, despite the fact that, for the time being, the doctor was to stay on in Busu Melo.

While Michael was home, we devised a new game with Loba. I could send her over to Michael's dispensary with a written message that she happily carried through our garden and across the road. All I had to do was hand her the mes-sage, mumble "*Uh*-huh," when she started stuffing it in her mouth, point her in the direction of the dispensary, and tell her, "Go, give this to Michael. Go, go!" Loba, who under-stood both French and Bangala, would immediately gallop away, and would soon return with a reply, a bit dirtied by the grass through which the chimp had dragged it. She would get a cookie, her reward, and would jump delightedly up and down on all fours, begging to play messenger again.

There was a slight drawback in this quick messenger service. Since Loba adored perfumed toilet soap, not only its scent, but its taste as well, one had to be careful not to use the soap just before writing the message, or the little chimp, evidently detecting the faint fragrance she liked, could not resist the temptation of eating the note on her way. She would come back after a while, sit in front of me, her arms crossed over her chest as usual when she was guilty of some mischief, and try to beg forgiveness with her irresistibly sad eyes and soft whimpering.

After Michael had left again, virtually all of my days were spent in "my" *mboka,* trying to learn and understand as much as possible about my African village friends.

I found that I had underestimated the villagers' resourcefulness in dealing with the elephants. For, following a general debate at the meetinghouse and considerable noise, one day the whole hamlet went to work and by nightfall two or three well-laid traps had been dug on the terrain of the probable retreat of the marauders. And in the middle of the night I was again awakened by a distant racket, and in the morning Jafke told me the news: two elephants had been trapped and slaughtered by the villagers.

An orgy of dark red *nyama,* which gave out an overpowering odor, followed for many days. It was in the soot-blackened pots suspended over the fires; slices of it were drying in the sun; they cured it with smoke; it was strewn on the ground and even the *basenji* dogs no longer would touch it; it was everywhere. But most of all it was in the expanded bellies of all these protein-starved people who lounged near their huts, radiating prosperity and contentment.

The *nyama* of two elephants proved a lot of meat even for the appetite of an entire village and the flock of vultures that kept hovering over the still partly full traps. At the end of the third day the evening breeze carried a waft of the nauseating smell of decay. From path to path, from hut to hut, first it filtered insidiously and then spread disastrously even up to the Busu Melo government post. At first none of the villagers gave any sign of minding this. Then, when the stench in the *mboka* grew so strong that no one could eat or sleep, it was too late to remedy the condition, for it was practically impossible to get within a few feet of the traps. Not that anybody had any real intention of doing anything about it anyway. The people forgot the pleasure and the taste of the delicious *nyama* that now stuck in their throats. They recalled what had brought on the elephants in the first place, and again they grumbled, "It is wrong to renounce the sun."

Nothing, however, not even the stench of death that was suffocating the village, could stop everyday life. Invariably the people gathered around their fires, told innumerable tales, quarreled, and drank. Although they did drink less than usual. Not that their thirst had in the least been affected by the events, but because the palm wine was only a small part of the brewing industry, and the sugarcane fields that supplied the ingredients for the manufacture of *masanga* had been largely destroyed by the elephants.

Oddly enough Molali's field had been spared, and he kept increasing his beer prices daily and neighing delightedly more and more frequently. When early one morning I followed him to his sugarcane field, I was surprised to discover that on a small mound of clay at the field's edge he had placed the primitive wooden statuette Molali Moke had carved in my likeness. This was most unusual in this village where I had never seen idols other than maybe a branch planted in a gourd or a rag tied to a stick or a feather stuck into a clay mound beneath a *monsese* (a thatched roof). This therefore struck me as a special tribute to me. But this illusion was short-lived.

"Why did you place my image here?" I asked Molali.

"To scare the elephants away if they should come," he replied with disarming candor.

Due to the shortage of *masanga*, Molali's customers sat for hours around his fire, waiting for him to finally declare the beer sufficiently fermented, eager to pay even his exorbitant prices. In all fairness to Molali, however, it must be said that despite his miserliness and his desire to sell as much beer as possible, he never watered his beer nor tried to sell it before it was ready. As a result of this beer famine, although Baloki's purchase price had been paid by Lisengo and all formalities attended to, she had not been given a celebration abounding in food and drink. This was a source of great unhappiness to her. There was no lack of food, but how could one honorably quench the thirst of friends and relatives at any important wedding feast with such a ludicrously small quantity of beer?

The problem was solved unexpectedly by Molali Moke and the other village children who offered Baloki the necessary *nsamba* (palm wine) and *masanga na nkoko* (sugarcane beer) to celebrate her marriage to Lisengo. Although *mboka moke* was really only a game, it nevertheless paid dividends, not only in the form of an occasional baby born to one of the older youngsters, but also in miniature fields of manioc, corn, and sugarcane. The combined alcoholic product of these midget fields, offered by the generous kids, would be enough for the feast. Molali, who went to look over this unsuspected wealth, stood gaping, and one could tell that he was mentally calculating how much profit he could make, were the crops his. Obviously I was not the only one who knew him well, for his daydreaming was abruptly shattered.

"None of all this is for sale," declared Ekomila. "This is our gift to Baloki for her wedding feast. If it were not for Baloki I would not give away my crop—that is, his crop," she corrected herself, indicating her rickety "husband."

"Nor me," he echoed.

"Nor us, either," chimed in the other children.

Molali hastily accepted. After all, this was for his daughter.

Furthermore, his triumph would not be complete if it were not the talk of the *mboka,* and he realized that they would never talk more than after their tongues had been loosened by plentiful *masanga.*

Though the wedding feast was a success and the people commented on Lisengo's winning Baloki in competition with Chief Mafuta because of only an empty gourd, a detail that made Molali neigh happily, still he was disappointed, since the people's derisive comments did not reach Mafuta's ears. The little chief had been in such a state of drunkenness for the last several days that the only thing he saw or heard were elephants in every corner of his hut—elephants that gracefully danced the *djibola,* that solo female dance he detested.

When Djito, white with *mpembe* paint, had performed the dance of *lela* to chase the bad spirits from Mafuta's hut and had finally drastically cut down the chief's palm wine and *masanga* rations, Mafuta plunged into a state of complete apathy. The villagers said that he lay flat on his back on his sleeping mat, with his short pudgy legs up in the air like a monstrous baby's, further stressing the resemblance by his persistence in sucking the key that hung from his neck. Molali had even considered sending Baloki to Mafuta's hut under some pretext, in a malicious attempt to rekindle the fat man's dying lust for the girl, but Lisengo would not have it. Since his marriage, which he liked so well, he never parted from his two-pronged spear. He worked hard every day on the building of a handsome new mud hut for Baloki, with the assistance of Bopoto, who put in unbelievably long hours, as though afraid that his privilege of being a slave might be taken away from him.

The children, who had been so good to Baloki and Lisengo, were equally generous with me. The council of *mboka moke,* in appreciation of my friendship, had set aside a hut in the little village, a sort of "guest room" for me to rest in on my visits. Shielded from the north wind by the adult *mboka* and the abandoned corn and sugarcane fields, the little village was not as exposed to the terrible stench of decay from the

elephant traps. Taking advantage of the children's standing
invitation, I attentively observed this junior beehive where the
differences between the little women, their *"mobali,"* and
their young neighbors were quickly settled by fisticuffs that
sometimes left a bleeding nose, or maybe a bruised eye, but
never a lasting grudge. I watched the tiny "housewives" preparing the rootstocks of manioc, bitter cassava. First they
allowed it to ferment for some days in the water of the surrounding swamps, then peeled off its black outer skin and removed its tough fibers. Finally they boiled it in a special clay
pot to make a thick, starchy paste they fashioned into long
rolls that, when tightly wrapped in the customary manioc
leaves, looked like sausages. The girls also cooked many other
dishes spiced with *pili-pili*, dishes of fish and, when available,
the highly prized *nyama*, which supplemented their daily diet
of the Congolese *mosenji's* staple food in this region, the cassava. The little girls' still somewhat clumsy hands, learning
skills to be used for the rest of their lives, made one realize
what infinite patience, physical stamina, and goodwill an un-
derprivileged African woman of the interior has to possess to
work, virtually around the clock, in the fields, attend to all her
domestic chores, and take care of her family and the forever
arriving new babies. Perhaps this explained why the women in
the *mboka* had no objection to polygamy and in many cases
encouraged their men to acquire additional wives and wel-
comed their rivals with open arms. The village custom allowed each wife a separate hut, so that there were as many
huts in a household as there were wives. The husbands fortunate enough to have more than one wife visited their wives'
huts on a sort of rotation basis, sometimes spending more
time with one than with the other or others. Since it was the
woman's duty to prepare all her *mobali's* meals, it gave the
other women of the man's household a chance for a much-
needed breather impossible for a single wife. Sex, although
totally uncomplicated, was paramount in the villagers' lives and

had a great deal to do with this custom. It originally grew out of the village women's refusal to have any sexual intercourse with their men during the whole period of pregnancy and lactation. This generally took a full twelve months, thus driving the men to have relations with other women. I was told that during the long equatorial nights local African men were addicted to nearly continuous coition, that eventually resulted in incomplete erections. Sometimes the prospective father appealed to the generosity of a friend, who loaned him his own wife for a night of love-making, or sought the paid services of a businessman like Mafuta, who would rent him one of his women. Therefore, if a man could afford a second dowry price, it was far simpler and more profitable for him to take another wife. But these adult considerations did not enter into the children's lives. The little girls were far more possessive than their mothers and did not tolerate competitors in their starkly realistic game of playing "house."

These little women spent hours gossiping about the happenings at the adult *mboka* as well as in their own dolls' houses. It seemed that the litigation between Motono and Siko, caused by Motono's chickens laying eggs in Siko's backyard, was going to be patched up "out of court." The girls giggled slyly in retelling the spicy bit about Muguntu's wife mixing the juice of *iika* (wild spinach) that was said to kill sexual desire, with her husband's meals. It was amusing to hear these little girls seriously discussing the importance of certain omens. I learned, for example, that one should not hesitate to conclude a business transaction on those days when small, playful fish come up to the surface of the stream, since this is definitely a favorable sign. Clearly, the best way to stand the unbearable pain caused by the blunt native chisel the village "dentist" used in shaping his patients' teeth into the highly fashionable triangles, was to concentrate on his navel. That set me to wondering if this simple method might not prove a good idea in our own dentists' chairs. I also heard that certain woods should never be used in building a fire. In an emergency, however, one could do almost anything, provided one did a *toto*. Doing a *toto* meant covering the left big toe with the right one. This, too, struck me as similar to our practice of crossing our fingers.

Instead of visiting the polluted adult village, I sat with the kids around their small fires and listened to their stories, which they told like their parents. The children themselves, probably also seeking to escape the stench of putrefaction, stayed away from their real homes now, and life at *mboka moke* began to resemble that of an ordinary village.

CHAPTER XXI

One early afternoon, while I was visiting *mboka moke,* excited shouting came echoing from the adult *mboka.* One of the kids, who had gone to investigate what was up, returned to tell us that it was in honor of a momentarily expected birth. But since it had failed to happen on schedule, the somewhat impatient friends and relations had begun drinking in the hope that this would speed up the appearance of the baby. My by now voracious interest in all regional customs made me decide to disregard the stench at the village and call on the prospective mother.

The celebration of the impending happy event had evidently begun well ahead of time, for most of the men around the fire appeared to have had more than their share of *masanga* and *nsamba.* These alcoholic beverages had been hoarded for days in advance for this special occasion and consequently were quite potent. Many of the inebriated guests, forgetting that the child had not yet been born, stubbornly demanded to see it. The baby, however, was slow in arriving.

In the stuffy little windowless hut, overheated by the

presence of many women, was the inevitable, gelatinous
Mula. The naked child mother to be was crouching in the
center of the hut, clutching her ankles with trembling hands in
a visibly desperate effort. She was whimpering plaintively, but
this was drowned out by the encouragements yelled by the
women around her. I had arrived at the crucial moment, for
only seconds later, when the suddenly compact circle of the
self-styled midwives had reopened, a tiny baby boy was lying
alongside his smiling young mother. Mula pulled on the navel
cord to form a small umbilical hernia—an embellishment she
was proud of, for it was her trademark, a lasting proof of her
part in the delivery. Then she severed the cord with a rusty
native blade, encasing the end of the cut cord in balls of soft
red clay.

Outside, the air by comparison with the suffocating hut
seemed delightfully pure. The news of the birth had made no
impression on the guests, since they had been celebrating this
event for hours. The intoxicated youthful father lifted his eyebrows in astonishment and hiccuped blissfully, "What, a second one?"

Before I left, the proud little mother came outside and
joined the others at the fire. She drank the palm wine toddy as
prescribed by custom, and her eyes did not budge from a certain spot in front of her new hut. It was here, at dawn, that
she probably intended to plant a banana sapling, symbol of a
happy birth.

The celebration should normally have also been at its
peak at *mboka moke,* when my two faithful lieutenants,
Molali Moke and Boboka, who had tracked behind me, had returned there with me from the adult village. But we were met
by an ominous silence instead. The children were all huddled
at one side of the tiny square, staring at something at their
feet. The "something" proved to be a little girl shaken by convulsions. She may have had an epileptic fit. However, she was
the third child stricken with a similar attack in the last two
days. I looked inquiringly at the children around me, and after

a moment's pause, one of the awed young voices whispered: "*Moloki* (the devil)!"

The villagers never brought convulsive children to the hospital. Not that they lacked confidence in the white *monganga*'s skill and free medicines. They came to him with wounds and snakebites; with yaws and malaria; they came with sleeping sickness and leprosy; they came with elephantiasis and all other kinds of ailments—but not with convulsions. This disorder, in their estimation, was something manifestly way over a white doctor's comprehension. Many theories were popular among the villagers to explain these fits. Two among these had been accepted by the serious and learned elders of the *mboka*, for they were not based on old wives' superstitious tales or pranksters' hoaxes, but on the experience of past generations and the knowledge of life's origin. One theory upheld the idea that this was a perfidious act of *moloki*, who attacked his natural enemies, the children. The second theory, favored by Molali Moke's grandfather, was founded upon an ancient belief that a dead person could leave behind an invisible but dangerous beast that would attack the living. Those in favor of the first theory shook their heads, pointing out that only children had convulsive attacks. But the old grandfather's faction derided this assertion for, they claimed, everyone knew that *moloki* carried his victims away with him and never left them on the spot where they had been felled by convulsions. Regardless of who was right and who was wrong, this was the beginning of a new period of prosperity for the witch doctors, for the people believed that they alone could help them.

Befeathered and strutting pompously, the witch doctors could be seen rushing from one hut to the next, to protect their owners from *moloki* or to kill the invisible "animal." Since the witch doctors invariably implied that someone among the villagers was responsible for the evil *likundu*, people were subjected to a new outbreak of tests. Fortunately for them the relative proximity of the government post made a vast difference in the witch doctors' choice of these tests. The practical medicine men did not resort to the gruesome ordeal by poison, for example, since after it cost them considerable time and effort it inevitably brought on a governmental crackdown.

If a child died in convulsions, the easiest and quickest test was that of the grave. The evil *likundu*-conjurer suspect was led before the child's grave and forced to proclaim loudly as he pounded his chest: "May I perish if I am guilty of the death of this *mwana*." The witnesses watched his face to assure themselves that he was not telling lies. Another seemingly harmless test was that of *libako*. As a rule this was used only in cases of theft, although occasionally it was also used in more complicated instances. This test consisted of placing a leaf inside a termite hill and calling the suspect's name. If following a two-day period the leaf was completely devoured, the accused was pronounced guilty as charged. Since the witch doctors supervising these tests obviously knew which leaf species would not be consumed by the termites, one could be exonerated by bribing them. This was another easy source of extra income for the *minganga*. Then, of course, there were those tests that could cause nothing less than permanent infirmity. They involved forcing splinters of wood and assorted juice extractions of poisonous plants underneath the victim's eyelids. But I had never seen these particular tests at "my" *mboka*, although from what the children said, these ordeals had apparently been occasionally practiced there.

"The baby born at the *mboka* this afternoon won't live very long," said Mosebe Moke.

"The newborn boy's mother has had one baby before, but Moeka conjured a bad *likundu* upon her and her *mwana* died," supplemented Bokumi.

"How did they know that it had been Moeka who had wished the bad luck upon her?" I asked.

"*Monganga* Djito and *Monganga* Mokolo poured some *mukungu* juice in his eyes. Everybody could see that he was the guilty one, because in a few days' time his eyes melted and ran out like bad water," Bokumi said.

"Did he confess then to conjuring the *likundu?*" I asked, shuddering.

"He was a very bad man," replied Bokumi. "He screamed that he was innocent and that the two *minganga* punished him because he refused to turn over to them the stone that gave off sparks when it was struck. That made the people very angry. He was so bad that everything he touched became bad and remained bad long after his death. Even Moeka's chickens were full of poison. The only ones who could eat them were the *minganga*. Others would have been poisoned."

"My father, who had been away hunting, did not know about all this, and he ate a chicken he had bought from Moeka's brother," said a boy named Mosebe Moke, "but he did not die from it."

"Mmmm, but he was very sick later," Bokumi reminded him. "His insides moved all the time but only blood came out."

"That was because of the *mobondo* that old Nsua conjured upon my father," Mosebe Moke retorted, heaving a sigh. "She also cast a bad spell upon my mother, who died later. And she would have cast it upon me, too, if I had not run away in time."

"She conjures the *mobondo* very often, old Nsua," Boboka said skeptically, "but very seldom does anyone die."

I thought I knew this Nsua, a poor old wretch who kept mumbling constantly under her breath and who brought to mind one of the witches in *Macbeth*. I happened to have seen her invoking the *mobondo* the day before. She stood beside a hut not far from Molali's house, and striking the ground with a stick called in a hoarse voice, "*Mobondo, mobondo.*" At the time I had imagined that she was calling some person instead of trying to curse one of her neighbors with fatal dysentery.

"He was a very bad man," Bokumi, whose thoughts were evidently still dwelling on luckless Moeka, repeated.

No one contested that, for the sap of the *mukungu* tree bark used in the test that had blinded the man had undeniably established his guilt in the eyes of his fellow villagers.

Three days later two more children had convulsions, and I dispatched a messenger on a bicycle to Michael, asking him to return sooner that week, in case these convulsions were some kind of an epidemic. But before Michael had a chance to come back, a sudden rumor swept the *mboka*. It was the old story—the story about the sun that, by punishing the whole village, revenged itself upon its chief. The people grumbled in open revolt. They had forgiven their chief the devastated fields; they had borne the polluted air that had ruined their pleasure of for once having an abundance of sweet *nyama*. This time, however, their daughters were getting sick and some even died, and this they would never forgive. Besides, their paternal love was intensified by the loss of the dowry that could have eventually been obtained from prospective husbands.

While I was taking cover under the low thatched roof of "my" tiny hut at the *mboka moke* from a fine drizzle that enveiled everything, Molali Moke crawled in to tell me that the enraged villagers were marching toward Mafuta's hut. Surmising that they were up to no good and realizing that there was no time to either summon the sergeant or run for my gun to help me in preventing bloodshed, I ran to join the crowd and found myself practically carried off by the human current, a silent and ominous throng that came to a halt in front of its chief's hut.

Djito stood outside the entrance, coolly surveying the menacing crowd. This time the witch doctor was not painted. He was anointed with oil, and rain tattooed his glistening skin with clinging beads. I was shivering with cold and apprehension. Djito glanced at me, and for a flitting moment a grin brightened his dour features. He and I, who had always distrusted each other, now found ourselves united in the same cause. For he, too, was evidently determined to protect Mafuta from the villagers' anger, although for an entirely different reason, I suspected. When the scattered oaths grew louder and then swelled into an almost unanimous roar, Djito, with an authoritative sign of his hand, quickly silenced the people. Then, without raising his voice, he said:

"Mokonji Mafuta has nothing to do with *moloki*'s crimes. He was wrong to turn away from the sun and he has been punished for this. Look—"

Djito raised the mat over the entranceway to Mafuta's hut and disappeared into it. Presently he came out, pushing the chief, obviously aroused from profound sleep, before him.

No one had seen Mafuta for the past few weeks. I had not been mistaken that day when I noticed the suspicious-looking spots on his back. Perhaps this was the normal evolution of his disease, or maybe it had been precipitated by heavy drinking that had lowered his physical resistance. His thickened ears, swollen nose, and deeply furrowed face left no doubt. Mafuta had been punished by the only malady the villagers truly dreaded—his body was ravaged by advanced leprosy.

The crowd dispersed shamefacedly, as if anxious to hide behind the steady curtain of rain, with me following in its wake, leaving before the hut only Djito and Mafuta. They both stood motionless and indifferent, like statues carved in ebony.

CHAPTER XXII

It was still raining the next day when, around noon, Leport appeared unexpectedly on his spluttering motorcycle. Michael's jalopy had broken down again somewhere along the road, Leport told me, and he was going to fetch Carlos. According to the local grapevine, Carlos, who had been away on business in the Nouvelle Anvers region, was back in our territory, having recrossed the Congo River a day or so before together with Almeida and Reverend Harrison, a young Protestant missionary from Bokula. All three were staying at the government stopover house about forty kilometers from Busu Melo.

"I'll bring Carlos to the *monganga*," Leport assured me confidently. "We may have to stop off at the Catholic mission to borrow a part for the doctor's *motuka*. I know what the trouble is this time—it's the cable for the choke."

"Oh, no, not again!" I exclaimed. "The Sisters have been hoping Carlos would repair their car."

"He will, he will," Leport said, "as soon as the new cable we'll order for them will arrive from Léo. The doctor has to bring the personnel back to Busu Melo this weekend, and the

Sisters never use their car anyway, even when it's running. Incidently, Madame," he changed the subject, "I think that Reverend Harrison will be coming this way, too."

"All right," I said, "bring him along. I'll have early dinner ready for all of you. I just got a large buffalo roast. And I'll bake my chocolate layer cake for the Reverend."

Leport was still laughing as he turned his motorcycle around in our driveway. My chocolate layer cake—really more a trifle than a cake—was a favorite of the Reverend Harrison's, and the Busu Melo Europeans could not make up their minds whether or not he was aware he was imbibing a little alcohol with every bite. The reverend, a small-town Englishman who lived in a region even more remote from any kind of European civilization than our own, without any roads except hairpin trails and narrow waterways and not a single trading post, was a modest man and a pious and self-sacrificing missionary. He had established his mission in the depths of the wilderness *because* of the challenge it offered. Occasionally, he crossed the Congo River to visit villages located quite a distance away from our Busu Melo road, where the influence of the Catholic mission was not as strongly felt as in most of the territory.

Jafke—who enjoyed receptions, not only because he was a big-city cook proud of his intricate dishes, but also because it provided him with a greater opportunity for robbing us blind in the pantry and invariably blaming it all on Loba—baked an exceptionally high cake. I did my best to saturate it with at least a pint of Michael's best whiskey. Perhaps the hours passed faster with all that work, or maybe the men were prompted by the prospect of a good home-cooked meal and my famous cake, but they made it in record time. I had barely finished changing into a fresh dress when Leport, Carlos, and Almeida arrived. They were all laughing and at first I imagined it had to do with the cake and Reverend Harrison, for his name was mentioned several times.

"The reverend will be here in about twenty minutes,"

said Leport, "he's changing at the stopover house. Carlos brought him on the back seat of his motorcycle, and you know what it's like on a rainy day like this."

I knew what it was like. All I had to do was look at the three of them. Soaking wet and splattered with the clay of the soft Busu Melo dirt road, they were leaving large puddles on the cement floor by the door of the front *baraza* that Loba was excitedly smearing into wider circles.

"Please don't tell the reverend about the whiskey in the cake," I asked them. "Let him enjoy it."

"He prefers milk, Madame, women's milk," said Leport, and broke into laughter.

"What are you talking about?" I said, but all three were laughing too hard to answer.

Finally they all settled down in the morris chairs arranged around the coffee table, and Albert got their undivided attention by setting a trayful of assorted bottles and glasses on it. Albert was wearing his houseboy's starched white uniform and cap for the occasion, but his poor training, which I had neglected in the past few weeks, was evident once again in his slight stoop and his unbuttoned trousers.

"The reverend was milking native women all last week," Leport presently explained to me.

He must have caught the reflection of shock and disbelief on my face, for he blushed and fidgeted uncomfortably.

"I swear it's true," he said. "Ask Carlos, Madame."

"It is true," Carlos said after draining his glass and refilling it at the table. "Almeida and I have just been to Reverend Harrison's village and we've heard the whole story from our *capita* there."

"Our clerk said that it all started when one of the village girls who had just had a baby ran off with her sweetheart, leaving her newborn at Harrison's dispensary. You know him, Madame; he's always playing the *monganga* in addition to his preaching," put in Leport.

"And naturally no woman in the region would breast-feed a child that is not her own, for fear of running dry, as is their belief," Carlos said.

"The girl who abandoned her baby boy in Reverend Harrison's lap, as it were, was his prize Sunday school pupil, too," Leport added gleefully.

"How do you know all those details?" I asked Leport. "You weren't there."

"We told him, Madame," said Almeida, "our *capita—*"

"Our *capita*'s wife, Nongu, was the first woman Reverend Harrison asked for milk," interrupted Carlos.

"Nongu has tremendous breasts," Leport explained appreciatively, "and she's just had a baby herself, maybe that's why."

All three laughed again, and I noticed that Leport had gold crowns not only on his front teeth, but all the way back on both sides of his mouth as well.

"If the reverend had only waited an hour or so until we had arrived he wouldn't have had to milk those women," said Almeida. "We had plenty of cans of condensed milk with us."

"Harrison had run out of canned milk, and the only milk-giving goat at the village had been carried away by a leopard. And the abandoned baby, after two days on some kind of a vagetable-and-flour concoction diet, was so weak it had even stopped crying," Carlos said.

"That's how the reverend came to milk Nongu," added Leport.

Once more the three men laughed, then all three, interrupting one another, reconstructed the incredible episode for me. And Leport, who had himself heard the story from Carlos and Almeida, who in turn had been told it by the husband of Nongu and other villagers, talked more than the two Portuguese traders, as if he had actually eyewitnessed the fantastic incident.

It happened at high noon on a very muggy, electricity-charged day. Reverend Harrison had approached Nongu at the mat-hung entranceway of her hut.

"Hmmm, hmmm, hmmm," he cleared his throat, and stammered, "Would you give me a little of your milk, Nongu?"

"It is not for that abandoned bastard?" she inquired suspiciously.

"No, no," the kindly reverend lied, "it's for me."

Nongu did not quite comprehend, but had looked down at her milk-glutted breasts, then at her equally milk-satiated and soundly sleeping baby straddling her right hip, and finally asked, "how do you want it, directly or in a gourd?"

"In a bottle that I've brought with me," the reverend told her. He was sweating profusely. But then, it was so hot and humid that day.

Nongu, who was supporting her baby astride her hip with one hand, made a conscientious effort to squeeze a little milk from her left breast into the small bottle that the Reverend had ready, but failed. "Try it with your hands," she suggested, "or drink it directly." According to her account, though, Reverend Harrison's hands were shaking so badly that when he tried he, too, failed.

It was then that Nongu's husband, who had undoubtedly been listening from inside the mud hut, came out. After asking the reverend whether he was not sick, for poor Reverend Harrison was ghostly pale, the man offered his advice.

"Try *her*," and he pointed to Lilenge, a neighbor, who was also nursing a baby.

By then, a small crowd had gathered around them, curiously watching the reverend milking Nongu. The prespiring reverend glanced at Lilenge who uttered an acquiescing "Mmmm," offering her breasts. He was visibly startled when a generous squirt came forth from her shriveled and pendulous breast. But she would not let the Reverend continue milking her very long. "I did not nurse my *mwana* yet," she explained. "But there are other women who have just had babies in the village."

Indeed there were others quite willing to participate in this odd pool. They would not move a finger to assist the reverend, but he was authorized to milk them each a little if he wished. They all smiled, and even pushed to get in line. His eyes downcast, as he went on trying one after another, he evidently developed a certain technique of his own. For when he unknowingly again tried Nongu, he obtained more than the few drops he had gotten the first time around. It was then only, when he had suddenly lifted his eyes, maybe to see what other woman, save Nongu, was the possessor of such large, heavy breasts that were so hard to milk, that he discovered they were Nongu's.

"Hmmm, hmmm," he stammered, "you've given your share already." By then his small bottle was full anyway.

"The other *basi* have also given twice," Nongu protested, indicating the other women.

Leport, Carlos, and Almeida started laughing again, and this time I joined in, in spite of myself. I could almost see the truly dedicated, modest, and so-easily-blushing Reverend Harrison on his errand of mercy, his curly blond hair drenched with the sweat of heat and embarrassment, milking with trembling hands all those willing women. . . .

Our laughter was so contagious that the reverend, who had walked in just then, started to smile himself.

"What's so funny?" he inquired after the usual amenities. "May I hear it?"

"Positively not," said Leport, "unless you have a little drink first."

"You know that I never touch the stuff," said Reverend Harrison.

However, after dinner, Leport changed his mind. "Now you may hear what we were laughing about before, Reverend Harrison. How about telling us a little more about your milking all those women?" he said, and started to guffaw again.

Apparently he was a bit high, as were the two Portuguese, for they had had a few drinks first, then red Burgundy with the roast, and finally my layer cake.

Unaccustomed to alcohol, Reverend Harrison was also slightly glassy-eyed, since he had been served the largest wedge of my whiskey-logged cake, but he remained serious.

"This is not a laughing matter," he said, almost sternly, and all three men abruptly stopped laughing. "The baby was dying of starvation and I was afraid to try any other food on him. On the morning that the baby was abandoned at my mission, my houseboy had thrown away what remained of my last tin of milk. It had turned a little sour, he said. I had preached to him and the others time and again not to waste any food while so many millions die of starvation around the world. . . That half tin of milk might have been life itself to the baby."

"But fortunately you found milk for him," I said. "You've saved the baby's life."

"Not exactly," said Reverend Harrison. "When I returned home, I found the baby's mother nursing it. Her conscience had made her come back to her child."

"So all that good milk you had collected from the women went to waste?" asked Carlos, his eyes twinkling. He was obviously on the verge of bursting into laughter.

"N-no," Reverend Harrison said, blushing violently. "You see, I'd always talked so much about the sin of wasting food, hmmm, hmmm, that I felt I shouldn't set such a bad example for my houseboy . . . hmmm, hmmm . . . I mean, I couldn't throw away a full bottle of milk, so I had it for lunch."

He remained serious while the other men laughed, but I could have sworn that in his eyes, too, there were mischievous sparks of amusement. Or maybe it was just that second generous helping of my cake.

And a little later, when we went out on the front *baraza* to see Leport and Carlos leave to put the part "borrowed" from the nuns on Michael's Chevy, and Leport's Mariette, who had been waiting for him near his motorcycle, noncha-

CHAPTER XXIII

The rainy season had come, and now it was pouring steadily. Michael had made me promise, before again starting out in his repaired car on his weekly tour early Monday morning, not to wade through the innumerable torrents that had only a short time before been hairpin bush trails leading from the main Busu Melo road to the old *mboka*.

How I wished I had a piano to be able to accompany myself, or still better, have Michael do it, when he was at the post. He was a true artist at the keyboard. I had even asked Carlos one day if it was possible to perhaps get a secondhand piano brought to Busu Melo. He reacted as if I had asked him to import the Eiffel Tower.

"No piano with all its woodworks would last even a month in this humidity," was his final verdict. "How about a guitar?"

So that was that, and all I could do was to keep on singing my solos to the accompaniment of the distant tom-toms.

One afternoon, nevertheless, Molali Moke and Boboka made me break my word to Michael by excitedly telling me that Molali had caught two magnificent wild ducks, and that everybody was preparing for a feast at Molali's house. Nobody had actually invited me, but it had abruptly stopped raining, and from past experience I knew that after the meal, when the men would light their pipes, one story would follow another, as usual, and that they wouldn't mind me at their smoky fire, since I was never a hungry guest.

When, somewhat winded—for the boys, hoping to get a bit of the forbidden-fruit *nyama*, had been rushing me all the way—we arrived at Molali's hut, everybody was about to "sit down" to dinner. There had been a brief delay, because of a preliminary discussion regarding these ducks. For a transparently obvious reason, self-styled ornithologist Molali had wanted to classify the birds with other domestic fowl that was forbidden to the women in the *mboka*. This stemmed from an ancient custom of Ngombe origin, accepted as spiritual law. In a moment of frankness, however, old Ngombe Bokoi had confessed to me that this law had originally been created for purely materialistic reasons. In the bygone days the Ngombe men returning from hunting and fishing in the jungle found that in their absence their gluttonous women invariably depleted the chicken coops. A strict law put an end to this scandalous practice, and all the chickens from that time on were for men alone.

Although Molali's attempt to triple his share of duck by officially disqualifying his wife and daughter had failed, he nonetheless still had a chance of winning his point, for no one had a mouth as large as his nor his boundless capacity for rapidly devouring huge mouthfuls of any food.

There were two guests at Molali's family fire: grandfather's blind friend Ndinga, and a neighbor. The latter was a strapping man equipped with uncommonly thick lips. He smacked them so loudly as he sucked the bones that it even slowed down the prodigious speed with which Molali ate. In fact, eating rapidly was a necessity for everyone. The only rule of etiquette abided by was that one should not snatch food from other people's mouths. But barring that single rule of courtesy, one could eat as much or for as long as there was anything left to eat. The faster one ate, the better one was served, even at this, an official dinner, at which important, notable friends were present. The neighbor had been invited to conclude a business transaction—the incorporation of two industries: palm wine and sugarcane beer production.

In a way these village gatherings seemed far pleasanter than most of the formal dinners of the European Congolese officialdom. For even though there the service and table manners were generally impeccable, the strict adherence to the seating protocol according to rank was not always easy to cope with, and often proved a downright nuisance, to say the least. Michael had once attended a dinner at which a high official had consistently refused course after course, only because he had felt slighted by the seating and serving arrangements.

While my mind had wandered off, my friends had finished the remaining food.

"Where is Ngombe Bokoi?" the grandfather inquired, evidently surprised by the unaccustomed absence of his closest friend.

"They have shaved his head," Boboka, who always knew everything, replied.

"Grandfather, Grandfather, tell us the story about the Ngombe," begged Molali Moke.

"No one cares to hear my stories." The oldster, who adored attention when he spoke, wanted to be coaxed, but didn't make them beg him too long this time. As soon as he began his story of the origin of the Ngombe, it became clear that I needn't have feared an ethnographic study.

"Years ago, when the big Congo River was so wide that no one dared to cross it, for it was necessary to paddle three days and three nights before coming within sight of the opposite shore, few people inhabited the earth. Instead of tribes ruled by great chiefs, there were only large families headed by the fathers. When these families went fishing, every member, including women and children, had to take part in the expedition, for the current in the river was mighty, the fish large and strong, and many hands were needed to hold onto the full nets. Often it was necessary to travel far upstream where the fish migrated each year before the big rainy season. Sometimes the families were absent for many weeks and returned with enormous hauls of fish.

"Then, it happened once that the fish, instead of swimming upstream as usual, did not move, and the families that had paddled a long way against the current had to come back home empty-handed. One family alone, the laziest in the village, that had straggled behind, had caught all the fish they had suddenly found within their arms' reach. When this family learned that all their neighbors had returned empty-handed, they feared they might be robbed of their easy catch, and they hid all their fish in deep pits they had dug behind their hut.

"After a while, when they had eaten all the fish they had kept in their house, they went to dig up their hidden supplies. But they could not find them, even though they dug and dug, anxiously rummaging in the earth. Where the earth had been stirred, plants sprouted and grew plentifully. This was how that family learned to cultivate the soil. They jealously guarded their secret, and while others starved to death around them, they grew fatter and fatter, feeding on the leaves and roots as nourishing as the fish from which they stemmed.

"Then, one day, their god Akongo decided to punish these selfish people. He made them crawl on all fours, hair grew on their bodies, and even their voices changed. They began howling in fear, for they had been turned into fat, wild dogs. Terrified, they fled into the thick forest where they went on digging the soil with their paws, just as all dogs do in our own time."

"But the Ngombe, the Ngombe, Grandfather," insisted Molali Moke.

"The Ngombe were none other than those wild dogs, *mwana*," the old man replied.

Evidently delighted with the exclamations of surprise

and approval all around him, he wet his deeply lined lips and went on, "As time passed, Akongo's wrath wore off and the Ngombe gradually lost the appearance of dogs and instead of hair, raffia grew around their loins." The grandfather reached out for a fresh *potongo,* took one puff, and concluded, "This is all. They had many children, these people of the woodlands, and the children of their children had many more. However, none had ever forgotten the place of their origin, neither the river, nor the taste of fish. That's why, one day, unable to bear the exile any longer, they returned to live as our neighbors."

"And nobody suspected that they had been dogs?" the blind Ndinga put in thoughtfully.

"Huh," scoffed Bokumi's father, a tall man who was as black as his son, who had just then approached the fire. "Have you ever listened to the Ngombe eating? They smack their lips and eat like hungry dogs."

"Is it not far better to smack one's lips like a dog than to cluck with one's tongue like a hen?" Ngombe Bokoi, who had also arrived unnoticed and had stood in the shadows, listening, rejoined.

I wondered how much he had heard of this fantastic legend about his people.

"*Losako,*" he greeted his old friend.

Grandfather nearly swallowed his pipe and could not reply in the customary manner, for he was choking and coughing with embarrassment. Ngombe Bokoi visibly enjoyed the situation, but he also seemed hurt, and apparently was determined not to allow the story to go unchallenged.

"And when these people of the woodlands, these Ngombe, these filthy dogs, had returned to the river, they taught their former neighbors a great many things," he said bitingly. "They taught them how to make fires and cook the fish which they had until then always eaten raw, and also how to make children, for the riverside people had remained as few in numbers as when the river was so very wide—"

He was unable to continue, for the laughter of the

assembled shook the whole neighborhood, attracting many others who came closer so as not to miss a good joke. And Ngombe Bokoi and the grandfather, who were inseparable friends, laughed louder than all the rest.

These banterings, although common between the Ngombe and the riverine men, never led to serious arguments, probably because these people, even though differing in their customs, nevertheless belonged to the same tribe. *Ngombe* means farmer, and the riverside people, the Bangala, are fishermen. It is the Ngombe, who live in the interior, who supply the riverside people with vegetables in exchange for fish. It was a different matter when a Bangala derided a Banza, a man of another tribe. A harmless joke, such as had tested Ngombe Bokoi's sense of humor just then, might easily have culminated in a poisoned arrow or a bloody skirmish.

Eventually, the conversation about the riverside people and the Ngombe turned to stories about dogs. Grandfather was fond of dogs, and so were many others, although in quite a different way—they liked them roasted. Grandfather did not own a dog now, for he was still loyal to the memory of his old *basenji* dog, which had given its life to save grandfather from a leopard. When one morning Molali had brought home a small *basenji* puppy, probably stolen, which he planned for his evening meal, grandfather had been so angered that, forgetting that his son was an adult and the father of a family, he had seized an iron rod that he kept in one corner and had tried to thrash Molali with it. Molali jumped from side to side like a little boy, trying to dodge his father's blows and begging his forgiveness, but his voice only guided the blind old man in the right direction. In fact, our shared love for animals made me overlook grandfather's leopard's tooth necklace. It was not surprising, therefore, to see his animation grow now, and hear him tell one dog story after another. The last legend of the evening was the most enjoyable.

"Dogs have not always belonged to men," grandfather,

who had become slightly hoarse, began his story. "Before belonging to anyone, the *mbwa* (dogs) were free and lived in the forest in long tunnels underneath the earth where no one could follow them. Only the males came up to catch fish that they brought back to the females and the puppies, for the females were forbidden to leave the tunnels. One day, however, a female, like so many other females everywhere, disobeyed the rule and was snatched by Assa, the Spirit of Wrath, whose tongue is as long and forked as that of a snake, and from which oozes a poisonous froth. He compelled her to lead him to the dogs' tunnels, where he viciously bit them all. Poisoned by the spirit of Assa, they fought among themselves and ended up by devouring one another. Alone the little bitch that had shown Assa the way was spared. In due time, she gave birth to a litter of puppies and from that time on dogs became the slaves of Assa. Assa mistreated the dogs; he starved and abused them and finally began eating them. All those dogs that had any strength left fled to villages, seeking protection from Assa, who now, having long since finished off his remaining dogs, tries to carry away our own. These days when a dog disappears from our *mboka* it is never certain whether it has been taken by a leopard or by Assa. Those who have followed their stolen dogs' bloody trails have often overheard their dying complaint and a wicked voice hissing, 'Assa, Assa!' Sometimes a dog manages to escape the venomous claws of the Spirit of Wrath. But the animal soon develops a forked tongue dripping with slaver, and attacks his master, for he is possessed by the angry spirit of Assa."

The grandfather sighed, and added astutely, probably for his son Molali's benefit, "And if the dogs should begin to fear that they might be eaten, they will return to Assa."

But Molali did not appear impressed.

"Did you not say, when you told us this story the last time, that dogs had first belonged to birds?" he remarked, and quickly retreated out of reach of his father's walking stick.

CHAPTER XXIV

Another attack of malaria, mild enough to permit me to keep on my feet but bad enough to make me feel miserable, forced me for the next few days to neglect my village friends. Besides, it was pouring again. And our bungalow, even without any windowpanes and with its cracked cement floor and the stubbornly growing termite mound in the middle of the living-room floor, (which Albert kept as stubbornly scraping off every morning) seemed nice and cozy by comparison with the dark, low, humid huts of the villagers.

It was Saturday afternoon. Resting on top of my bed, one of my hands hanging over its side, I was petting Loba. Reeking of wet wool, she was curled up on the bedside rug. Suddenly something or someone rapped on the closed shutters from the outside. Loba pricked up her ears, and I listened for a short while to make sure that it was not my own buzzing ears, but the rhythmical tapping had started once more. I took my hand away from Loba's head, and the chimp protested instantly by whining like a spoiled baby, and the noise stopped. Then it started again, and I put my hand on my gun lying beside me on the bed. I knew it was rather ridiculous, but I

could not help feeling insecure and afraid. And to Jafke's and
Albert's puzzlement, for the past three days I had not let the
gun out of my sight. It was lying alongside me even when I
slept, occupying, it seemed, the whole bed. It is incredible
how much space a gun can take up when you have to sleep
with it. In fact, I had felt so jittery the day before that I had
even considered accepting Madame Van Derveer's invitation
to stay at her house till Michael's return.

"We whites must stick together," she had told me, instantly making me change my mind about being her house-
guest.

Monsieur Van Derveer was again in Busu Djanoa, surveying the brick-making for their future home there. Maybe
Madame Van Derveer, too, felt lonely and scared in the quiet,
rain-flooded post. Or maybe she was really not as mean and
hard as we all thought.

The rapping sound resumed once again, and Loba began
to whimper. "Jafke!" I called. But nobody answered.

Since I am not particularly brave, perhaps it was nothing
but fear that, without any further nerve-racking delay, made
me face whatever was waiting for me under the window. My
gun pointing forward, I slowly opened the door. It was still
too early in the afternoon to be completely dark, but the leaden
clouds cast deep shadows beneath the thatched, sloping
overhang of the bungalow roof, and I did not immediately recognize the indistinct figure standing under it.

"It is I, Lisengo," said Lisengo's voice.

"Anything happen to Baloki?"

"Baloki?" he echoed, sounding baffled. "It was not Baloki; it was a *mwana moke* (a little child), a *mwana mwasi* (a
little girl)."

It was my turn to be mystified. "Come on in," I invited
him, "what are you talking about?"

Lisengo took his time explaining himself. Without parting from his spear, he accepted with dignity my invitation to

sit down and, stiffly erect, sat on the edge of the chair. And it struck me that sitting there all tense in front of each other, armed as we were, we must have made a funny picture. But even though Loba, who was smearing the wet prints of Lisengo's big, bare feet on the floor, was very amusing, Lisengo did not return my smile.

"Now, will you not tell me what's happened to the little girl? And who is this child?"

"I do not know who she was," he said. "She is too disfigured."

A new chill pierced my bones. "Won't you tell me everything?" I said.

"Chief Mafuta is a chief and yet not a chief," he began with a new riddle, but I thought I knew what he was trying to tell me.

The gravely ill little chief, who had sunk into a state of constant drunkenness, was once again a fat, placid man who snored, laughed, drank, and totally lacked any initiative. But that still did not explain what Lisengo had come to tell me.

"It is *Monganga* Djito who is the real chief now. Is it not he who brings the chief all that the chief can drink? Is it not he who gives the chief anything that the chief wants? But, except for *masanga*, Chief Mafuta wants only one thing . . ." I saw Lisengo's hand tighten around his spear, ". . . he still wants Baloki."

"Why did you come to tell it to me? And what has it got to do with the little *mwana* you mentioned before?"

He appeared not to have heard my last question. "The chief cannot have Baloki as long as I live. But *Monganga* Djito told him that I shall not live long," he said angrily.

"How do you know?"

"*Nayebi* (I know)." He remained sitting very quietly, then continued, "Your husband is a *monganga mokonji* of the white king. Tell him to tell *Mondele Nkoi* and *Mondele Alembi te*? to hang *Monganga* Djito."

"Why would they hang *Monganga* Djito? Because he's made some vague threats against you? You know the laws of the white king—"

"Because," he interrupted triumphantly, "today *Monganga* Djito killed a small girl, and he and *Monganga* Mokolo ate her!"

For a moment I hoped that he wasn't in earnest, but he was. "They wouldn't dare," I said without conviction. "They wouldn't dare. At Busu Melo, the headquarters of the men of the white king—"

"You know the island of *moloki?*" he again interrupted me.

"Mmmm," I nodded. It was the small island lying in the channel above the far end of the village, that looked menacing because of its thick vegetation hanging low over the shallow water. It had never occurred to me to explore it, for there were swarms of tsetse flies around it, and they frightened me more than leopards, snakes, or even mice. Although only one or two in a thousand among these flies were infected and could transmit the ghastly disease, there were a few advanced cases of sleeping sickness in the village, treated at the hospital, and it was probable that there were many other early cases that only repeated examinations could track down. Anxious not to be stung by those flies if it could be helped, I kept fanning myself with a large palm leaf every time there was a possibility they might be around. Michael, who had been to the mouth of the low Giri River near the Ubangi River before my arrival, had had previous experience with the tsetse flies. The tsetses were so numerous there, Michael said, that one was stung constantly, despite careful precautions. He considered himself lucky not to have caught the disease in a region where over ninety percent of its native population was said to be suffering from it.

According to the children, the real danger of the postage-stamp-sized island was far greater than the flies infected with the much dreaded *bokono na mpongi* (sleeping sickness).

"Who lives on the island?" I had once asked Boboka when, during one of our usual walks in the jungle, the boys had practically come to a standstill, quite obviously unwilling to go upstream.

Boboka's laconic reply had explained everything. "It is *moloki.*"

Despite Boboka's uncharacteristic reticence I managed to worm out of him all that he knew about the "Island of the devil." The devil who lived on it was, above all, the enemy of children. In the past he had snatched them from the *mboka*, and their cries had been heard on many moonless nights afterwards. The way to protect oneself from him was to wear a *sepo* (a bit of pierced wood on a string) that could be purchased from the witch doctors. Each of the children in the *mboka* wore such an amulet resembling an identification tag. Boboka wore two of these talismans on his leg that day, probably just in case. Quite unexpectedly, evidently thawed out somewhat, Boboka had become more communicative.

"The father of Bolompo did not want to buy a *sepo* for his son. He claimed that even those bought from Djito were worthless, and he made one for his son himself. But it proved that this *sepo* was powerless also, for one evening when Bolompo went to *mboka moke*, a huge *esulungutu* (owl) pounced upon him and carried him off. Old Nsua, you know, the one who conjures the *mobondo* all the time, saw the owl flying over the huts with Bolompo in its claws, and the father of Mosebe heard the *esulungutu* laugh like a man."

"The owl is a small bird. How could it possibly carry away a big boy like Bolompo?" I had chaffed Boboka.

"The *esulungutu* is really *moloki* who disguises himself as a bird," Boboka had explained patiently. "Everyone knows this."

"Did anyone ever go to the island to see just what's happening there?"

"No one dares to go near the house of the devil," Boboka had said emphatically. "Moeka, the bad man, wanted to go and find out what had happened, for he said that he saw a fire on the island, and since *moloki* dislikes both fire and water, it had to be a man. But he did not go, for no one would go with him, and Djito said that any man who went to the island would die before two moons were over. But Moeka died even though he had not gone to the island but had only thought of going."

"I have been to the island of *moloki*," Lisengo interrupted my thoughts as if reading them.

"You have?" I asked incredulously, to make him feel important.

"I saw *Monganga* Djito going there. If he can, so can I."

"Isn't he a *monganga?*" I teased him.

But although he looked scared he only shrugged his broad shoulders. Despite his shrug, meant to indicate that he no longer believed in the faith of his childhood, he was still as afraid of spirits as ever. He simply no longer associated them with witch doctors. He looked quite a few times over his shoulder while relating to me his adventures at *moloki*'s residence.

As he was slowly circling the island in a small dugout, he told me, he was amazed to find at the island's other tip an open hut, a roof of *monsese* on four poles, fenced in by a low *potopoto* wall. He had nearly left the island without looking inside the open hut, when his nose had suddenly smelled smoke. This could not be the devil's house, not the devil's who hates both fire and water, as everybody knows, and so he had finally furtively approached the hut and looked over the low wall inside it. The two *minganga*, Djito and Mokolo, were sleeping beside the spent fire. Whether the witch doctors were simply exhausted and fast asleep or drugged, Lisengo did not know, for both were very still. Near one of the walls was lying a child, a little girl, and she was dead. He could not recognize the child, for her face was horribly mutilated, and some other parts of her body were missing.

"If what you say is true," I said, shuddering, "both *minganga* will hang for it, all right."

"It is true," said Lisengo. "Tell your *monganga* when he comes home—he will be back soon."

"No, he won't," I said. "I'm expecting him only tomorrow morning."

"*Lobi na ntongo wapi* (tomorrow morning, nothing)!" he shrugged. "He will be back tonight. Did he not already leave Pimu?"

He didn't accompany the Bangala word "*lobi*" by pointing ahead to indicate that he meant tomorrow, although the same word "*lobi*" also means yesterday when one points over one's shoulder. Perhaps he was simply tired, or maybe he felt that gesticulating wasn't necessary when it was clear from what he said that *lobi* in this instance was tomorrow. However, I didn't dwell on this Bangala finesse, and didn't argue the matter of Michael's homecoming any further. The Africans had their own way of preceding the fastest travelers with the tom-toms.

After surprising me by refusing an apple, Lisengo left. Maybe he didn't know what it was, or maybe he was just too preoccupied.

Momentarily I remained standing at the open door, listening to the thousand voices of the stirring jungle, and the tom-toms that seemed to make part of it, thinking of how strange the beat of the African drum was to the uninitiated ear, especially at night. Sometimes it sounded so alien and disquieting, while at other times I thought I almost understood it. The way one almost understands a foreign tongue, when all at once, after living in a foreign land for a while, one day it suddenly becomes familiar and acquires meaning. It reminded me that I wanted to mention to Michael that in his abandoned study on the relation of the two sounds of the jungle drum to the dot and dash of the Morse code, he might have perhaps overlooked the rhythm; that the same combination of sounds drummed at different intervals could mean different words.

And I also thought of how much Lisengo had changed since his marriage to Baloki. Only a short time before, ignoring all elementary common sense, he had tried to kill his powerful rival. Now he came to ask for the protection of the white man's law. There was no question that he was doing the right thing and that I was being foolish. But still I couldn't help wondering if I did not prefer the old, less sensible, but bold and brave Lisengo.

CHAPTER XXV

As I might have known, Michael, who returned to Busu Melo that same evening just as Lisengo had predicted, did not believe Lisengo's story.

"If you weren't feverish, you would realize how preposterous Lisengo's story is," he told me.

It incensed me, for why would Lisengo go and invent it all? But with Michael home, the shadows chased away by gasoline lamps hissing gaily in all the rooms, and both Jafke and Albert miraculously reappearing and busying themselves around the dinner table, Lisengo's story did seem a shade less credible—quite incredible, in fact. My growing doubts about the truth of Lisengo's story were borne out a little later, when Michael, who had gone over to the hospital to run a malaria test from a few blood smears he had taken from my finger despite my loud objections, had returned home.

"You do have malaria, *mon bébé*," he said. "You'll have to get an intensive course of treatment."

"I don't feel sick, and my fever's down," I protested.

"Not quite. And Lisengo evidently had a bit of fever himself, for that matter. Those fantasies of his!"

"Maybe he did see that child," I said musingly. "Don't you believe Djito and Mokolo capable of killing a child?"

"From what you've told me about them, of course they're capable of it. They sound like a pair of blackguards. But they didn't."

"Because this's Busu Melo, the seat of the territorial government, hunh? I said sarcastically, using almost exactly the same words I had said in earnest to Lisengo earlier.

"Honestly," Michael said, "soon you'll talk like the villagers. 'Hunh? Mmmm,'" he mimicked me. "No, not because it's Busu Melo, but because no child has disappeared from the village."

"Hunh?"

"Mmmm," he teased me. "Your friend Lisengo, who has a long tongue, has made confidences to others, and you know how a rumor spreads around here. The villagers have made a quick inventory of their kids, and nobody's missing. My *infirmiers* had quite a laugh about it at the hospital. I think that your Lisengo will have the devil to pay to the witch doctors."

"Stop saying 'Your Lisengo,' will you?" I said. I was furious at that big bullock of Lisengo for making an ass out of me, and scaring me besides. But what an imagination!

"Unless—" Michael began.

"Dinner, is it not served?" announced Albert, trying his best to remember my lessons. He had on his starched white uniform, complete with cap and white gloves, in Michael's honor, and, miracle of miracles, he was all buttoned up.

With Albert hanging about, and Jafke coming and going, I did not ask Michael what he had meant, but as soon as we were alone on the *baraza,* sipping our demitasses, I went back to Lisengo's problem.

"What did you mean, 'Unless,' just then? Unless what?"

"Did I say that?"

I nearly "Mmmm'ed" but caught myself in time. "You probably wanted to say something about that allegedly killed little girl."

"Oh, that . . . I meant to say that perhaps the witch doctors had dug up a dead child's body."

maybe because I was worn out; or maybe it was the drug Michael had given me; or Michael's reassuring nearness; or simply that I did not take the gun to bed, but as soon as my head touched the pillow I fell asleep and slept deeply all night.

Piercing the still low, leaden clouds, the morning sunrays had found their way through the small cracks in the closed shutters and woke me.

Although my face looked a bit peaked it was amazing how well I felt. Not a trace of my previous evening's gloom remained and my interest in "my" villagers was an enthusiastic as ever.

Later that morning Baloki came to see me. Lisengo was in a jam again, this time because of his wagging tongue. The medicine men were infuriated against him, and prophesied that he would be carried off by a *nkoi*. But Baloki did not appear overly concerned. Perhaps this first sunny morning after days of uninterrupted downpour had made her, too, feel more confident. Moreover, was not her Lisengo a strong *mobali* who had the best spear in the *mboka*? And early that morning did she not see quantities of lively little fish in the creek, and was it not a good omen? And she remembered to make a *toto*, to insure its magic effect.

The following morning, however, despite reasonably good weather, Baloki felt quite differently. Lisengo had been attacked by a leopard the night before, just as she and her *mobali* were about to retire to their hut. It was only because Lisengo could see in the dark like a cat himself, and because he never parted from his spear, that he had been able to ward off the animal which had unexpectedly leaped into the air from the black darkness of the night. While Baloki hastily stirred the embers to rekindle the fire, the struggle between the two had continued. When the fire had finally blazed up, the growling *nkoi* was lying on its side, combing the air with its sharp-clawed paws, yet still trying to get nearer Lisengo who had pinned it down with his spear. Then, as Lisengo had pulled back his spear to deal the mortal blow, the leopard had suddenly sprung to its feet and had again leaped at Lisengo. The spear had struck the leopard in mid-air. The wooden shaft split and, although fatally wounded, with Lisengo's spearhead embedded in its spotted body, the animal had made one last powerful leap and had clutched the edge of the *monsese* roof of their hut with its claws. It had hung there suspended for a few seconds, then had finally dropped to the ground and had stirred no more.

Now, after telling of her harrowing experience, Baloki was crying. Ordinarily, a leopard is intimidated by human presence and flees back into the jungle. But this, she wailed, had not been an ordinary *nkoi*.

Baloki's fears made me also feel uneasy. Not because I shared her superstitions, but because I remembered what Michael had told me earlier that morning, before getting into his as usual top-heavy jalopy.

"Incidentally," he had said, just before kissing me good-bye, "maybe Lisengo wasn't lying about that hut on the island; maybe it was there, as he described it. I sent the sergeant and two soldiers to the 'Devil's Residence' to have a look, but all they found were ashes. Somebody had evidently just burned the hut down, for the ashes were still hot, the sergeant said." Michael had added something else, but it got drowned out by the roar of the motor. Perhaps it was a reminder to for God's sake stay away from the *mboka*.

Now it was days later, and it had been raining again for forty-eight hours. I had been giving a lot of thought to the burned-down hut on *moloki*'s island, and to Lisengo's story. If his story of the hut was true, then it was conceiveable that the rest was also not a lie. However, there was absolutely no way of proving it, so that was that. I still felt too dispirited to go to the village, and none of the villagers came to visit me. On the third day, the sun suddenly came out again. Maybe sheer boredom made me pull on my boots, from which Albert had to scrape a layer of green mold, and face the sticky, water-logged mud of the village trail.

There had been no thought of Lisengo's problem in my mind until I reached his hut. Surprisingly, not only Lisengo and Baloki, but their whole family, were sitting around the fire, brooding. That first leopard had not been a coincidence, Lisengo informed me. Silent shadows with greenish eyes prowled about his hut in the dark. At night he and Baloki heard clawing at the *eboli* (mats) that barricaded their hut entrance. On many other occasions, Lisengo had noticed spotted forms unexpectedly appearing against the background of the thick jungle, even in the daytime. Finally last night he had been attacked again right in his own hut. But the fact that he had killed this leopard, too, without getting a single scratch, did not seem to cheer him. He readily explained the situation. "It is the same *nkoi*. It possesses multiple lives," he said glumly. "It does not matter how many times I kill it."

Nothing one could say would reassure Lisengo. Without being conscious of it he again was at the mercy of the witch doctors. One had to admit, though, that there was something frightening in the way these cats kept singling him out. It was at the same time absurd and depressing. Plainly, Djito would not let this opportunity of enhancing his prestige slip through his clever fingers. And I was fully aware of the influence exercised by the witch doctors on their gullible people. Lisengo's predicament brought to mind an instance of witchcraft in the region of Budjala, where a man had been made to believe by a sorcerer that he had willed him to turn into an elephant. And the following day this man began to walk with a heavy gait reminiscent of an elephant's, munched leaves, and had finally disappeared into the forest, never to be seen again. Then there was the case of another man who, threatened with blindness by a witch doctor, found himself totally blind shortly thereafter, although his eyes and optic nerves were pronounced organically sound by the baffled physicians in Coquilhatville.

Unfortunately, there was nothing fanciful about the leopards. And the villagers' loudly voiced sympathy was not exactly comforting to the shaken Lisengo. Frankly, I was becoming more and more alarmed myself. The only one pleased by it all was Molali Moke's and Baloki's grandfather. He strutted about in a new *lukusu* and an over-the-shoulder sash that Baloki had made for him out of the first leopard skin. Both the *lukusu* and sash were emblems of importance.

A clue to the leopard mystery was perhaps supplied the grownups by the children. Boboka, who was dawdling on the threshold of Lisengo's hut, suddenly began inhaling vigorously, which after a little while became exasperating. Something was unmistakably bothering him for he wrinkled his nose and sniffed like a rabbit.

"What is it that stinks like this in the hut?" he finally asked nobody in particular.

Molali Moke got up from the ground and walked over to his friend. "It smells like the *mono Monganga* Djita was preparing a few days ago," he said. "The wind carried the odor to me as I was running by his hut."

"*Monganga* Djito knows how to lure a leopard into a trap without any bait," said Lisengo. All at once he no longer looked scared, joined the kids and also took a few whiffs, then entered the hut.

The odor floating in the air was reminiscent of something, and when I approached the threshold of Lisengo's hut and bent over it the smell grew so pronounced that I suddenly knew what it reminded me of. It was the odor of valerian, the drug a friend of mine in Brussels used to take to calm her girlish nerves. One day when the bottle fell accidentally, spilling the valerian all over, my friend's cat had greedily licked the drug off the floor. Could there be any connection whatsoever between the tastes of a domesticated cat and one of the jungle?

Lisengo reappeared, looking downright pleased. "Everything smells of the *mono* in there," he said, pointing to his hut. "Somebody has made bait out of me." He gave the impression of having completely recovered his normal faculties. "I will wash my house and everything in it," he added, his eyes widening with amazement at hearing himself say that.

"Maybe we could use your loincloth to bait the trap?" suggested the practical Molali.

Lisengo would not agree to this, but since it was probable that other leopards were prowling around, they decided to set a trap with real lure, a small sheep maybe. And after a while Lisengo generously let himself be talked into allowing the sheep to be rubbed with his belongings before he had washed them clean of Djito's devilish *mono*.

Perhaps the witch doctor's medicine had some kind of *likundu* (magic) powers in more ways than one, for the rubbing of the sheep with Lisengo's loincloth seemed to have brought new troubles. Anyway, the next morning the children came running to inform me that the trap had been sprung but that the sacrificed sheep had vanished. We all hurried to Lisengo's hut behind which the trap had been carefully set. It was a small, shacklike roofless cage of bamboo stems, equipped with a door designed to drop shut when the prey stepped on the wooden bottom. Nobody could explain how the sheep could have gotten out from inside the shut trap, since its walls were far too high even for a *nkoi* to leap over.

To begin with, Lisengo questioned his father-in-law, Molali, but Molali swore he knew nothing about this matter. Then Lisengo examined the embers of the fire for traces of the previous night's feast, the bushes for possible bones, and even his father-in-law's belly which bulged more than normally.

When we came back to the trap, Lisengo pointed to something he had noticed in the grass. At first I saw nothing, but as my eyes grew accustomed to the varied greens of the jungle, I detected a wide trail leading from the trap into the tangled underbrush—a series of lightly marked depressions in the grass, and broken branches. With Lisengo leading the way, we advanced stealthily, and had not far to go to find the aggressor—an enormous python, the largest I had ever seen. He was sleeping peacefully, digesting the small sheep that considerably rounded out its beautifully patterned, scaly body. The python slept so soundly that it was killed by Lisengo's hatchet before it even had a chance to fight for its life.

Molali, cleared of the suspicion of having consumed the sheep while everyone else slept, walked around with a long face, although his remarks made it plain that his unhappiness was not due to wounded dignity. "It would have been as well if I had the sheep in my belly, instead of its being in that of the accursed *nyoka*," he kept repeating, obviously unable to forgive himself for not having conceived the idea sooner.

His recriminations only brought him more trouble from where he least expected it. The morning was not far gone when a neighbor inquired if Nyoka had not stolen the sheep, and Molali had innocently replied that indeed it had. Then sometime later another neighbor came up and asked the same question, and Molali again nodded agreement.

"You should have seen its stomach. It was as round and tight as a drum!" he said.

The neighbor walked away muttering, "Who would have believed it—Nyoka, a thief!"

Clearly, it was some kind of misunderstanding, but unfortunately Molali's brain worked too slowly to grasp its implications. And, sure enough, presently Nyoka himself—who turned out to be none other than the young neighborhood witch doctor who had one day not so long ago administered Molali Moke the peppery enema—arrived to discuss the slander. Nyoka, judging by his appearance, must have prospered since his last visit to Molali's house when he had humbly blown into the large straw lodged in Molali Moke's posterior. Recent events had called for extensive spiritual treatments, offering lucrative opportunities to a budding witch doctor of Nyoka's talents. Garbed in a brand-new costume unmistakably copied from Djito, with his arms folded across his chest, Nyoka challenged Molali:

"Why do you go around telling our neighbors that I am a thief?"

Molali, choking with indignation over this second unde-served accusation in a single day, rejoined, "I have always thought it, but I have never said it to anyone!"

Nyoka, who received the insult without twitching a mus-cle, spoke without raising his voice. "When one man accuses another of theft and cannot prove it, he must pay for it."

"Pay" was a most loathsome word to Molali's ear. He lost all self-control and, grabbing the unfortunate Nyoka by his mixture of hair and feathers, pushed him aside, howling, "Pay? I shall pay you, snake, son of a snake! I shall pay you!"

Upon which Nyoka departed, but not before threatening dire vengenance.

The Molali family definitely did not have much luck with witch doctors. Nyoka's threat—even though it arrived in the form of a gift for Molali—materialized a little later. It was a young marabou, which was delivered by a helper of Nyoka's along with the witch doctor's warning.

"This bird is a lucky charm. The one who kills it will die during the same moon. The one who tethers it under the open sky or even under a *monsese* will become a slave himself. The one who allows it to get away, will lose all his riches. The marabou's name is Koku." And depositing Koku in Molali's hut, the messenger walked away.

It looked as though grandfather's dream about a mara-bou threatening Molali Moke was prophetic. Only it turned out to be the wrong Molali.

Molali's first impulse was to fasten the *eboli* over his hut's entrance to keep the bird from getting out, because its loss would bring his ruin. But, on the other hand, since keep-ing Koku confined under a roof equally jeopardized his wel-fare, Molali helplessly scratched his head, trying to figure this thing out.

Koku was not an enviable bedroom companion by any standard. Molali Moke told me the next morning that none of them had been able to sleep all that first night, and that his father had fretted till dawn, striving to work out some solution to his predicament. Then at sunup, evidently as a result of all that nocturnal pondering and muttering, Molali began putting up a fence around his hut and yard—the first of its kind in the village, where fencing in one's house or garden was regarded as unneighborly, if not downright unethical and unlawful.

In the next couple of days the situation appeared to be well in hand and, satisfied that he had outwitted Nyoka, Molali went about smirking to himself. The true extent of the young witch doctor's subtle vengeance, however, was to crystallize fully only in the days that followed.

CHAPTER XXVI

Michael did not return home on Saturday as we had agreed. Instead, a perspiring village policeman brought me a small crushed and dirtied piece of wrapping paper on which Michael had scribbled a few words, telegraphic style: "Have emergency, unable return this weekend. Send some sugar, flour and a . . ." The remainder of the note was illegible.

"What's happened?" I asked the policeman. "Where is *Monganga Mokonji*, and why did he not come back to Busu Melo himself?"

The policeman drew a deep breath before answering. After hours of riding his bicycle, his bare legs and even the pale blue shorts of his police uniform were all covered with mud.

"Did not a hippopotamus upset the dugout?" he finally said.

"*Monganga Mokonji*'s dugout?" I asked, feeling myself turning pale.

"*Te,* no, the *mosenji*'s whom *Monganga Mokonji* is now sewing up."

"Oh," I said, feeling the blood returning to my cheeks. "Mmmm," he nodded.

There was nothing unusual about a hippopotamus overturning a dugout. Sometimes they did it deliberately. I had heard about a hippo in the Giri River which the Africans from the Catholic mission had nicknamed "Albert." Provided no arms were aboard a dugout, one was certain to encounter this hippo on the two-kilometer stretch between the government post and the mission. Old Albert had good eyesight and a familiarity with firearms, gained through several bullets lost somewhere in his thick hide, and sound judgment in addition to his innate instinct. It was impossible to get close to him while carrying arms. And when wily hunters hid their guns on the bottoms of their pirogues, Albert seemed to sense it and swam at a distance, out of gun range, disappearing beneath the surface. The unarmed, however, were inevitably subjected to his pranks. Albert would upset the dugout and then calmly swim alongside his victims who were a long way from the shore, since there was no firm ground between the post and the mission during the high water season. Although Albert never harmed anyone, according to a missionary whose pirogue had been overturned many times, Albert appeared to mock those he frightened, snorting and blowing large bubbles through his partly submerged snout as he swam and dived all around them.

"Did the *ngubu* hurt the man very badly?" I asked the policeman, since not all hippos are blessed with Albert's sunny disposition. I had seen a man whose leg had been crushed at the thigh by an angered hippo. I had also been shown a small whaleboat in whose metal bottom was embedded a broken tusk, suggesting that the blow had not been a playful one.

Jafke, who had evidently interviewed the messenger before calling me outside, answered. "Was it not a crocodile that bit the *motu?*"

"The policeman said the man had been bitten by a *ngubu,*" I corrected Jafke.

"*Te,* no," said Jafke. "*Ngubu wapi* (a hippo, nothing)!"

"Mmmm," mumbled the policeman.

"Then it was a hippopotamus?"

"*Te,* it was a crocodile," he replied.

"But didn't you just say 'Mmmm,' that it was a hippo?" I insisted.

"I said, 'Mmmm,' yes it was not a hippo," he said patiently.

"The hippo turned over the dugout, but it was the crocodile that bit the *motu,*" clarified Jafke. "The two *nyama* are good friends."

This was reminiscent of the story about a hippo's and a crocodile's "gentleman's agreement." The hippopotamus was invited to feast on the plantlife in the crocodile's domain, and in return he was to capsize all the dugouts to provide the crocodile with regular meals. There were hundreds of crocodiles, lazily stretched on the sandy shores of the Ubangi River, which at the approach of any craft awoke and unhurriedly slid into the water. It was a common sight to find flocks of small white crocodile birds calmly picking the crocodiles' well-armed jaws without ever being devoured. Naturally, it would have been difficult to grow fond of the ugly *nkoli,* but in the deceptive security of a large dugout one did not experience fear. The Africans went swimming and bathing in both the large and small rivers of the Congo. They splashed and laughed and made a lot of noise to scare away the crocodiles. One of the old Congo hands told the story of one reptile, nicknamed Joseph, supposedly the pet of a witch doctor from Nouvelle Anvers, one of the oldest outposts on the right bank of the Congo River. Every day before sundown the witch doctor paddled out into the middle of the river and fed Joseph fish, in return for which Joseph ate all his enemies. The Africans did not challenge this fantastic story, and whenever somebody fell victim to a crocodile they attributed it to Joseph and the witch doctor.

There were other stories about men taken by crocodiles.

Scarcely a riverside village had been spared. Most likely many of these accounts had been somewhat exaggerated, but there existed recorded instances of such repeated accidents in Bukama during the construction of the railroad bridge there. Michael had told me of a ghastly incident he had witnessed himself.

It happened one day on a high bank of the Giri at the point where it empties its murky waters into the Ubangi, while Michael was considering buying a rifle from a professional buffalo hunter. The man claimed that the powerful weapon had almost no kick, and wanted to demonstrate it by firing a couple of shots. While he was pointing the gun toward the river, a small, low dugout was heading downstream quite close to where he and Michael were standing. An aged Congolese woman was seated on the stern of the dugout, slowly propelling it with the usual single paddle held with both hands. Her weight submerged the small craft so much that she appeared to be sitting on the water itself. Abruptly, a crocodile came to the surface and, with a mighty swish of its tail, swept the old woman from the dugout. While she shrieked and struggled, the reptile seized her and submerged in a whirlpool of bubbles and foam.

"Why didn't you fire!" Michael shouted, since the hunter, a reputed crack shot, had already been aiming at the crocodile.

"If I had fired without taking careful aim, I might have injured the woman," he calmly explained, ignoring Michael's indignation. "Why should I risk having problems with the authorities? I have plenty of troubles as it is."

The life of an old African woman carried off by a crocodile on the Giri River meant little to this callous white hireling, who probably would never again recall her agonized cries.

Now it looked as though we had an authenticated crocodile case right in our own backyard. "How badly is the *motu* hurt?" I asked the policeman.

It was Jafke once again who went into a detailed description of the man's wounds. "It will take your *monganga* many hours to repair this *motu*," he concluded. "And your *monganga* does not even have his big book which tells him how to do it."

I cast him a covert glance to see if he was being sarcastic, but he evidently wasn't. Jafke had great respect for books. That is, the only two kinds of books he knew probably: prayer books that helped save souls, and Michael's medical books that helped to repair human bodies. Maybe it was a book, that third illegible item in Michael's note, for which he was asking? Since there was no way of being certain, however, the policeman left loaded down with two dozen items, any one of which might have been Michael's mysterious request.

That Saturday dragged on even more slowly than a weekday. Its monotony was interrupted only by a short visit from Leport, who had come to get some small change for his bearers at the Busu Melo government office. One could tell that Leport was at the stopover house, which he occupied while at the post, by the sound of his portable phonograph blaring unmercifully on the stopover house's *baraza*.

"It's getting harder and harder finding eggs in this damned hole," Leport complained to me after we had exchanged other news in front of his temporary home. "I sent a boy to the village over an hour ago."

It wasn't hard to get eggs, even fresh ones, in Busu Melo, as I had learned by that time, if one was willing to pay a decent price for them. Leport stuck to the regulation price, however, which was considerably lower than the one paid by the Portuguese traders. It was the duty of the government-appointed village chief to supply the local European personnel with enough chickens and eggs for their daily needs, and the villagers complied grudgingly, but not before deciding on a certain quota among themselves.

To my surprise, it was a very stooped Molali who glumly shuffled up to the stopover house, carrying a dozen eggs in a bit of old fish net.

"Listen to this," said Leport, brightening things up with

his golden smile. He changed the record on his phonograph and cranked it up a little. It was one of those early-morning-on-the-farm recordings, with roosters crowing, turkeys gobbling, and cows mooing. Perhaps Molali did not understand most of the unfamiliar noises, but he was obviously impressed with the strange box from whose insides these extraordinary effects originated, for he kept gaping and emitting incredulous sounds. The recording was climaxed by a mounting crescendo of a hen's cackling, and when it was over Leport reached into the large old-fashioned loudspeaker and produced an egg, which he had evidently put there while changing the record. Molali's eyes nearly popped out, and he started making noises as if he were about to lay an egg himself.

"I do it all the time," Leport explained to me, visibly quite pleased with his innocent little joke. "You should have seen the natives in Munkongo . . . Hey you!" he turned to Molali, who had apparently recovered from his surprise and was slowly backing away. "The eggs, take them over to my cook."

"You do not need the *make*," said Molali. "You have a *likundu* box that lays them." And turning around he left briskly, without paying attention to Leport's loud protests.

Laughing, I followed Molali to allow Leport to swear his fill at ease, and overtook my village friend halfway to the *mboka*. The eggs, which he was taking back home and that he would sell me or Carlos for twice the price Leport would have paid him, gave him no pleasure. He had troubles, bad troubles, at home; Nyoka's curse was working, he dolefully informed me.

The marabou was a huge bird, and since it did not eat bananas or manioc and was forever hungry, persistently demanding meat and fish, the question of feeding this insatiable creature had become Molali's constant nightmare. Koku had rapidly grown accustomed to his new surroundings and showed signs of satisfaction with them. He stuck his long nose wherever traces of food could be found, and cunningly filched all that was unwatched for even a minute. On two different occasions Koku had devoured the whole family's evening meal. One morning, when he had been chased away from the fire, he went quietly into the backyard where soon the hens started cackling hysterically. When Molali, led by a hunch, followed the marabou he saw something that set him to yelling as if he were getting the *chicotte*. They all scurried to his rescue, only to find Koku tossing into the air the last of the baby chicks that he then quickly gulped down, following the meal with gurgling and cooing, probably to express his satisfaction. From then on Molali did not know a moment's peace. From early morning when the chickens were let out of their coop to nibble on whatever they could find in the yard, Koku followed them. Heartbroken, Molali had to trade salable *masanga* for fish that regardless of their size Koku gulped down like tiny pills. The whole *mboka* took turns watching Molali's plight, and Nyoka himself came by at least twice daily to gloat over his victory. Molali was losing more and more sleep trying to think of a way out of all this. But, since he dared not take the simplest way out—get rid of Koku—he was losing not only sleep but lots of weight as well, while Koku was growing lazier and fatter. It looked as though poor Molali would worry himself sick.

Anyone who has ever tried to raise a marabou has had somewhat similar problems. I thought of how the arrogant stealing of these birds differed from my Loba's subtle ways of raiding our table. I could easily imagine that the still very young Koku would be even harder to control when he grew bigger and stronger.

Koku had sensed my fear of him from the first and when the impertinent bird saw me coming he spread his wings and ran at me hissing in a most disconcerting manner. Molali Moke, on the contrary, was not afraid of the marabou and they had frequent wrestling matches. These were not always to Molali Moke's advantage, since Koku put all his heart into the combats with the little boy who so often fed him fish stuffed with the fiery *pili-pili*.

CHAPTER XXVII

When Molali and I arrived at the *mboka* we found Molali
Moke busily carving a small new ebony figure, with his best
friend Boboka assisting him by sticking out his tongue and
moving it rhythmically with each new whittling. Boboka, who
was having problems of his own, looked drawn and puffy-
eyed. He had recently lost a second front tooth and now had a
symmetrical hole in his upper front teeth, that for some reason gave him a rodent-like expression. He had difficulty in
keeping his tongue in his mouth and, even unintentionally, it
kept sticking out like that of a Pekingese.

"What's wrong?" I inquired.

"Nothing," he said, just as his mother came to fetch him
home.

"Who does he think he is, this pretentious little rascal, to
cover up his bottom at his age?" the chagrined Eluo yelled.

Boboka turned away, scowling like an old man. He was
in a bad mood. He had received a good spanking from his
mother earlier that morning for having tried to put on his
father's breechcloth, Molali Moke told me when Boboka and
his mother had left. And judging by the way everyone exam-

ined Boboka's swollen buttocks as he followed his mother, this news of his vanity must already have spread around. The real reason for Boboka's attempt to don his father's loincloth, Molali Moke told me, was that for the first time in his life Boboka was truly interested in a girl, and it was she he had wanted to impress by wearing a grownup's breechcloth.

"Above all, say nothing about this to anyone," Molali Moke cautioned me. "Not to a female, in any event. Females have long tongues—" He tactfully caught himself.

"You'd better go to the stream and wash. You look like a dirty little pig," I countered, smiling.

"Baloki made me wash three days ago," he protested indignantly.

That same afternoon, at a meeting of the "Secret Society" the childlren had invited me to attend, I had an opportunity to meet Boboka's girl friend.

"Who is the president, you or Boboka?" I could not help teasing Molali Moke on our way to the *mboka moke* (the children's village).

"Boboka is," he said indifferently. "I am his assistant."

The purpose of the society was to keep informed about all that happened in the Busu Melo region, and members were under oath to keep all information confidential. Both the president and vice-president of this society decided that they had told me so much about it that it was high time to make me a member in good standing. The name of their society was *"Mompepe"* (wind), and I chuckled to myself at the thought of important secrets confided to the wind.

Molali Moke and I were surrounded by many old acquaintances when we reached the *Mompepe* meeting place. Bokumi, who seemed blacker than usual, Mosebe, Bokula and his sister, Ekomila, both lighter than the others, and other children I knew, were there. There were ten of them in all, in addition to their president, Boboka, and his second-in-command, Molali Moke. They were all so busy greeting me that none paid any attention to the undignified behavior of their president. Leaning his body against a tree, he stood on his head. Even had I not known of his being in love, that had already cost him a spanking, I could easily have guessed everything after one look at a little girl standing alongside the tree, in whose honor he was obviously grandstanding. Like Boboka, the girl was missing some front teeth, and stood gaping at him delightedly. She was somewhat taller than Boboka and had already begun to mature. Despite her nakedness, a plain hairdo suggestive of pigtails made her resemble any little girl anywhere in the world. Boboka nearly lost his balance in the process of resuming a normal position. And I knew that Boboka's affection was requited when the little girl cried out, pressing her hand against her budding breasts.

After the *Mompepe* president was finally back on his feet, the meeting was called to order. A few initiation tests had to be given me. These tests were not too complicated or difficult, the kids explained. I was only required: first, to chew without grimacing a dozen *pili-pili;* second, to put my hand into a column of marching red ants while the president counted to ten; third, to pitch a spear into a tree trunk from an approximately ten-foot distance, and other such insignificant exercises that, despite my best intentions, I could never have executed. There was only one thing I could do: offer to pay a high fine for release from each test. This amounted to bribing the children, of course, but there was no other choice, since it was a certainty that not only would I be unable to get down all those pungent peppercorns without grimacing, but that they most decidedly would make me quite ill even if I managed to swallow them. While the *Mompepe* membership was considering my offer, I took Boboka's girl friend aside for a chat, since being a new member herself she had no right to vote. Her name was Ikoko, like that of the small fish Mokolo cooked for medicinal purposes. She had successfully passed all the tests, and what had seemed most difficult to her, she told me, was being unable to say *"te,"* for six full days. In addition to the boys laughing at her while they asked her for things she would have liked to refuse, it also cost her a painful spanking at her father's hands. He had accused her of stealing a corn cake, and she could not deny it, because it would have disqualified her for the *Mompepe* membership. She said she suspected the boys of having done all those things on purpose. Ikoko was a sweet and exceptionally bright child.

We were waiting under an imposing ceiba tree which stood alone, towering over the brush that had repossessed the abandoned sugarcane fields. It was an odd old tree, a close relative of the baobab, with its gourd-like pods, filled with seeds that tasted like grapefruit, hanging from husky limbs, and its top often dressed in the mist floating around it. According to a legend, its master, old Chief Likomi, whose soul lived in its massive trunk, was evidently asleep this morning, for not a whisper came from its silent branches. The villagers claimed that sometimes, by pressing one's ear against the old trunk, one could hear Likomi's grouchy voice grumbling in the tree's *libumu* (belly). Ikoko said that those who had the patience to listen for awhile, could distinctly hear Chief Likomi's lament, "*Naoki motu, naoki motu* (I have a headache)." After all those years, the old chief still complained of a headache, caused by a deadly blow, owing to which his nephew, the now dead father of the present Chief Mafuta, had inherited his chiefdom. The villagers said that when Chief Mafuta was not too drunk, he came to this tree to implore forgiveness for his father, who roamed the forests of the west as a great pale-faced chimpanzee.

At last the children announced acceptance of my offer. They had already conferred upon me the nickname of *Muteniteni* (Firefly), and I considered that itself worth the initiation fee of three big jars of strawberry preserves. I could get the latest report available exclusively to *Mompepe* members right then: there was a meeting scheduled to be held by the elders of the *mboka* at Molali Moke's grandfather's place. The old man had done something wrong, something very,

very wrong; they didn't know exactly what it was; maybe the meeting was already in progress . . .

I rushed to the village without waiting for the end of the news bulletin. Poor old grandfather! Whatever on earth could the wise, blind old man have done?

The meeting was indeed already in session. It was a large gathering, held in the open around a fire, and although it had not rained since early that morning, because of the penetrating humidity grandfather's guests, all as old as he himself, were trying to get as close to the fire as possible without getting singed by it. Perhaps this was also to tighten the circle for a more confidential discussion of the matter. But their voices rose more and more excitedly as their palaver progressed and became clearly audible from a distance. Some of the men spoke Ngombe, and since I was not familiar with the dialect it would have done me little good, had not Baloki and Lisengo joined me, taking turns in translating for me everything into Bangala.

The notables had come to accuse Lulango of introducing into the *mboka* something that could not be tolerated by any self-respecting man, they claimed. Specifically, he was accused of lending his approval to the partitioning of land belonging to everyone and not to anyone in particular, and appropriating part of it.

"Since time immemorial," said a provoked voice, "the land has belonged to no one person. The whole village had only one common field which everybody cultivated and benefited from."

"But—" grandfather began.

He was not given an opportunity to speak, for someone else pursued the argument.

"All our people went hunting and fishing together and smoked the fish over a common fire. Gradually, those possessing more wives to send out to work than other men began to plant their own fields. Until now, however, nobody has ever openly admitted that he has separated his interests from those of the *mboka;* that he had contempt for the laws of our fore-bears and has appropriated the soil which belongs to all."

"But—" the blind old grandfather again unsuccessfully tried to put in a word.

Once again, the accusing voice would not let him. "How is it possible that Lulango, the most respected member of our group of elders, who in the past had always opposed the inno-vations of a few upstarts, has suddenly gone over to their side, the side that cannot even boast of the birth of a single chief among them dating back prior to the founding of this vil-lage?"

"But you are all mad!" the poor old man shrilly man-aged for the first time. In desperation, he had torn off his *lu-kusu,* exposing his bald head for all to see. "You are all as mad as old Bikimi, who tries to feed his drum bananas. What did I do?"

Total silence replaced the strident voices for a long minute. I thought that grandfather must have done something foolish and felt sorry for the old man who in his bewilderment was ripping his *lukusu* to shreds. Then once again the accusing voice calmly resumed the charges, this time adding a note of gravity.

"When your son Molali planted his field of sugarcane and separated it from the community, nothing was said for it was taken into consideration that to manufacture his beer he needed more cane than did the rest of us. His *masanga,* ahem-mmm, was very good, and many people were invited to taste it. This was as if at least part of the soil was being re-turned to the community."

"Mmmm," echoed the assembled.

"A few days ago, however," the man went on, "your son erected a barrier which outlines the boundaries of land that does not belong to him. He has surrounded a part of the land on which his house is built with a fence, and you tolerate it. Today it is a small plot around your son's house; tomorrow it will be fields, and soon it will mean no land for our children's children, who, when they grow up, will want to build their own houses."

So it was Koku's fence that was causing all this hurrah! Molali, who stood listening, was quite visibly stunned. Although it was a hardship to have to feed the big, lazy, and greedy Koku, the destruction of the fence would mean the bird's escape and Molali's consequent ruin. But Molali's father was smart and astute, and after only a brief deliberation, his reply nearly resulted in Molali's heart failure.

"I am deeply saddened," he said in a gloom-choked voice, "that my honorable friends could have thought that I, Lulango, would approve of partitioning the land for my and my family's personal use. My son Molali likes marabous; not only his own, but all marabous, and this enclosure is open to all the birds belonging to any and all of you. This enclosure is meant as a public place for the raising of marabous."

Molali need not have worried, for this declaration was purely theoretical, since Koku was the only marabou in the *mboka*. Nevertheless, this kept up the appearances and safeguarded the principles dear to the old notables' hearts. Molali Moke's grandfather had the satisfaction of receiving the apologies of all those assembled, and the compliments of being *na mayele mingi* (very smart).

Peace was celebrated in the usual manner—with a little *masanga* as sour as the face of Molali who poured it.

CHAPTER XXVIII

The gathering, which had lost much of its initial formality, went on late into the night, despite the absence of good *masanga*. Several other people, including myself, as well as Baloki and her Lisengo, had joined the merrymakers, and the conversation centered around the palaver of the week that resulted in a poor man's turning into a slave only because of his inability to pay an outraged husband. Recalling the trap set for Ngele by Mafuta and his oversized wife, I wondered if this case, too, had been the consequence of a similar ruse. The events of that evening proved me wrong.

The odor of grilled corn had scarcely begun to tickle our nostrils and the sour *masanga* had hardly gone the second time round, when loud shouting interrupted the villagers' favorite discussion on the subject of female passion and infidelity that invariably thrilled the old men. The clamor came from Ikinza's house. He was the man who had surprised his wife with her lover. The swiftness with which the news reached us no longer amazed me, for I now knew how it worked. These people enjoyed spreading any news as much as hearing it. Butu, Lisengo's best friend, had probably raced all the way to be the first to tell us what was happening. He told us with great relish, while trying to catch his breath, that there had been a friendly meeting at Ikinza's house to celebrate the fair and profitable verdict of the elders that had made Malimbo, his wife's lover, Ikinza's slave for an indefinite period.

Since all the men present were Ikinza's intimate friends who knew of his wife Mokua's habitual infidelity, they talked freely of her passionate nature and her many past escapades, as well as of her clumsiness that enabled her husband unfailingly to catch her in the act.

"Ikinza is very pleased, for this is the first time that his wife has had the good sense of choosing a lover among the free males," explained Butu. "Until now Ikinza had always caught her with his own slaves, and that was unprofitable."

"This will set a good example," the grandfather observed.

"When you were young," cackled Ndinga, "nothing would have prevented you from seeing a woman, whether she was married or not; not even the loss of one ear, as was the penalty for such a crime in those times."

Old grandfather Lulango, the unsuspected Casanova, looked considerably embarrassed, and Molali Moke shrieked delightedly at hearing this about his grandparent. Then they all remembered Butu, standing there, and the story he had started to tell them, and they all urged him to continue.

"When Ikinza's guests had emptied the first gourd of *nsamba* and there was no one there to serve them more, Ikinza rose and went to get another gourd from Mokua's hut. But he and his guests had had no more than a few sips when they all became quite ill. They had frightful cramps, vomited, and two among them fell and lay still on the ground. When Mokua came and saw what had occurred, she started to run away. But they caught her and beat her until she had confessed everything. She said that she had bought some *mono* from Nyoka to whom she had promised to pay a high price for it. She had not intended to use the *mono* that night, but because

Ikinza had found the gourd in her hut and had offered the palm wine to his guests, he uncovered everything."

"Mokua could have paid Nyoka handsomely after Ikinza's death," remarked Ngombe Bokoi, "for there are no heirs other than the children she has borne Ikinza. And she would have been in charge until they grew up and could divide the inheritance among themselves. But tell us, what did Ikinza and his friends do?" he asked Butu.

"Those who were able to walk went to find Nyoka. But they could not find him, so they are waiting for him near his house."

Molali Moke and all the other kids belonging to *Mompepe* looked significantly at Boboka. Evidenlty they all knew where Nyoka was, and had a prearranged signal, for suddenly Bokumi said with feigned innocence:

"I saw Nyoka leave downstream in his dugout. He was carrying a large fish net."

At hearing this, Butu rushed off to tell the others where they might find Nyoka, for the witch doctor's large pirogue could never make it over a tall tree felled by lightning and lying across the stream at some distance below the *mboka*. Nyoka would not go far.

A little later we learned that Mokua had fled into the forest. I had often noticed this woman with a strikingly low brow and a rather skinny body. She was better known by her nickname of *Monkuwa Mpamba* (Nothing but a Bone) given her by women envious of her romantic adventures. Her success among men in this village, where corpulence was a measure of feminine allure, was surprising.

"Why do you think men like Mokua so well?" I asked, looking at everybody around the fire.

General laughter was the reply, and then somebody explained, "Men like any woman they can get."

It struck me that Mokua had ended her amorous adventures rather dismally, but the others did not share my view.

"Mokua will not perish in the forest," said one of the men whose name I did not recall. "Neither will she be unhappy, for perhaps even there she will find a male, though he may only be a chimpanzee."

This joke did not provoke laughter. As it developed from the ensuing conversation, it had not been meant as a joke at all.

"If the big apes remember her mother, she will have an easy life," said grandfather.

Intrigued, I asked him for an explanation of what he had meant, and he told the weirdest story.

"A long time ago," the old man began, "when Mokua's mother was only a small *mwana*, Mokua's grandfather found a young wounded male *kumbusu* (chimpanzee) and decided to take him into the village to nurse him, believing that one of his deceased relatives inhabited this animal's body. The *nkema's* (ape's) weight, that was nearly equal to his own, forced him to proceed slowly, and darkness overtook him far from his *mboka*. He and the animal spent that night between the large old roots of an ancient tree which protected them from leopards and other nocturnal predators. When a tornado unleashed, Mokua's grandfather congratulated himself for selecting such a fortunate spot, for even the pounding rain could not penetrate the tree's thick foliage.

"Nonetheless, although hardly able to stand on his feet, the chimpanzee kept trying to get away from under the tree. The animal crawled with difficulty, but when Mokua's grandfather attempted to hold him back, the *kumbusu* almost bit him. The chimpanzee kept crawling away and whimpering pleadingly as though inviting Mokua's grandfather to follow him. The old man was wise and he knew the forest well. In the end, without knowing why, he finally gave in and followed the ape into the cold downpour, leaving the comfortable shelter. They had scarcely left the spot when fire fell from the angry sky, blackening the tree like coal and burning and breaking the huge roots that had served them as refuge. Mokua's grandfather plainly owed his life to his ancestor who lived in the body of this wounded *kumbusu*."

Old Lulango stopped to get his breath, and everybody waited silently for him to continue.

"Mokua's grandfather brought the *nkema* into the *mboka* and called the *monganga* reputed for his *mono*, and the *nkema* was cared for like a member of the family. The ape recovered rapidly and would have gone back into the forest at the end of that same moon, had Mokua's grandfather not had a dream. His deceased uncle had come back from the Land of the Spirits to tell him that his fate was bound to that of the ape, since they owed their respective lives to each other. He advised him to take good care of the animal, for the moon of the animal's death would also be his own. When he awakened, he kept thinking about his dream. How could he protect the ape's life that also meant his own, if the ape returned to the forest?

"Finally, he thought of building a large cage of sturdy logs and he imprisoned the *kumbusu* in it. He planned to keep the chimpanzee thus forever, so as to be able to take care of him till the end of his own days. No one had as much to eat or drink, and the big animal, which already was quite large, began to grow bigger and stronger with each passing day. Nevertheless, the ape's was an unhappy life, since he had lost his freedom. For hours he tried to shake his strong prison bars, he grew vicious and wicked and nobody dared to go into his cage for fear of him. When a village slave was condemned to death for theft one day he was pushed into the ape's cage and the animal killed him before the crowd had had a chance to witness a struggle between the two, because the man was old and weak and could not defend himself.

"From that day on the *kumbusu* became completely wild, and Mokua's grandfather had to repair the cage daily, for the animal had become huge and powerful and the old man himself had never felt better and he did not wish to risk

death. Then one day, when nobody was about to stop her,
Mokua's mother, who was a small, thin girl, had approached
the cage and before you could say 'iye!' the *kumbusu* had
grabbed her with his mighty paws through the bars and had
dragged her inside. When the neighbors, who had expected to
see the child mangled to death, arrived armed with spears and
hatchets, they witnessed something very strange. Hooting in a
friendly way, the chimpanzee held the little girl tenderly in his
arms close to his chest, caressing her with his huge paws. Not
in the least afraid, the child appeared to enjoy the ape's ca-
resses. She giggled and tickled the animal which laughed like
a man who had had too much *masanga*. When she wanted to
go, he let her, but the following morning she was back in his
cage, and they played for hours. Many seasons of high waters
came and went and she was still the only one who could come
near the *kumbusu*. She had by now grown so much that she
no longer could squeeze herself through the long bars. She
was now a *likombe* (an adult unmarried young woman), a
peculiar *likombe* who spoke little and roamed alone in the
jungle.

"She was married finally, and gave birth to Mokua,
but even then she often returned to her father's *ndako*
(house) and was seen hugging the *kumbusu* through the bars.
Then one day, they found the cage broken and the chimpanzee gone. And although Mokua's mother also disappeared a
few days later, no one thought of connecting her disappear-
ance with that of the ape at the time. They searched for her a
little, and finally even her husband forgot about his incorrigi-
ble wife, and no one ever thought of her any further.

"Not until ten or twelve moons later, when a Banza
hunter shot a poisoned arrow into something skulking in the
thick tree branches and killed a huge *kumbusu*. Then a woman
appeared out of nowhere, and falling upon the animal's
body wept disconsolately. This woman was Mokua's mother
who had left her husband and child to follow the big ape into
the forest. After shouting something in a tongue that no long-

er was ours, she vanished into the bush, never to be seen again. Nikomo's son claimed to have seen her once in the midst of a pack of apes, carrying a baby on her back. Nikomo's son was a notorious liar, however, and no one took him seriously."

Grandfather was a master raconteur. And, just as it had to me, it must have occurred to all those present how closely Mokua had followed in her mother's strange footsteps.

"And what became of Mokua's grandfather after the ape's death?" inquired Ngombe Bokoi, obviously leading on the old man, since being his closest friend he probably knew the outcome of the story by heart.

"When he learned of the ape's death, he realized that his own time had come too. He consulted all the *minganga*, trying to fight off the evil spirits that surrounded him, but nothing could save him. He rapidly lost weight, coughed without interruption night after night, and finally died before the end of the moon, as everybody expected."

"Yesterday we chased away a big *kumbusu* from *mboka moke*," announced Molali Moke, evidently uncertain as to whether or not he should be proud of the deed.

"Have I not told you that it was one such ape that taught us how to make good spears?" his grandfather scolded him.

Molali Moke squirmed uneasily and, after a brief pause during which some more *masanga* was quaffed and new *potongo* lit, grandfather told us the story about the clever and friendly chimpanzee that had taught the people how to temper iron.

"All this happened a long, long time ago, when our people did not know that their iron spears, which always bent against the wild animals' tough hides, causing the deaths of many of our ancestors, could be made so hard as to become brittle as old clay pots—"

"What is the good of iron which breaks like an old pot?" Molali spat disdainfully.

Grandfather appeared to be groping for something he

might hurl at his son's stupid head for having so rudely interrupted him, but somebody hastened to put a freshly lit *potongo* into his shaking hand, and he calmed down. (Why the villagers enjoyed the local tobacco was a puzzle, since it had only one quality: it grew faster than bad weed). Anyway, after several puffs on his *potongo*, grandfather explained, in a manner and tone of a schoolmaster addressing a retarded pupil:

"When a bone is young, it is soft; it bends and the infant cannot walk. When the bone is old, it is brittle and breaks. Therefore, old people break their limbs when they fall. This is why bones give men good support when they are neither too soft nor too hard."

Lisengo had elbowed his way nearer to grandfather. But since everybody knew that if he should engage the old man in a discussion about metals no one would ever hear the story about the ape, they stuck a gourd of *masanga*, and even a pipe, into Lisengo's hands. And before he could recover from this flattering show of attention, had swallowed some of the beer, and had puffed at least three times on the *potongo*, as was the custom, grandfather had resumed his tale.

"One day, the children of that faraway time who were as foolish as our own are today chased a tremendous old *kumbusu* unable to run fast enough to elude all their spears. When one of the spears had barely missed it, the ape picked up the weapon and examined it critically. 'Do you call this iron fit for hunting?' it yelled to the children, bursting into loud guffaws. 'Give me a good fire to heat this spear, a pot of good palm oil to dip it into when it is red hot, and I shall show you a good spear!' Then the old chimpanzee threw the spear on the ground and left, spitting disgustedly.

"This shamed and awed the children, for they realized that in this old ape's hide lived one of their wise and learned forefathers, and when they returned to the *mboka* they told this incident to their fathers who from then on began tempering their spearheads in the manner suggested by the *kumbusu*.

It is thanks to this that never again did anyone die because his spear was softer than the animals' hides."

At that moment Molali Moke whispered jocularly in my ear, "They enjoy this sour *masanga* just fine, do you not think?"

His eyes twinkled mischievously, undoubtedly in great fun at a new practical joke at his father's expense, even though it would most certainly cost him another spanking. The guests had apparently grown accustomed to the taste of the spoiled beverage for they had stopped grimacing and instead greedily downed the generous stream of beer offered by Molali. Molali Moke's glee was puzzling. His father was visibly delighted to be able so elegantly to get rid of a stock he could not sell and yet had not the heart to throw away. With a smug grin, he kept bringing fresh supplies of gourds, and when one of the long-spouted gourds that never touched anyone's lips was passed around to me, I sampled the *masanga* myself. Rather than the sourish liquid I had expected, it was delicious, freshly brewed beer. It was exactly right and I, too, drank it with thirsty pleasure.

Molali's stifled howl when he finally discovered that somebody had switched beers, substituting the fresh gourdfuls he had set aside to put on sale the next morning for the sour *masanga* he had intended for the guests, explained the mystery to me. That someone did not bother to wait for the outcome of his father's investigation, but disappeared into the protective shadows of the night.

Now, after Molali had been serving all that delectable fresh *masanga*, he could not possibly follow it up with the spoiled beer without giving himself away and losing face. Fortunately for him, fate saved Molali from almost certain apoplectic death. For when he reappeared, dejectedly carrying a fresh gourd, a distant hubbub, so loud that it reminded me of my first evening in the *mboka*, brusquely put an end to the night's festivities.

Nyoka had been captured.

CHAPTER XXIX

Sleep eluded me that evening. Malaria was not the only thing one picked up in an African *mboka*. One of my toes itched unbearably, and from past experience I knew that it was a chigoe, the minute sand flea, a common Congolese nuisance.

The first warning of the flea's presence is a tickling sensation. If the chigoe is not instantly removed, the impregnated female, its abdomen packed with eggs, grows to the size of a pea in a matter of a few days. Then, leaving her eggs behind, the flea shrinks back to her minute size and drops out. The condition is then not only painful but also dangerous. It often leads to a bacterial infection that could result in suppuration and possible loss of a toe, for which the chigoe has a definite predilection. Fastidious people never allow this sort of thing to develop, naturally, extracting the sand flea at the first significant itching. The Congolese are quite adept at removing these fleas with an ordinary pin or any pointed instrument.

It was Jafke, proud of his skill and the speed with which he removed the little pest without ever leaving any part of it behind, who usually removed my chigoes. But now it was very late. My last petrol lamp had petered out, and for a while, sitting on my bed, I tried to remove the chigoe myself, holding a pin in one hand, a flashlight in the other, and wishing I had a third hand. It was unbearably hot inside the mosquito net, and the sticky humid air made breathing difficult.

Perspiring and shivering at the same time, I got into Michael's pyjamas (laid out on his pillow by Albert) probably more to give me comfort than to keep me from catching cold during the night. Through the cracks in the shutters, one could see the nearly continuous flashing of lightning. Thunder rumbled like a distant battle, and the muffled beat of tom-toms in the *mboka* indicated that the excitement of the crowd there was mounting.

Presently my toe began to bleed. I hoped that perhaps the blood would flush out both the flea and its eggs that I had not succeeded in removing. Jafke, the chigoe expert, would inspect my toe in the morning. Worn out, I lay quietly for a while, and some time later fell asleep from exhaustion. I had a nightmare that I was running away from Djito who, armed with a Banza bow, shot poisoned arrows which reached me everywhere I went, wounding me and causing me sharp pain. I called out to Michael, but he was not with me, and all at once everything blacked out.

I opened my eyes, drowsily trying to penetrate the darkness. I was back in Busu Melo, under my stifling mosquito net. Djito had vanished together with my bad dream, but the arrows continued to burn my flesh. I lay still for a few minutes, expecting the pain to go like the rest of my nightmare, but it grew so acute that it awakened me completely. The room was full of light patter and there was a low murmur in the *monsese* of the roof, and the walls. Wide awake now, I realized that the red ants had invaded my house, and all the other insects, which shared it with Michael and me, cockroaches, spiders, and black ants, were attempting to flee. Almost tearing the mosquito net as I jumped out of bed, anxious to get out myself, I must undoubtedly have stepped into a marching mass of ants, for it felt as though boiling water had climbed from my ankles up to my knees. Hundreds of red ants were clinging to me. I heard Loba protesting loudly against the biting ants. She nearly tripped me as soon as I opened the back door, and scooted out, screaming indignantly while taking refuge in one of the trees in our backyard.

Outside I found unexpected activity. Jafke, Albert, and a few others, including the sentry who had abandoned his post in front of the Administration Office, were waging a hopeless war against the *mafumba* (red ants). The chicken coop door was wide open, probably to save our chickens, and I could hear them cackling and flapping their wings somewhere in the dark. They must have also picked up some of the ants before escaping.

"*Mafumba, mafumba!*" Jafke kept repeating almost jubilantly, even though he had already been forced out of his own quarters and the kitchen.

It was the first time that I had ever seen him in a loincloth. Maybe this was how he dressed after shedding his Western clothes along with his duties. Or maybe he had just been caught off guard, with his trousers already invaded by the *mafumba*. Reflecting on this made me think of my own state of undress, and with relief I complimented myself on wearing Michael's pyjamas.

I ran toward the fire that the boys had started in the middle of the backyard and proceeded to pluck off the ants which preferred to leave their heads embedded in my skin rather than loosen their hold. A strong, dank wind was blowing from the swamps and, after the warmth of my bed, I shivered with cold. It was not necessary to be a professional strategist to evaluate and understand the battle in progress. A compact column of red ants about three or four feet wide was making its way from the surrounding grassland. Near the back of the kitchen house the column split; one kept on marching, describing a semicircle around our bungalow, and the second column dispersed and attacked in broken formations. Jafke and Albert were trying to protect their quarters by building a barrier of hot coals in front of their door, doing their best to add the coals as quickly as the ants advanced. But it was a losing battle, for they were blocking the progress of only the original column which simply went around the glowing coals to continue encircling the bungalow. And there was of course neither enough coals nor time to enable the men to cut off the invading enemy from all sides.

All at once, several oddly shaped lumps flew out from beneath the roof of the bungalow, but fell to the ground instantly, landing heavily, like ripened fruit falling from a tree. Squirming slightly, one of these strange objects dropped at my feet. It was a bat completely coated with red ants. Caught in the area between the ceiling and thatched roof, it had had the strength to leave it, but weighted down by the ants, had collapsed to die on the ground. I myself was still trying desperately to pluck out all the ants which had invaded me, grabbing them through Michael's slippery silk pyjamas, unable to hold back the tears that ran from my smarting eyes. Some of the ants had already reached my neck.

It was then that I noticed a huge, fantastic figure advancing rapidly out of the shadows. It was Madame Van Derveer in a bright red kimono rushing to my rescue. I allowed myself to be led to her house like a small girl, and I'll never know if I was more bewildered by my predicament or her unexpected kindness to me that memorable night.

When a little later, the commotion somewhat subsided, all of my ants extracted and my skin tingling pleasantly after a cologne rub, Madame Van Derveer and I were relaxing on the *baraza* of her old bungalow, she still was the new, unfamiliar-to-me, friendly, motherly woman. Nursing my hot tea laced with cognac, delaying retirement to the guest room prepared for me, my eyes harder and harder to keep open, I was listening to her stories of when she first came to the Congo some fifteen years before. And as minutes passed, the ordeal I had just come through somehow began to seem almost worthwhile. For in those few brief moments of confidence, from be-

hind the mask of the bossy and calculating wife of the chief of
the territory had emerged another person—an unhappy, frustrated, and lonely woman, afraid of aging, who looked over
her shoulder rather than into the future that she believed held
nothing more for her.

Then I was again trying to get to sleep in a strange bed,
listening to the unyielding tom-toms and thinking about my
little chimp that would have to spend a lonely night in a tree.
But of course Loba was safe up there, and would come down
in the morning with her stomach bulging with the fruits of
whatever tree she had taken refuge in. I also thought of the
red ants—the true masters of the African jungle. I had encountered their compact column on quite a number of occasions as it marched across the Busu Melo road, or the narrow
trail leading to the old village. The column was never very
wide, one could easily jump over it, but it certainly was long,
for it could keep on marching for days. It was impossible to
determine where the red ants came from or where they were
heading, for the column always emerged from thick bush and
disappeared into an equally impenetrable vegetation on the
opposite side of the road. But it clearly had a purposeful des-
tination, for one could stand rather close to it without changing the ants' direction and without being attacked.

Now, after having personally experienced the savagery
of their onslaught on anything flesh and blood, when that was
their objective, I was inclined to be far less skeptical about the
many red-ant stories, particularly the one concerning an
habitual drunk who kept being locked up in a jungle post jail for
disorderly conduct. As in the case of most structures in the
interior, it was a crude construction of clay and thatch, with the
exception of its doors, made of heavy hardwood. Because
during each lockup this African had had screaming fits and on
several occasions had attempted to break down his cell door,
that particular night the guard had ceased to pay any heed to
the prisoner's screams for help, and eventually the screaming
stopped. But the following morning, when they came to re-

lease the man, pitiful remains consisting of a few bones and the man's breechcloth testified to the visit of the *mafumba* and the inhuman agony the poor fellow had gone through as he was being devoured alive by the tiny cannibals.

Only recently I had witnessed a struggle between red ants and termites defending their hill. Someone had sliced off the top of a high mound standing by the side of the road, and before the agile termite workers had had a chance to seal it again, swarms of red ants had attacked it. In a split second the termite workers were replaced by soldiers armed with powerful and, in proportion to their bodies, immense jaws. The battle did not last long. The defenders were outnumbered, overpowered, and destroyed, and the red ants flooded the subterranean tunnels of the colony. For four or five days thereafter, endless caravans of red ants were carrying off eggs and larvae of termites from the conquered mound. When the last red ant had gone, the termite mound remained open and still—a mute reminder of the end of a small world.

Now I was sorry at not having thought of knocking down the little termite hill in our living room before rushing out of the house. The red ants would not have missed the opportunity of invading the subterranean termite community and would have rid us of our uninvited boarders.

Madame Van Derveer was still asleep when I left the following morning, and in broad daylight the new image she had created of herself the night before seemed absurdly unrealistic. My own bungalow was still invaded by the *mafumba,* and Jafke had mobilized quite an army of volunteers to help him in cutting off the arriving reinforcements of the tenacious enemy.

I had practically no pain left from the multiple *mafumba* bites. Although it was annoying to be driven out of my house for who could tell how long, there was a small compensation for this inconvenience. I knew that after they would finally go, the red ants would leave a clean house, with not a single insect left behind. I even suggested to Jafke that perhaps some brave man might agree to dash into the invaded house and cut off the tip of our living room termite hill. But Jafke couldn't think of who such a brave man might be.

"If this mound leads to a large termite village," he said, "the *mafumba* may live in your *ndako* for a long, long time."

"Forget it," I said. If this had to be the choice, I preferred to coexist with the termites.

Jafke also inspected my toe, and proclaimed that I had successfully removed the sand flea. I had the impression that he was a bit disappointed that I had managed to do it without his expert help.

The tarnished sun occasionally pierced the low ceiling of gray clouds and the humid air was still saturated with electricity. There was no place for me to go except back to Madame Van Derveer's house or to the *mboka*, and I chose my village friends. The last thing I saw on the Busu Melo road before leaving was Loba. Seemingly unaffected by the red ants, she was taking a free ride, hanging by one hand from the bamboo pole of the "Water Brigade" that was carrying water to one of the bungalows. The little chimp had discovered this new game a few days ago, and the prisoners apparently did not mind her at all, despite the added weight they had to carry in this suffocating heat.

A couple of hours later that morning, at the *mboka*, I found that I was not the only one who suffered from the weather, so unusual in a period when the rains should have been pouring virtually around the clock. It also affected the villagers. A number of them had gathered in the main village square to witness the trial of Nyoka. He sat on a low stool and, although his nervous fingers betrayed his inner agitation, his face expressed an incomprehensible self-assurance. The oppressive humid heat was becoming untenable and nearly caused me to faint, despite the shade provided by the *monsese* from under which I was watching the proceedings.

The charges against Nyoka were being preferred in the customary manner. They established the fact that Nyoka had knowingly sold poison to Mokua for the purpose of murdering her husband. They also accused him of complicity in the crime, since he could have counted on generous payment for the *mono* only after Mokua's husband's death, when she would have come into ample wealth. His eyes nearly closed, Nyoka was listening to the accusations without uttering a word, and his silence was interpreted as an admission of guilt.

All this was outstandingly interesting and it inevitably prompted a curious parallel and a favorable comparison of these jungle dwellers with the so-called civilized people I had lived among all my life. In their own way these Africans had an infallible sense of justice and fairness, sometimes to a point seemingly inconceivable in such a remote Congolese community. I was reflecting on this intriguing subject when a new man joined the debate, proving, on the other hand, that corruption in politics was not necessarily the exclusive product of our civilization. The man was an elderly notable, whose mobile face was topped with a rakishly worn *lukusu*. His alert little eyes wandered over the assembly, twinkling shrewdly.

"My client does not claim that he did not sell the *mono* to the woman Mokua, nor will he deny that the *mono* was a poison," he shrilled in a high, nasal squeak. "He positively does deny, however, that it was intended for her husband or any other person." He bared his teeth sarcastically at the gathering, and went on, "The poison was meant for rats. There was such a quantity of it because it has no value whatsoever. That is why all sixteen of my good friends who have partaken of it have lived to accuse Nyoka. As to the price agreed upon, it has been paid in full. The woman Mokua spent some time in *Monganga* Nyoka's hut," he concluded, casting a sizable fagot of sticks, which buried those of the prosecution, into the middle of the "courtroom."

These sticks, each representing a conclusive argument on either side, were symbols of victory. Mokua herself was not present and therefore could not be questioned. Nyoka rose, indicating unequivocally that the attempted murder trial was closed.

Baloki explained to me excitedly that the funny old man, who enjoyed the reputation of the best orator in the *mboka*, by unexpectedly undertaking Nyoka's defense, had upset the whole procedure. The murder case had turned into one of adultery, and Nyoka was rich enough to pay an outraged husband for his wife's favors. But for that Mokua had to be found first. In the meantime, it was apparent that the old rogue's skillful defense had won everybody's approval. Some notables patted the old man on the back, some expressed their admiration by smacking their own naked thighs, some came to congratulate Nyoka with a flow of adjectives. The witch doctor's name was on everyone's lips. Nyoka would become a great *monganga*, the people were saying. And Molali Moke's grandfather must probably have realized how fast Nyoka's prestige was growing following his victorious weathering of the brief crisis. For, led by his grandson, he shuffled over to where we were standing and started to whisper to Molali, loudly enough to be heard by all the neighbors:

"Why make an enemy of someone who will be powerful when I no longer am here to protect you? Go on and tell him you regret to have beaten him the other day. He will appreciate it and everything will be forgotten."

But as it soon became obvious, the old man, in his eagerness to help his son, had unwittingly offered him poor advice.

For this once, the pigheaded Molali heeded his father's counsel, and walking up to Nyoka told him, "Do you recall the day when you came to ask if I had said that you were a thief?"

Clearly not desiring to discuss this embarrassing matter publicly, Nyoka replied that he recalled nothing of the kind. But Molali, who was anything but diplomatic, having made up his mind to ask Nyoka's forgiveness, was at a loss in the face of the witch doctor's denials.

"Have you forgotten the morning when I dragged you out of my house by your hair?" he insisted.

Nyoka, visibly annoyed and more and more nervous, maintained that he did not know what Molali was talking about. Molali, who was irritated by Nyoka's sudden loss of memory, could not drop the subject, since several people who had gathered around them had begun to snicker.

"Do you not remember," Molali went on with the insistence of a fly, "when I did this?" And he reached out with his large paw to grab Nyoka's bushy hair.

At this, the ambitious little man completely lost composure and began hurling insults at Molali, calling him a *nsombo* (wild pig). And Molali evidently had decided that there was nothing else to do but seize Nyoka by his elaborate headdress, and this he did as though he were catching a rare bird. It quickly degenerated into a real brawl. The white-striped Nyoka emerged out of this scuffle somewhat bedraggled, smeared, stripped of his feathers, and quite unmistakably no longer quite certain of his being selected to replace Djito. One thing appeared indisputable: Molali could fully expect retaliation from Nyoka, and this time probably of a far more unpleasant nature.

This arrived even sooner than any of us had anticipated, and its subtlety confirmed once more that Molali had made himself an enemy he would have a hard time outwitting.

A messenger from Nyoka had arrived while Molali was resting on his threshold, to inform him that Molali could release Koku, since Koku was just an ordinary marabou anyway, and not a charmed bird.

For a moment it appeared that Molali would suffer a stroke. He was probably thinking of all that fish he had been feeding the insatiable bird. Glumly, too nakedly confounded to swear, Molali went about the task of dismantling the "public" enclosure for the village marabous.

And I was thinking that although I had not made a single friend among the local witch doctors, I had to admit that they undoubtedly were the smartest members of the community, for they were reaching their goals by their wits and applied psychology, and were certainly entitled to my grudging admiration.

Perhaps the people—in a village where each and every public meeting, every trial or marriage, were so many pretexts for noisy celebrations—were not entirely satisfied with the spectacular but brief trial of Nyoka. When I started for home there were several small clusters of men and women still loitering and debating in the main square. Once on the decay-permeated trail, I sang as usual. And the melancholy words set to the romantic music of Chopin's second étude were punctuated by the unceasing beat of tom-toms all the way to the government post. At home I found that the ants had vacated the bungalow, leaving the characteristic vinegary odor of formic acid in the air.

CHAPTER XXX

The next morning I slept very late, exhausted by all my experiences of the previous day. After a leisurely brunch, I was thumbing through a pocket magazine on the front *baraza*, with Loba snoring in my lap, when a soldier on a bike, his bare legs and uniform shorts splattered with mud, rolled up to the steps. He had some mail for me.

The mailbag was an important event in the jungle. In Busu Melo it came twice monthly and represented many things—letters from home, news from friends, and a sense of connection with the distant continent left far behind, sometimes for what seemed like centuries.

But this was not the usual mail the soldier had brought me. He was a special messenger from Michael whose letter was two days old. Michael wasn't too far away, so maybe the soldier had taken a brief vacation en route. Or perhaps Michael had left the Busu Melo road to call on some riverine village, and not wanting to worry me about his going to a tsetse-infested region again, had not let me know. He was fine, he said. And he was also sending me other news in an enclosed letter from Léopoldville that for some reason instead of coming directly in the Busu Melo mailbag, that generally arrived through the navigable Busu Kwanga *chenal,* had come through Lisala. This letter was from a fellow doctor who said he had heard rumors that the *Médecin en Chef* intended to transfer Michael to Katanga, in the upper Congo, where he would be in charge of a medical district. Most likely it would be Jadotville, one of the headquarters of the *Union Minière,* the large and important copper mining company in the Congo. Aside from the promotion and a good laboratory Michael missed so much, it meant living in a big town. It meant a comfortable brick house with adequate plumbing, good stores, country clubs and golf, people to see, and a lot of other appealing features. The main attraction to me, however, was that I could have a piano and would be able to sing again. Really sing, before an audience in an auditorium, and not just "keep my vocal chords in" on a jungle trail, scaring the birds and monkeys in the trees. But it also meant farewell to the jungle, the *mboka,* and my dear village friends. It also meant that poor Michael would have to intensify his jungle travel even more now to wind up the work he had mapped out in the territory.

Michael had from time to time been gone for a whole week before, but I imagined that now this would be his constant routine and I would be seeing him only once a week for a few brief hours that would go so swiftly.

There was also a note from Mongana, the seat of the big palm-oil company, where we had thought of spending our weekends before learning on our arrival in the territory how impossible it would actually be. So now maybe we would be going there soon after all, if only once, to spend a few days in more comfortable surroundings. The note was an invitation from a Mongana executive and his wife. The guest house would be ours any time we chose to come, and they would make sure that their tennis court was kept in condition during this rainy season.

The third and last letter was from that nice couple in Léo who had taken such good care of me when I arrived from Europe. They had already heard via the capital's own grapevine, apparently as efficient as the jungle drums, of our projected transfer to Katanga. They had a present waiting for me that I would receive on our way through Léo, en route to Michael's new assignment. The precious gift was one of my friends' two adorable Tenerife terriers, smart fluffy little white creatures with incredibly beautiful black eyes and shiny black noses. I had my choice of either the tinier Whiskey, or his somewhat larger brother, Soda, as the month-old puppies were called. And without even seeing them, I instantly decided on the smaller Whiskey, whom I already renamed Vicki. I had always wanted such a little pup, but didn't know then that I had just acquired a loved friend that for the next fifteen years would become my inseparable companion and an important part of my life all over the world.

While I was thinking about this news, the secret *Mompepe* society burst onto the veranda past the haughtily protesting Jafke and met by the welcoming hoo-hoo'ing of the wakened Loba. Jumping off my lap, she was trying to get the kids to play with her by running past them and slapping their legs on her way. Only after a good half-hour of pursuit, wrestling, shouting, and overturned chairs, when Loba grew tired of being the center of attention, and after noticing the "Water Brigade," did she quit the game and run off to take another ride suspended by one hand from the water carriers' bamboo pole. It took the children a moment to regain their breath before they could explain what news they had brought me from the village.

There would be a celebration at the *mboka* after all, Molali Moke explained. It was still because of Nyoka, but instead of celebrating his punishment for attempted murder it would be held to honor his having been entrusted with a special mission by Ibanza, the god of the rich, a fact that had temporarily been overshadowed by his trial. The children, constantly interrupting one another, chattered like sparrows, but finally told me the gist of the story.

A few days ago, Nyoka had announced that from now on he would be dispatching the dead to Ibanza, despite the lack of traditional food supposed to accompany them to the beyond, into the land of the rich. Naturally, he could not decide upon such a drastic departure from secular customs, but Ibanza himself had appeared to him in his sleep. The divinity had complained to Nyoka of the scarcity of new arrivals into his kingdom for most of the dead were ending up in the domain of his brother Nsungu, the god of the poor. Nyoka alone was authorized to determine the proper amount of food to satisfy Ibanza. Although the Africans' life span in an equatorial hamlet was a very brief candle indeed, there were relatively few people dying at the *mboka*, and apparently Ibanza's choice of Nyoka would eliminate all future competition of the other two *minganga*. They were consumed with envy that Nyoka had been singled out to receive the divine message. Boboka claimed that Djito and Mokolo took up the habit of retiring much earlier, hoping that Ibanza would visit them too. But all was in vain—Ibanza had made his choice.

While we were on our way to the *mboka*, with all the members of the *Mompepe* still licking their sticky fingers after feasting on a jar of honey at my house, the kids filled me in on other news gathered by the "secret" society.

"Djito has a *monkole* (a boil) very low on his back," Boboka whispered confidentially.

"He mixes water into the *nsamba* he sends to Chief Mafuta," reported Bokumi.

It was amazing how in just a few days these children had changed their attitude toward the most feared witch doctor in the *mboka*. Djito, like all humans, had his foibles and vices, and evidently a close scrutiny of his personal life did little toward enhancing the respect of the youngsters, whose minds were susceptible to new impressions far more than were those of their parents. The older generation carried formed images fixed in their minds like old, familiar photographs, while the children's gift of observation and logical deduction was remarkable. Much of the news was trivial, but some appeared germane. Ekomila had seen Djito sprinkling the strong-smelling liquid which attracted leopards on Nyoka's porch. Djito had been in such a hurry to leave the scene that he had nearly tripped over Ekomila, and she proudly showed off a lump on the back of her head, sustained when she had bumped her head against a post in dodging Djito. The *sepo* (amulet) she was wearing that evening had been no good and she had thrown it away. In fact, the children did not particularly respect these talismans and often discarded them, as Ekomila had, in favor of others they happened to take a fancy to.

When we reached the village's main square it was crowded with people who had begun to assemble to secure ringside places. Here, as anywhere in the world, only a few privileged could occupy "reserved seats." The fires had not yet been lit and the large fagots of firewood with the dark outlines of the pots suspended over them projected illusory shadows. Particular attention was being devoted to the area where the fighting matches were to be held. Several women scraped the ground with an assortment of tools in an effort to level it out. As usual, the ethical sportsmen demonstrated their good will and honest intentions by allowing their wives to do most of the work.

The whole Lulango family, which had made an obvious effort at sartorial elegance, was at "ringside." Baloki and her mother had painted their lids white and had coated their bodies with fresh *ngola*. Grandfather was wearing his leopard *lukusu* and over-one-shoulder sash. But most of all I was dazzled by Molali. He was superb—he was clean. For this once, instead of having himself scraped with the usual iron scraper, he had consented to wash, using water that had been heated in a large pot similar to the one I saw at the feast on my first visit to the *mboka*, and lots of black, homemade soap. Molali was unmistakably self-conscious, embarrassed, and awkward.

Evidently being clean was not an altogether unpleasant sensation, but his expression indicated that he considered the procedure itself sheer torture.

The festivities began with the *ebinela* (public dance). But soon only a few people showing off their special talents remained in the round. A lot of the tribal dances were unfamiliar to me, and I was absorbed by what was obviously an erotic dance performed by two women. It represented a dispute of two rivals for the affections of the same man, and ended in a make-believe tearing off of the raffia skirts. This performance had considerable success. Many in the audience could not keep still and followed in slow motion all the movements of the two dancers who performed a combination of something akin to the rhumba and the belly dance.

The fighting competition followed. First, the witch doctor chased the *likundu* (evil spirits) from the arena, since they could easily enter the bodies of the losers. Then several "promoters," resembling ghosts, for they were completely coated with *mpembe*, argued about the contestants, all the while trying to hold back the women who encouraged their men by yelling at the top of their lungs. The fighters wore only small breechcloths of woven raffia tightly wound about their loins. Baloki explained that these were not worn merely for conventional purposes, but to afford protection. In addition to this, each of the contestants wore one or more cumbersome objects that were the only things on their thickly oiled and slippery bodies an opponent might hold onto. The inconvenience of these assorted heavy objects was compensated by the spiritual advantage, since each of these was an amulet certain to assure its wearer of victory. These objects were so extraordinary that I wished for a closer look at them. There were animal teeth, nuts, pieces of carved wood and bits of metal; a dried lizard's head, an elephant's tail and an attractive tuft that, it turned out, was nothing other than a bunch of tarantula's legs. All these charms, of course, meant additional income for the witch doctors who, I supposed, manufactured and sold them.

At last the fights began. The man who succeeded in throwing his adversary onto the ground on his back or stomach, no matter by what means, was proclaimed the winner. Everything was permissible to accomplish this: choking, every possible blow, even tripping. At first I expected to see one or the other of the fighters downed immediately, but these young men were as agile as cats, and even when everything seemed lost, they managed to escape a stranglehold and regain their balance almost as they fell. When in the end one of the men was thrown down, there followed an interesting demonstration. Those of the women who had supported the winner now sang to celebrate his feat. He was the strongest and most nimble of men who had brought honor and glory not only to his own family, but to the tribe, the village, the whole world. This chanting was accompanied by approbatory yells of the spectators. In the meantime, the women belonging to the defeated man's family, in an attempt to comfort their contestant, began to chant that this was nothing but an accident and that a return match would prove their man to be the strongest and the most dexterous of all men. The chanters did not attempt to interfere with one another, but rather sang alternately, providing their rival group with a kind of musical background and creating a most striking harmony.

While the *mpembe*-coated "promoters" cleared the arena for the next fight, I mixed with the excited crowd, which had again formed a wide, thick circle, and unnoticed slipped into the village street that seemed quite dark after the bright firelight in the square and slowly started for home. Unexpectedly there was a loud, jarring noise behind me that soon rose to a shrill crescendo. Even in casual conversation among themselves, when not inhibited by a white person's presence, the Africans, adults and children alike, particularly the females, spoke very rapidly, in an abrupt succession of high and low-pitched voices, creating an impression of constant agitation. But the growing clamor seemed to be something out of the ordinary, something like a collective outcry of indignation. Curious, I turned around and once again walked to the main square. A new wave of noise greeted me. This time it was brief and followed by total silence, broken only by the crackling of twigs in the fire. Looking over the heads of the crowd I saw Mafuta in the center of the square, wearing his best clothes—his velvet vest. He was as drunk as usual, but gone was the placidity of a few days before. He was spluttering like a tired motor. In spite of his huge belly and pendulous breasts, there was nothing ludicrous in his wrath. He was holding a spear with which he had just slashed the large *mbonda*'s skin drumhead. This gesture, followed by a flow of oaths, provoked general consternation.

Baloki and Lisengo, who saw me standing across the square, pushed their way toward me and explained to me in low whispers that the purpose of this big drum was to stress everything said and done. That was why when they performed the dance of war and shouted "*Etumba*" they struck the *mbonda* to lend the word "war" more forcefulness. And now the drunken chief was emphasizing his threats to the heavens with the aid of the biggest *mbonda* in the whole *mboka*.

Even before there had been a rumor that Chief Mafuta had defied Djakomba, the god of the universe, and it had aroused in the village a premonition of impending danger. And now Mafuta confirmed it publicly. He shouted something, but the momentary silence created by his unthinkable audacity had instantly given way to a buzzing of voices so intense it became impossible to hear any one person in particular. Grandfather had once said that Djakomba was too great in stature to punish a single little man. For, as he had put it, "A man cannot crush with his foot a single ant in a column of marching ants." Now the villagers knew that they would have to pay dearly for their drunken little chief's arrogance.

Perhaps Djakomba's foot was even larger than the villagers imagined, since back home Jafke was waiting for me with bad news he had received by way of the jungle grapevine. Michael, who was coming home that afternoon, was ill, very seriously ill.

CHAPTER XXXI

It was close to midnight when, leaning weakly on Leport who had driven him home, Michael stepped out of his Chevy. Even before talking to Leport I knew by the scared faces of the villagers that Michael was indeed a sick man. It was positively not malaria, Leport, who for once did not bare his gold-capped teeth, declared. There was a slight flu epidemic in the territory and Michael had been working extremely hard lately; that's probably what he had, a bad case of flu. Leport most likely did not tell me how high Michael's temperature actually was. It had undoubtedly been higher than 103°, he had admitted to me, for Michael was half delirious, only occasionally recognizing us to mumble something about his life insurance policy. The frightened faces of our neighbors were adding to my panic. And Jafke finally exploded the fragile bubble of my self-imposed composure by inquiring in respectfully hushed tones:

"When *Monganga Mokonji* dies and you leave, could I have the portable iron bathtub and the *monganga*'s mosquito boots?"

"For heavens's sake, do something!" I screamed at Leport, who was doing his best by looking through Michael's medical books. "Take him to Lisala, to a physician, any physician."

I would have gratefully accepted even the doctor from Bomboma, a lanky Frenchman who was the constant target of jokes because he was so afraid of catching a tropical disease that he never came near an African patient (for which he was eventually fired) and even washed peeled bananas in a permanganate solution.

"He couldn't be moved in his present condition," Leport objected, "not on our roads."

"Then get the doctor from Lisala to come here!"

"We've sent word by runner already," he said. "Believe me, Madame, there's nothing to do but wait for the fever to break. It usually takes several days for the flu to run its course."

Michael had probably kept on working for a few days while he was already sick, for the fever went down on the second day of his return home. It crawled down degree by degree, and by the third day he was sleeping peacefully. And my hopes skyrocketed when I caught a disappointed look Jafke had furtively sneaked at Michael's boots. It was also that same day that Fallet, back from Busu Djanoa, brought the answer to the message sent to Lisala. The doctor was very sorry he was unable to come. The district physician was somewhere on inspection in the Bomboma Territory, and he was all alone in Lisala to take care of the hospital. Why didn't we send Michael to Lisala?

So that was that. I glanced at Michael who was resting quietly, and went out on the front *baraza*—for the first time in three days. The rain that had been coming down for the past forty-eight hours had abruptly stopped, and the sun had unexpectedly appeared fleetingly and then had swiftly dropped into the jungle.

"We shall leave here as soon as *Monganga Mokonji* is a little stronger," I told Jafke. "Maybe in a day or so. You'd better start packing." Then recalling that he had faithfully gone almost without any sleep always to be there day and night in answer to my call, I added to his agitation by fulfilling his frustrated dreams. "You may have the portable iron tub and all the kitchen utensils, the dishes and the tableware. *Monganga Mokonji* will give you his boots when we get to Léopoldville."

Jafke's blissful face and his effusive gratitude made me realize how happy I was myself to be able to give it all to him. It was certain that we would not have any use for all this equipment specially designed for the bush. In the large centers of Katanga one could take a real bath; one didn't need break-proof crockery but could use elegant bone china for dinner parties. And most important of all, one could get medical help when one was seriously ill.

I was on the point of going back into the house when Lisengo dropped in to bring me up on the latest village news. The crushing foot of the wrathful Djakomba had come down heavily on the *mboka*. It had all begun a couple days before, while the kids were playing in the big stream behind the village. A few small fish were floating on its surface, their white bellies turned upward, and the children had fished them out and had thrown them upon the shore. It developed into a speed contest, in the midst of giggling and yelling. Someone had been fishing upstream, they thought, using *botoko* leaves which had healing properties but also killed fish, and fish dead of *botoko* were good to eat. The one who had thrown the leaves into the stream must have been a fool, for he should have done it farther downstream where the channel was narrower. It was stupid to allow the killed fish to float away. Anyhow, later the news spread around and quite a few adults had joined the children in fishing out the free food, the fish tasted wonderful and they all gorged themselves on them, but shortly after everybody had become desperately sick. Even Molali, who could digest practically anything, was as sick as the rest of them. And Koku, who was still around and had managed to steal a whole fish and all the tidbits he could beg, was not his own cocky self. The following morning the dead fish were still floating downstream, but even though they knew by this time that nobody was dropping *botoko* leaves into the stream, more people, lured by the unexpected abundance of the forever scarce *nyama*, ate it and became ill. And now the natives feared that it was Djakomba's wrath. But Mafuta had nothing to fear from the villagers. Two of his slaves had been netting dead fish for him, and he had evidently eaten more of these bad fish than anybody, for he was sicker now than anybody else. Although it was true that Mafuta was not as sick as one of his old slaves, Mobulu, who had obviously eaten even more, for he had died the previous night.

Lisengo turned around just as I was reentering the door, and shouted the last bit of news to me: "Molali Moke and Boboka are sick, too."

He had disappeared before I could ask him for more details. And back in the house, I forgot all about the villagers' plight, including my two little friends, for Michael was again mumbling something in his troubled sleep.

His fever went down later in the day, and I slept uninterruptedly that night, for the first in three days, in a morris chair beside Michael's bed.

It was only the next afternoon, while the European residents of Busu Melo were calling on their quite pale and quite shaky *Monganga Mokonji* propped up in bed, that I remembered about Boboka and Molali Moke. And because the mood in our bungalow was so effervescent, with everybody such good friends, drinking that extra toast to Michael's convalescence and speedy recovery; with Fallet making everyone laugh with the latest spicy gossip about the amorous adventures of the aging director of the Mbinga plantation; and Leport proudly taking credit for Michael's early recovery; and Jafke's happiness, that he translated into new masterpieces of canapés whipped up from recklessly uncounted cans of pâté and shrimp, the message from the *mboka* affected me all the more deeply. At noon, despite all the drugs from the hospital dispensary and all the expensive medicines purchased from the village witch doctors, Molali Moke died, followed only two hours later by his inseparable friend Boboka.

I went on listening to the gay stories, some of them repeated for the second time for Carlos and Almeida, the latecomers. Perhaps worn out and harassed as I was, I did not quite realize just then how greatly I had grown attached to the two youngsters. Or maybe I was still too preoccupied about Michael who, unaware of the noise our guests were making out on the front *baraza*, was sleeping restfully. It was not until later, in the privacy of the black tropical night, that I wept for the first time, and continued to weep on and off while packing our belongings in the long iron colonial trunks that were badly in need of a fresh coat of paint.

It was nearly reveille time when, exhausted, I had padlocked the last trunk and opened the door to the front *baraza*, admitting along with the fresh morning breeze a swarm of hungry mosquitoes. The bent, naked flagpole was already silhouetted against the reddening sky, and the fire in front of the territorial office was out. A hoarse rooster, down in Carlos's backyard, roused the sentry, asleep on the office steps. A dark figure I had at first failed to notice on our own steps startled me, but I almost immediately recognized Lisengo by his inevitable two-pronged spear. He stood up and I expected him to tell me something about the *mboka*, perhaps about the family or maybe something more about the dead boys, but he didn't.

"Is it true," he asked, taking me aback, "that life is easy in Kinshasa, and no one has to work for the magic iron is plentiful and does everything by itself?"

"Kinshasa" was the African name for Léopoldville.

"There's no place in the world where no one has to work," I told him, trying to understand what was behind his question. "The iron cannot work itself. Human hands have to build the machines and someone has to operate them. This is work, hard work, Lisengo."

He gazed at me as at an ignorant child and explained patiently, "To work means to watch the women while they labor in the fields; to build a *monsese;* to carve a dugout or to dry or smoke fish. Work is what we must do every day all of our lives. To handle iron is a pleasure. Besides, no one has enough of it to keep working every day with it."

He grinned dreamily at his own thoughts in which men did nothing all day except play with iron.

"Now that Molali Moke is not here any more, Baloki will go to Kinshasa with me," he went on, his grin spreading broadly all over his face. "And who knows, maybe some day I will go to the faraway land of the white king; the land that is like the land of the people of the sky where everybody is a chief; where everybody is rich; where everybody knows everything and everybody is better than all our people here. Someday soon, all of our young people will leave the *mboka.* And the *bana* when they grow older will also go to Kinshasa, or to the faraway land where life is so nice and easy. Only the very old ones will stay behind, and when they die, there will be no *mboka* left," Lisengo added before starting on his way back, perhaps anxious to try on the gift I had bought for him at the local store, the first pair of pants and silk shirt he had ever owned.

I wanted to tell Lisengo that his exalted idea about the people in the "faraway land" had little to do with reality. But feeling that I had dampened enough of his illusions for one day, I let him go without another word.

It was nearly ten in the morning when Michael woke up. He was still too wobbly to walk, but strong enough to make the trip—so said his attending physician, Leport, who had his dream coming true, too: he was inheriting Loba. We had reached this decision after long and painful consideration. We both were deeply attached to the affectionate and bright little animal, but common sense told us that should we take her to the much cooler climate of Katanga, and later on to even colder temperatures away from the African soil, sooner or later she would end up in some zoo, or still worse, die of pneumonia. It was then best to leave her with Leport who loved her almost as much as we did.

There were strings attached to the bequest. He was also inheriting my two other neglected friends, the white Desdemona and the black Othello. But not before he had given his word twice that neither the hen nor the rooster would ever end up on his, or any, table. And I instinctively watched his feet to make sure that he was not doing a *toto* while he solemnly promised that my feathered pets would be allowed to live out the full span of their chicken lives. Leport would probably also get Michael's jalopy, which after its very long and glorious past had apparently lost its marketable value even in Busu Melo. Besides, Michael's replacement had not yet arrived in the territory, so there was nobody to sell the jalopy to in any case.

Before our neighbors, whom we expected to drop in to wish us bon voyage, started to arrive, I quickly ran down the soggy and by now so familiar trail leading to the *mboka*. The downpour that had come earlier that morning had evidently shortened the ceremony of the burial, for everything was over when I had reached Molali's hut. Alone Baloki still sustained an uninterrupted and plaintive keen. But I also beheld something ever sadder than Baloki's wailing and mournful chanting. Grandfather was squatting all alone by the dying fire. His whole body weighted down with grief, he was weeping bitterly. Only Molali seemed little affected by his young son's death, and his heavy wooden pestle sang while it crushed the sugarcane for fresh *masanga,* although this was his own way of expressing his sorrow: the beer was intended for the wake that would last as long as there remained anything to drink.

I gave Baloki a couple of flowery silk *pagnes* I had ordered for her from Léo some time ago. And the delight on her beautiful, still tear-stained face momentarily took my mind off my sadness at never having had the chance of giving Molali Moke and Boboka their presents—some fishing equipment I had ordered through Carlos—that had only just arrived. I wasn't quite sure if the meerschaum pipes and the tobacco I got for Baloki's grandfather and her father, Molali, could replace the *potongo* they liked so well. And I also wondered whether Baloki's mother would ever try to wear over her *ngola*-coated body the calico *pagne* I had brought for her.

I said adieu to all of them, although I don't think they understood that I was leaving for good, probably never to return.

Baloki, who walked to *mboka moke* with me, told me a little more about the dead boys. In order that they might have an untroubled journey to the great beyond and reach the land of Ibanza without delay, the other children of the little village had contributed much food to accompany Molali Moke and Boboka. The two little boys were buried in the shade of the giant tree which served as the *Mompepe*'s "clubhouse." On our way there, in front of Mafuta's house, we saw old Nsua striking the ground with her stick and calling, "*Mobondo, mobondo.*" She was practicing her witchcraft against Mobulu, Mafuta's dead slave, so one of Nsua's neighbors, who was weaving a net on his threshold, told us.

"Nsua, who hated Mobulu, had been too afraid of Chief Mafuta to use the *mobondo* before, even against his slave, while the *mokonji* was strong and powerful," he explained. "But now that the *mokonji* is a dying man himself and his slave is dead, Nsua hopes to curse with dysentery the ape in whose body Mobulu will return to live on earth. This way he shall have died twice, and Nsua does not think this would be often enough."

Practically the whole *Mompepe* membership was at the little village, and most of the kids stopped me to inquire if I wished to attend a general meeting held to elect their new president and his assistant. Depressed, I fled to avoid having to participate in their *likambo* (palaver).

As I neared the old ceiba tree, I heard stifled sobbing. A small form was stretched face down on the freshly dug soil. Her funny little pigtails trembling pitifully, Ikoko's spread arms embraced Boboka's grave. Squatting down beside her, I did my best to console her. And while soothing her I realized as never before the extent of my attachment to the two boys and the depth of my affection for them. Wistfully I remembered Molali Moke's contagious, pixieish exuberance, Boboka's strangely mature, thoughtful reserve, and their touching trust and their devotion to me.

A surge of fresh breeze, which shook the branches of the ceiba tree, reminded me that it was growing late. Ikoko insisted that she could hear chief Likomi's low lament in the whispering foliage.

On my way home through the *mboka* I saw quite a crowd in the main square, and Lisengo, trying not to betray his excitement, explained to me that the council of notables would meet to discuss the forthcoming election of a new chief. Mafuta was still alive, but when he died he would leave fourteen sons, none among whom were old enough to assume the responsibilities and the intricate duties of a chief. It was more than likely, therefore, that while awaiting Mafuta's death and the official election of a new chief, the council wished to prevent the forever scheming witch doctors from taking this opportunity to seize even more power. Or perhaps it was not for political but financial reasons that the elders had called this meeting, since Mafuta was leaving a great fortune and they wanted to make certain that it would be equally divided among his children, and administered by the children's mothers or close relatives, in accordance with the time-honored custom of their tribe. Thus, a great fortune that had temporarily accumulated in one man's hands would be divided among many, as it should be.

Lisengo seemed to have completely forgotten about his recent Kinshasa dreams. He was titillated by the topic of the impending discussions.

When I got home I found a small gathering of villagers forming a semicircle around our *baraza* to stare at their pale *monganga mokonji* reclining limply in a morris chair. Leport was nearby, keeping a watchful eye on Michael and possessively rocking Loba on his knee. There were other visitors. Madame Van Derveer looked dangerously close to crying. And briefly I again glimpsed the woman beneath the mask, who was capable of kindness and generosity. Perhaps, had she spent more time at the post, I might have had a chance of getting to know her better, and we might have become good friends, despite the difference in our tastes and mentalities. Or maybe it was just as well that I was leaving on this note of good will.

Paulette Fallet appeared with red and swollen eyes. But Leport whispered to me, favoring me perhaps for the last time with his golden smile, that it was not on our account, but because Paulette had just discovered she was not to become a prospective mother that month. The Portuguese contingent was well represented by two traders, but Carlos was not in sight. I learned that he had left ahead on his crazy motorcycle to arrange in Mongana the ferrying of our car on the company's boat across the Congo River, in order to get Michael directly to Lisala. Another trader from Lisala would bring the car back. So it looked as if Michael and I were not fated to spend any time in Mongana after all. Everybody helped themselves to the drinks, since Jafke and Albert were busy saying their own goodbyes.

The Busu Melo villagers in front of the *baraza* had started to chatter loudly and by the way some of them were cocking their heads to one side and turning to look in the same direction, it was clear they were listening to the distant sound of tom-toms. Perhaps the rhythmical beats proclaimed some new developments at the *mboka*. Or maybe they were telegraphing the villages lining the road to Mongana that *Monganga Mokonji* from Busu Melo would soon be passing their way.

But besides the uncoded message, the two melodious wooden sounds, one sharp and piercing, the other grave and hoarse, brought back the memory of the fragile huts and their occupants who were so difficult to understand because their brutality could live side by side with incredibly subtle ethics, and their prejudices with good common sense. And once again I heard the laughter of my little friends, already gone, and the sobs of the heartbroken old man left behind.

All at once it occurred to me that "my" *mboka*, this tiny African community with its joys that were so different and its sorrows that were like those of men everywhere, this village in the swampy equatorial wilderness, was a rare link between the Congo of *lobi* (yesterday) and *lobi* (tomorrow).

I also thought that in spite of the encroaching tide of outside modernization, that no doubt would be stepped up with the passage of time, all this wealth of tribal folklore, this unique marriage of everyday life and the charm of age-old legends, should not be allowed to pass from existence without a trace. I considered the possibility of one day perhaps meeting again some of my young village friends grown to adulthood as free citizens of a new and independent Congo. But I could not help wondering if even they would remember, or wish to remember, the village of their fathers as it had once been—with its poverty and good fortune equally shared by all, unspoiled and untouched by the new and borrowed ways of an alien life. But I knew that on many a nostalgic day I myself would leaf back the years to relive the past.

A breath of warm breeze gently shook the purple bougainvillea arching over the *baraza* steps. And riding on its fragrant mixture of wet grasses, wild orange blossoms, and the smoky village fires, the distant sound of tom-toms came closer and closer—a jungle tongue I now believed I understood.

(continued from front flap)

their "secret society." She provided a unique solution to Baloki's problem when the chief tried to take her away from Lisengo. In village celebrations, like an enraptured child herself, she remained unnoticed, sitting by smoky fires and listening to old legends and stories of the past told by the village elders.

Providing a rare firsthand glimpse into an ancient culture, Мвока is a warm, poignant, often humorous recollection of a little-known people and their proud heritage.

Lona B. Kenney was educated in England, France, Germany, and Italy. After she finished her musical studies in Milan, and had a successful operatic debut at sixteen, she sang major roles in many of the cities of Europe. In her second career of writing, she has produced articles, short stories, and television plays, as well as a novel called *A Caste of Heroes*, before writing her latest book, *Mboka*. She and her doctor husband reside in New York City.